Effective Classroom Teacher

LEADERSHIP SKILLS IN EDUCATION MANAGEMENT

Series Editor: Professor Trevor Kerry

Other titles in this series

Mastering Deputy Headship
Acquiring the skills for future leadership
by Trevor Kerry

The Head Teacher in the 21st Century
Being a successful school leader
by Frank Green

From Teacher to Middle Manager
Making the next step
by Susan Tranter

The Special Educational Needs Coordinator
Maximising your potential
by Vic Shuttleworth

Effective Classroom Teacher

Developing the skills you need in the classroom

Trevor Kerry and Mandy Wilding

London • New York • Toronto • Sydney • Tokyo • Singapore
Hong Kong • Cape Town • Madrid • Paris • Amsterdam • Munich • Milan

PEARSON EDUCATION LIMITED

Head Office:
Edinburgh Gate
Harlow CM20 2JE
Tel: +44 (0)1279 623623
Fax: +44 (0)1279 431059
Website: www.pearsoned.co.uk

First published in Great Britain in 2004

ISBN 0 273 66326 7

British Library Cataloguing in Publication Data
A CIP catalogue record for this book can be obtained from the British Library.

10 9 8 7 6 5 4 3 2 1

Typeset by Pantek Arts Ltd, Maidstone, Kent
Printed and bound in Great Britain by Bell & Bain Limited, Glasgow

The publishers' policy is to use paper manufactured from sustainable forests.

About the authors

TREVOR KERRY is Visiting Professor at the International Institute of Educational Leadership in the University of Lincoln. In 2002 he was appointed the University of Lincoln's first Emeritus Professor. He is also Professor in Education at the College of Teachers and a former Dean and former Senior Vice President of the College, and for five years edited the College's journal *Education Today*. He has had a long career in teaching and education management, which has included teaching posts in the primary, secondary and further education sectors, as well as several spells as a teacher trainer. He was also Senior General Adviser (INSET) for Norfolk LEA. Trevor is well known as an author of texts on education management issues (including *Mastering Deputy Headship* and *Working with Support Staff* for Pearson Education). He has written prolifically on teaching skills and in education journals. He is a member of the Court of the Guild of Educators and, with his wife Carolle, operates TK Consultancy (Lincoln) Ltd – an education consultancy providing training for schools and LEAs. He belongs unashamedly to the school of applied research and believes passionately that what matters most in education occurs at the interface between teacher and students, at whatever level the learning is taking place.

MANDY WILDING is head teacher of a successful small primary school. She still has a considerable teaching commitment across the whole primary age range, which keeps her in touch with the issues and concerns of classroom teachers, as well as being responsible for the performance and development of others. Her experience took her in rapid succession from teacher, to deputy, through acting headship to running her own school. During this time she had significant experience of Ofsted inspection. Mandy is a graduate with a first class honours BA from the Open University. She was one of the OU's first cohort of PGCE graduates; she also holds an MA in Primary Education and an Advanced Diploma in Education Management from the Open University, and the NPQH qualification. She had a short but interesting term of office as Vice-President of the College of Teachers. She has written several articles and reviews for education journals.

Contents

Series editor's introduction

The nature of schools and the educative process is changing. Indications are that the first decade of the twenty-first century will see the fastest and the most far-reaching changes in schools and schooling since the compulsory education system was established. The signs are there if we have eyes to see them:

- Advances in technology will alter the nature of learning. While school has been characterised by the need for groups of people to assemble together to listen to a teacher, the computer, its software and the internet are making learning accessible to anyone, according to need and inclination, without this assembly.

- Technology, through the computer and through video-conferencing, gives access on a local level to global opportunities. Given the technology, pupils in Britain can access the very best lessons and the very best teachers from anywhere in the world. In place of thousands of teachers teaching thousands of different, more or less good, lessons on a topic, the student will be able to access the most complete and dynamic lesson regardless of where it is taught.

- Computers even threaten the concept of school time. Since the computer gives access at unlimited times and in unlimited places, learning no longer needs to be associated with time slots at all.

- It is not just computers that are driving the forces of education into new channels. Economics also plays a part. School buildings are inflexible and costly, yet they often remain unused for more than 80 per cent of the time – during vacations, evenings, nights and so on. Costly plant lying idle is a luxury that society may feel unable to afford.

- Increasingly, we can see support staff of various kinds becoming more central to the education process. There was a time when no adult but a teacher would have been found in a classroom. Now schools often have a greater complement of technicians, administrators, nursery assistants, special needs assistants, students from care courses, voluntary helpers and counsellors than they do of teaching staff.

So in key areas – how learning takes place, where it takes place, when, its quality, the type of plant required, the nature of the people who deliver it – are all in the melting pot in this new millennium. If ever there was a moment for developing a new breed of teachers who could span the effective practice of the present system and forge a path into the future, this is it.

This series is therefore dedicated to achieving those ends: to help education managers and leaders at various levels in the system to become more effective now and the pioneers of the future. The present title is concerned specifically with the teacher in the classroom, but above all with those who want to become 'master teachers', i.e. the best the profession has. This process takes in knowledge, understanding and skill: no one is sufficient alone. The title will also be of interest to all who manage teachers and who want to encourage them to be the best.

The titles in the series are all written by people with proven track records of innovation. The style is intended to be direct and the reader is asked to engage with the text in order to maximise the training benefit the books can deliver.

Change is rarely comfortable, but it can be exciting. This series hopes to communicate to teachers and school leaders something of the confidence that is needed to manage change, and something of the fulfilment that comes from meeting challenge successfully.

Within the text, Chapters 1, 2, 5, 9 and 10 have been written by Trevor Kerry. Chapters 3, 7 and 8 have been written by Mandy Wilding. Chapters 4, 6 and 11 have been collaborative. In addition, each author has read the other's work and made suggestions. Editorial shortcomings remain my responsibility.

Professor Trevor Kerry

List of activities

List of tables

List of figures

Preface

We share a deeply held conviction about the value of the teaching profession and the importance to society and its children of getting educational experiences right.

This book is not for the faint-hearted. It is a book for teachers who share our conviction – teachers for whom their daily lives are driven by the imperatives of helping children to learn more effectively and of gaining satisfaction from a job carried out professionally, not merely from achieving yet more 'results'.

Even in promoted posts we have each sustained our roots as teachers of young people, hopefully as effective and thinking practitioners: that connection with the reality of classroom life is important to us. So this text is addressed to teachers who want to be at the very apex of their profession *as teachers* first and foremost. The best teachers understand the intricacies and intimacies of the job they do; they shun the modern pressure to teach by numbers and dumb down their calling to a trade. In the text we call these teachers 'master teachers'. To quote Mayo, master teachers are:

> Continually engaged in a reflective and reflexive act of enquiry, making instructional decisions based upon research and using theory to inform school level decisions.
>
> (Mayo 2002: 29–33)

If one had to sum up such teachers in a single phrase it would have to be: *they care*. They care about pupils first and above all. They care about their subject matter, whether they are primary generalists or secondary specialists. They care about their colleagues, especially those just entering the profession whom they may be able to influence, help and guide. They care about society. They care enough to deliver what society needs to make it strong and improve the lives of its citizens.

Such teachers are not dewy-eyed idealists, they are intellectuals. They demand to know not just what works and how it works, but why it works and whether it can be made better. They are malleable, not to fashion but to the positive changes that blend learning to new eras and lifestyles.

We meet such teachers in our work. They do not sport haloes or the insipid glow of self-satisfaction. Indeed, they are often self-questioning, even self-doubting. The intention of this book is to make them strong; to give them theoretical bases for their behaviour, the professional encouragement for their convictions and the evidence-based rationale for their actions. In this, we hope both to challenge and supersede many of the current political constructions of teachers and teaching.

Reference

Mayo, K. (2002) 'Teacher leadership: the management model', *Management in Education*, 16(13): 29–33.

How to use this book

This is a book about the knowledge, understanding and skills required of a teacher in a primary or secondary school. The book uses a variety of means through which to set out, examine and exemplify these skills:

- *text* to provide information, discussion and continuity

- *tables and figures* to convey data quickly or in graphic form

- *lists* to set out key issues or skills

- *activities* to involve the reader in practice

- *reflections* to encourage the reader to apply the text to their own situations

- *case studies* to provide real examples of teaching situations.

The book can be used in a variety of ways. It can be read as a textbook: the reader will then simply read over but not carry out the activities. It can be used as a source book. You can consult the relevant sections (such as accessing professional development more effectively or thinking through approaches to learning) as the need arises. It can be used as a training manual by an individual; in which case you will work through it systematically, pausing to carry out each reflection and each activity as you come to it. Finally, the book can be used as a training manual for personal self-development. To get the most from the book we would recommend you use the reflections and activities and keep a log of the outcomes from them.

The book is based on the philosophy that teachers need specific skills for the job. These skills can be identified, analysed, refined, broken down into subskills, taught, learned and even assessed. We hope that the book will be seen by busy teachers as a kind of *vade-mecum* – a source of comfort and inspiration. It would be useful too as the basis of a systematic dialogue between a teacher and a mentor.

This book stresses the importance of the links between the practice of teaching and the theory that underpins specific aspects of the role. We believe that practice without a theory is a house built on sand and that theory without translation into sound practice is an empty vessel.

We trust that this manual of skills, based as it is upon grounded theory and experience, will bridge the gap that often exists for teachers who want to improve their effectiveness.

chapter one

The aware teacher

Professionalism, professional values and professional practice

In this chapter you are invited to:

- Engage with definitions of professionalism
- Examine some sociological insights into teachers and teaching
- Reflect on the socio-political implications of education policy and approaches to teaching
- Develop awareness based on current debates about professionalism, society and political control in education

Professionalism

It is surprisingly difficult to offer a satisfactory definition – a definition, that is, as opposed to examples, descriptions or codes – of professionalism as it applies to teaching. Throughout much of the teacher-related literature professionalism is treated less as a state or as a philosophy, and more as a process that needs a context within which to define itself. Thus Møller states:

Teachers and administrators, at various levels within schools, have different functions and knowledge, but they have a joint responsibility for providing pupils with a quality education. The professional identity one develops, becomes apparent through interaction with others working at the same school, with other schools and other areas of the education system ...

There is a tension between the teachers' demand for autonomy, for an independent right to draw up and discuss the ethics of professional practice, and the control of this practice by the democratic state ... A professional role entails professional responsibility, and this implies that teachers make their experience more visible [i.e. within an accountable, self-managing school].

(Møller 2002: 204, 213)

The dictionary definition (Chambers) of a profession as 'an occupation requiring special training in the liberal arts or sciences ... the body of people in such an occupation' is clearly no longer adequate. Indeed the close juxtaposition of professionalism and accountability is reaffirmed by Powell (2000: 41). She examines the business excellence model on which school self-assessment in the UK is largely based. She identifies three 'grammars' of this accountability process which she claims are procedurally distinct:

S1 – *self-review*: a process that 'combines imposed external accountability, under the illusion of self-assessment, with a reduction in the cost of external inspection'.

S2 – *self-evaluation*: involves teachers in action planning and target setting and, though outcomes-led, is more participative.

S3 – *self-assessment*: a process-led collaborative enterprise in which individual teachers share a common purpose and are committed to change in themselves and their institutions.

Teachers' professionalism, the argument goes, is realised not by managing change but when 'teachers themselves become the originators of change and professional learning' (Powell 2000: 47).

REFLECTION

Look at Powell's three definitions (S1–S3) above. How, and to what extent, does each apply to you in your own job?

Although Powell's conceptual map of the route to professionalism is essentially uncomplicated in its form, not everyone would accept it. MacLure (2001) is certainly resistant. She uses biographical accounts of teachers' lives to support her conclusions:

> *The pervasive pre-occupation with the nature and adequacy of the self may also be a reflection of teaching's continuing status as a 'semi-profession', whose claims to professional status revolve around the investment of the self in the occupational sphere. What is clear is that there is considerable unease among teachers about the restricted range of culturally endorsed professional identities available to them, and widespread resistance to the old iconographies of the dedicated carer.*
>
> (MacLure 2001: 178)

MacLure's reservations, then, highlight the sociological problem that status – including professional status – is ascribed, at least in part. It is a matter of how one views oneself and also how one is viewed by others. There is an interplay between these forces, a reality brought to life in an address to the Australian College of Education by David Kemp (1997):

> *I believe that teachers can gain immense respect and standing within the community if they are given the opportunity to articulate their own professional standards. Identifying what a profession rewards as accomplished practice for its members is a necessary prerequisite to making decisions about many other professional issues including teacher education, selection and induction.*
>
> (Kemp 1997: 8)

This kind of professionalism – the professionalism of control over the profession's standards and activities – has been progressively eroded in the UK over the past two decades.

REFLECTION

Teachers are now required to be members of the General Teaching Council (GTC). It controls professional behaviour. How has the GTC impacted on your professional life and the professional lives of your colleagues?

This is a topic to revisit, but first it is instructive to follow Hargreaves (1997) in an historical review of the concept of professionalism. Hargreaves defines four historical 'ages' of professionalism:

- the pre-professional age
- the age of the autonomous professional
- the age of the collegial professional
- the post-professional age.

In the pre-professional age teaching was seen as 'managerially demanding, but technically simple' (Hargreaves 1997: 90). In other words, children were organised into classes, class control was established (sometimes with difficulty), material was transmitted through didactic methods and recitation models, learning to teach was based on the apprenticeship model, and professionalism was judged on the extent to which the individuals devoted themselves to the craft.

The autonomous professional (a status achieved in many areas from about the 1960s) was paid substantially more, was trained in prescribed ways (often with graduate status), had autonomy over curriculum and had choices about pedagogical methods. The autonomous professional was free to experiment but also inhabited what I have elsewhere labelled the 'fine and private place' of the classroom (an echo of Marvel's description of the grave). Hargreaves traces many of the current problems of the profession to this era of autonomy, including at the level of the teacher:

- lack of confidence about their effectiveness
- lack of opportunities for shared learning with peers
- horizons limited to one's own classroom
- lack of consistency and coherence in the broader educational programmes
- the realisation that isolation leads to monotony not excitement.

At the level of the school:

- the egg-box nature of buildings
- a feeling of being trapped within traditional procedures
- a sense of foreboding about external scrutiny.

Gratch (2000: 120), a teacher trainer, identifies the isolation of teachers, arguing that the voices of teachers must be made more central to the dialogue on teaching and learning. She concludes that teachers are 'not able to critically reflect [sic] without discourse with peers'.

However, from the 1980s there was an increasing imposition of requirements from outside the school. This was coupled with a growing suspicion by those in political authority of the 'expert advice' offered by trainers beyond the school. Thus a sense of collaboration and self-help emerged within schools, producing the age of the collegiate professional. Furthermore, shared professional development seemed to bear fruit. But there was also a more negative side to this collegiate approach in that it was arguably a response to the growing problems of teaching:

- rapid change
- integration of special needs into mainstream classes
- multiculturalism
- the growing alienation of secondary school pupils
- changing patterns of school leadership and management.

Finally, we move into contemporary times, Hargreaves argues, and we need to construct a postmodern view of teachers' professionalism for a post-professional age. This postmodernism has to take into account social factors (consumerism, shifting social and economic patterns, changing relations with government). Schools are more market orientated. Pupils come from more diverse family structures. Traditional neighbourhoods have broken down. Accountability operates at a variety of levels, requiring from teachers new communications skills with parents and others. There are specific areas of public controversy such as discipline and assessment. In the field of teacher training, education faculties are often geographically marginalised. Schools look down on them as repositories of questionable theory; other university faculties see them as intellectually low-level. While governments have tried to reduce the influence of the training institutions, there has been an increasing emphasis on competence models and the gaining of government-approved qualifications (NVQs, NPQH and so on). Thus Hargreaves concludes:

So we are now on the edge of an age of postmodern professionalism where teachers deal with a diverse and complex clientele, in conditions of increasing moral uncertainty, where many methods of approach are possible, and where more and more social groups have an influence and say. Whether this postmodern age will see exciting and positive new partnerships being created with groups and institutions beyond the school, and teachers learning to work effectively, openly and authoritatively with those partners; or whether it will witness the deprofessionalisation of teaching as teachers crumble under multiple pressures, intensified work demands and reduced opportunities to learn from colleagues is something that is still to be decided.

(Hargreaves 1997: 108)

REFLECTION

Do you feel deprofessionalised in your teaching? How? To what extent? Why? Are you views shared by your colleagues?

What is clear from a wholly UK perspective is that these processes described by Hargreaves are not myth: every teacher of sufficient age could exemplify these movements in professionalism from their own experience. While these 'ages of professionalism' overlap to a degree, it is possible to argue that the governmental impositions on teachers since the mid-1980s have lowered teachers' professionalism. Among such impositions have been:

- increasing powers of school governors
- local management of schools
- increased marketisation of schools coupled to parental choice
- the National Curriculum
- Standard Assessment Tasks (SATs)
- Ofsted inspections
- requirement to publish tables of results in public examinations
- teacher appraisal
- imposition of compulsory targets for schools and local education authorities (LEAs)
- strong steer provided by the National Literacy and Numeracy Strategies
- performance-related pay.

Hoyle and John (1995) argue that, while teachers were relatively unaccountable before these changes, their autonomy embraced high levels of professional integrity and responsibility. The erosion of autonomy has led to the undermining of professionalism and a consequent lowering of morale. There is an irony at the heart of the process. The government felt obligated to assert:

> *The time has long gone when isolated, unaccountable professionals made curriculum and pedagogical decisions alone, without reference to the outside world.*
>
> (Department for Education and Employment (DfEE) 1998: 3)

Yet the 'effective school' movement and the 'world class school' aspiration of New Labour has arguably led not to improved teacher professionalism but to its erosion, even its denial.

— The teaching profession from a sociological perspective —

The history of the struggle for professional status for teachers has been a long and by no means successful one. Whitty (2002) rehearses a number of the issues we have visited above, but does so from an overtly sociological perspective. To take up the story from where we left it in the previous section, he notes that professionalism is often defined by a 'sort of bargain' between the state and a profession – a licence to pursue the profession under the participants' own rules. But in the case of education, teachers were thought to have violated the code from the 1950s to the 1980s, and thence a succession of events and figures questioned their licence: Callaghan's Ruskin College speech, the Great Debate, the William Tyndale enquiry, and the reforms of successive Secretaries of State for Education – Sir Keith Joseph, Kenneth Baker, Gillian Shepherd, and others.

Under New Labour, the result has been an increasing takeover by the government of areas of teacher professionalism. Whitty notes that, while governments can appear to be handing over autonomy to a profession (as in the case of the establishment of the General Teaching Council – of which more below), they may retain control in reality. The professionalism then consists of delivering according to the government's specifications. This includes managing schools in a prescribed way. Managers who do this (by, for example, improving performance levels) may see their professionalism rewarded by government, while those who pursue other agendas (such as social inclusion at the expense of results) may be penalised. The professional influence of teachers may likewise be eroded by such ploys as employing non-qualified staff, the introduction of support personnel to take over some traditional roles, and the employment of more part-time personnel and fewer full-timers.

Not only existing teachers are affected by these trends, but even those in training are drawn into these scenarios. Just as schools now have a National Curriculum, so teacher education has a prescribed training curriculum. It is subject to inspection. The traditional university departments and colleges have been partly superseded by schemes such as the Standing Council for Intial Teacher Training (SCITT), schemes of on-the-job training on the apprenticeship model, and at best are controlled by a government department in the form of the Teacher Training Agency (TTA). Entrants to the profession are thus affected and conditioned from the outset into new modes of thinking about their roles and employment.

Whether the process just outlined is accurately described as deprofessionalising teachers is a matter of debate. Some would argue that is more precisely a reprofessionalisation. The new professionalism is a model that is appropriate for the new society in which teachers work, and this new context was spelled out in the Green Paper (Department for Education and Employment (DfEE) 1998). This would be the postmodernist view, notably that reforms of teacher education and professionalism are about teachers operating in a modern, changing and open society and in a more responsive and accountable way.

These debates about professionalism are not value-free. Underlying the conflicting opinions are codes of belief about what teachers and teaching are and should be. In one sense, the whole of this volume is designed to address these issues. But this might be an opportune moment for you to take stock of your values at this point in time: it is a question that you can revisit from time to time as you read the text. To this end you should proceed to Activity 1.1.

ACTIVITY 1.1

Identifying your beliefs and values about teaching as a profession

What precisely is education for? What purpose does it serve in society?

Who are the stakeholders and how exactly should they benefit from it?

What motivates you to be a teacher?

How do you define your job? What words best describe your approach to it: e.g. occupation, vocation, craft, science, employment – any others?

What to you are the rewards?

What are the penalties? What would you change to make your job better?

What do you hope to achieve (for yourself, for your school, for your pupils) by the time you leave the profession?

In a sentence, how would you encapsulate your attitudes and feelings towards this role?

Who are teachers?

This question could have a number of different meanings, but in the present context it is construed sociologically – how can we define the group that goes by that name and exercises their profession in the nation's schools?

We need to speculate a little about that question because values do not come out of nowhere. Who we are has a bearing on what we believe, and the beliefs you have articulated under Activity 1.1 are almost certainly influenced by your sociological background and resulting cultural milieu. Furthermore, part of the awareness of the chapter title is understanding ourselves and our colleagues. With this in mind, the intention is to examine four propositions:

1 Teachers epitomise high social class

2 Social class is a factor in pupils' experience and perception of education and its relevance

3 To understand and pursue their profession, teachers must understand the social class implications of today's society

4 Social awareness is simply one aspect of a broader political awareness

Before you read the section that follows, ask yourself how you categorise yourself in social terms – what social class, values, behaviours, etc. epitomise you?

Proposition 1: Teachers epitomise high social class

Where do teachers come in the social pecking order? The answer, according to the revised classification system used by the Registrar General, is in social class two of eight (see Table 1.1). This classification is based largely on their professional status: they are trained, graduate, white collar, working under conditions of service contracts, with access to salaries that are well above the minimum wage and that have potential for expansion through promotion.

Teachers do not necessarily see themselves in the same way as society sees them. Many probably feel that they are first-generation educated, self-made, originating from modest neighbourhoods, and with values more readily described by the vernacular term 'working class' than 'middle class'.

Research evidence shows, however, that most students accessing further and higher education (which all teachers do) are drawn from the higher social classes (see Table 1.2, which is taken from data provided by the National Statistics Office and uses a slightly different social classification from that in Table 1.1, though the parallels are clear). Students entering such training, particularly towards professional qualification, may not view themselves as of high social class initially, but inevitably are ascribed that status by society on qualification. This leads Hargreaves (2002) to note that teachers are 'physically, socially and culturally removed from the communities in which they teach'.

TABLE 1.1 2001 social classification system

Class 1: higher managerial and professional (about 11% of the population), doctors, dentists, lawyers, university lecturers and employers of over 25 people

Class 2: lower managerial and professional (about 23.5%), teachers, social workers, journalists, police sergeants and junior managers

Class 3: intermediate (about 14%), police constables, fire-fighters, prison officers

Class 4: small employers/own account workers (about 9.9%), non-professionals such as self-employed plumbers and carpenters

Class 5: lower supervisory and technical workers (about 9.8%), foremen, train drivers

Class 6: semi-routine employees (about 18.6%), shop assistants, call-centre workers

Class 7: routine workers (about 12.7%), drivers, cleaners

Class 8: unemployed, long-term sick

TABLE 1.2 Entrants to full-time further/higher education by social class

Social class	% of participants
1 Professional	72
2 Intermediate	45
3 Skilled non-manual	29
4 Skilled manual	18
5 Partly skilled	17
6 Unskilled	13
7 Across all social classes	31

So professionalism is a determinant of social class and class, like professional status, is something that can be ascribed to an individual by others regardless of the individual's self-image.

Proposition 2: Social class is a factor in pupils' experience and perception of education and its relevance

The classic comedy sketch featuring John Cleese, Ronnie Barker and Ronnie Corbett had the tall, bowler-hatted Cleese as the upper-class man literally and metaphorically looking down on trilby-clad Barker, the middle-class man. Barker looked up to Cleese 'because he is upper class', and down on Corbett 'because he is working class'. The diminutive, working-class Corbett in his flat cap could only look up. A good visual joke, but less good for the health of society.

In the pre-comprehensive school era this stratification of society was perpetuated by the tripartite school system: secondary moderns, central/technical schools and grammars or private education (according to income). The government Circular 10/65 put an end to all that – or did it? An international study certainly suggests the value of comprehensive education in minimising social differences (Hirsch 2002); but in a society as stratified as the UK we should not be complacent. Indeed, the late John Eggleston surveyed staying-on rates at 16 as recently as 2000 and concluded:

> *Of all the key life determining decisions in education, the decision to 'stay on' after the minimum leaving age is probably the most important. It is at this point that the major distribution of career opportunities takes place ... It is the point of entry to professional training, higher education and a more certain prospect of employment, higher earning, professional status and enhanced and desired life style...For those who leave at minimum age a diminution of prospects, though not inescapable, becomes probable ... [One perspective] favoured by social scientists is that social reproduction is endemic in most areas of society; that covert and overt processes tend to preserve the distribution of class, status and power from generation to generation and, without interventionist strategies, are therefore subversive to any labour market driven educational initiatives that threaten to modify this transmission.*
>
> (Eggleston 2000:1)

With support from a Leverhulme grant Eggleston surveyed stay-on rates and practices in a range of comprehensive schools. A summary of his conclusions may cause a sharp intake of breath:

- Motivated, able students were courted for their tonic effect on numbers and results.
- Teachers were conveying to their students the link between ambition and deferred gratification – work now, rewards later.
- Students were aware of the schools' economic motives in cultivating them – increased revenue for staffing, enhanced school reputation.
- Virtually all the alienated, the troublemakers, the unmotivated and the low achievers quickly disappeared.
- A majority of students of middle-class origin stayed on.
- Only small, albeit growing, groups of working-class students stayed on.
- Schools hid other opportunities for 'staying on' beyond the school gates (e.g. the option for further education courses).
- Of the families and their students who wanted to cross the class divide by seizing educational opportunities, the numbers were small and mostly from the ethnic minority communities.
- The school with a majority of white working-class origin displayed the highest proportion of students wanting to leave at 16.

Eggleston concluded that 'little had changed since the *Early Leaving Report* of the 1950s' (2000: 16). He urged:

> *Remember that positive achievement, aspiration and self-esteem should always be enhanced not diminished by teacher expectation ... Sadly, this still requires a fundamental change in the professional approach of many teachers*
>
> (Eggleston 2000: 22)

While teachers themselves have crossed the social divide, many of their pupils have not and may not. But social class effects in teaching are more endemic even than staying-on rates. Consider each of the following:

- The language that teachers use separates them, in many instances, from the pupils they teach.
- Within classrooms the range of cultures across pupils is immense.
- Access to learning (for example, ownership of a laptop, opportunities for out-of-school visits, access to books) may be dependent on income and thus social class.
- In 1996 the bottom 30 LEAs in league table performances at GCSE were in 'substantially deprived urban areas' (Plummer 2000: 25); thus compounding the self-fulfilling prophecy of failure.
- As we entered the year 2003, in response to the government's debate about top-up fees, potential higher-education students were complaining: 'Just because I am not rich, does not mean I'm entitled to less education' (White 2002: 14).
- Students from less advantaged backgrounds are likely to go to worse performing schools (Hirsch 2002).

So what are the messages that underlie this proposition that social class is a factor in pupils' experience and perception of education and its relevance? Clearly, that the influence of social class has identifiable and even quantifiable effects on pupils' performance, and thus that part of the professional awareness of teachers is to attempt to bridge the class divides that distance them from the pupils and the pupils from the culture of the school. As Hill and Cole (2001: 140) put it: 'Children from Hackney stand less chance of getting to university, or learning to read, than do children from Huntingdon.' While teachers have to be wary of prejudging issues by lowering expectations for pupils from deprived areas, they cannot turn their backs on the realities that poverty engenders (Pyke

2002); nor can they be insensitive to the increasing divide between best and worst schools (Tomlinson and Edwards 2002).

So in a more than usually useful feature in the *Times Educational Supplement*, Gold (2003) explored the latest research on the relationship between poverty and the effectiveness of schooling and concluded that 'intake limits what schools can achieve'. Similarly, latest data on school performance (for 2002) show a correlation between ethnicity and achievement, with black Caribbean students performing poorly at GCSE and Indian and Chinese students doing exceptionally well (Shaw 2003). This leads us to our third proposition, which is about social background and education.

Proposition 3: To understand and pursue their profession, teachers must understand the social class implications of today's society and how to respond to them

In examining this proposition we shall take just two examples, one somewhat negative and the other rather more positive. On the negative issue we draw attention to the government's resolve that the parents of school truants should be punished by fines (Passmore 2002). Examine for a moment the logic of this proposal using Activity 1.2.

ACTIVITY 1.2

Analysing a truancy scenario for socio-political undertones

Read the scenario presented below. Ask yourself these questions:

- How valuable to the school will be the outcome of the head's action?

- What effect is this action likely to have on the home–school relations in this case?

- How likely is it that this action will be effective in promoting positive learning attitudes in the pupil concerned?

- What are the socio-political messages that are conveyed in this scenario?

- What are the alternatives?

Truancy affects relatively underperforming schools, which are frequently in deprived areas. Many truants are picked up by truancy squads actually in the presence of their parents, who are conniving at the offence. It would seem reasonable to suggest that the motivation for the offence depends in part on the perceived need of pupil and parent to engage in an alternative activity of signifi-cance to them, and in part because of a perception about the relative unimportance of school. Truancy squads represent the face of officialdom (wel-fare officers) and oppression (the police). Truants and parents are returned to school, where the parent (who maybe poor, unemployed, inadequately edu-cated, working-class, linguistically limited) is further disadvantaged by a fine imposed by the (rich, middle-class, educated, linguistically fluent) head.

Our second scenario is more positive. It consists of a plan to educate all trainee teachers in essential socio-political skills during their progress towards Qualified Teacher Status (QTS). Here is a quotation from the document that sets up this approach:

The new module gives trainee teachers the knowledge, skills and understanding to play an effective role in society at local, national and international levels. It helps them to become informed, thoughtful and responsible ... aware of their duties and rights. It promotes their spiritual, moral, social and cultural develop-ment, making them more self-confident and responsible both in and beyond the classroom ... It teaches about our economy and democratic institutions...

[It provides] a vision of schools as democratic cornerstones of the community ... and [aims] 'at no less than a change in the political culture of this country'.

REFLECTION

Spend a moment reflecting on the implications of this new course for trainee teachers, what difference it will make to their work and how this scenario con-trasts with the one in Activity 1.2.

Now be aware that this two-part quotation is a spoof. The first paragraph is the text of the National Curriculum document *The Importance of Citizenship*; the second is part of an article about teaching citizenship in school by Lee Jerome (2001), Education Director of the Institute for Citizenship, and the Crick Report (1998). While citizenship is destined to become a 'new subject' in schools, many teachers remain all too unaware of it as an academic discipline and even naive about the implications of the socio-political messages in practice in schools.

Ask yourself how a teacher promoting the citizenship lessons described in this spoof quotation could even begin to countenance the actions depicted in the scenario in Activity 1.2. One problem is that in the new context of a controlled curriculum for teacher trainees there is no room for studying the sociology of education courses, which, until their demise in the 1980s, provided all teachers with insights into the kinds of issues we have outlined in this chapter. In the past, teachers would have been aware of sociological factors, and we have to concur (Kerry 2000) with Whitty's concise summary (no spoof this time), which is in turn supported by Hill and Cole (2001):

> *Many studies have drawn attention to the cumulative effects of low social class, poor educational achievement, reduced employment prospects, and poor physical and mental health. Notwithstanding Giddens' arguments in his most recent work (Giddens 2000), there are not many families who are education rich but poor in other respects ... Although Secretary of State David Blunkett apparently dismissed his views as 'claptrap' (Pyke 1997), [we concur with] Robinson's (1997) suggestion that an attack on poverty would be more effective in reducing educational inequalities than school-focused reforms.*
>
> (Whitty 2002: 123)

Proposition 4: Social awareness is simply one aspect of a broader political awareness

Out of the discussion above, it seems to us that there are three compelling reasons why teachers need to be politically aware. First, education is, and has become progressively, a domain in which governments intervene on behalf of the tax-payer (value-for-money debates) and in order to achieve political goals (to effect a 'world class education system' to quote New Labour).

Second, schools operate within society, and society is a political phenomenon. The place of schools in meeting the needs of citizens, in laying the foundations for employment, in sustaining the nation's economy and so on – that place is crucial. Unless teachers understand their place in society they cannot operate intelligently. Indeed, the inevitable links between education and politics were noted as long ago as Dewey who, according to Crocco, Munroe and Weiler (1999: 8), 'inspired the practice of education as the mechanism democracy would use to sustain and regenerate itself'.

Third, professionalism is itself a socio-political phenomenon. Professional status is part of the make-up of society; professional behaviour cannot be exercised without an intelligent understanding of socio-political context.

REFLECTION

What have you learned so far in this chapter about teachers as sociological and political animals?

With these reflections behind us, the time has come to look more closely at professional behaviour.

Codes of professionalism

We have seen that professionalism can be defined, albeit controversially, and that professional status can be both assumed and ascribed. One dimension of professionalism is admittance to the professional 'club' – the body that controls work in the area of one's expertise. There may be hurdles to entry into that 'club' such as graduate status and specific qualification (Qualified Teacher Status, QTS). Another hurdle is acceptance into an appropriate professional body, such as the British Medical Association in the case of doctors. Teachers laboured until very recently with no such body to act as the focus of its professionalism. This changed in 2001, when the General Teaching Council (GTC) was formed.

The early history of this body (Docking 2000: 153–4) was unfortunate. Many teachers refused to pay the subscription to join and enthusiasm is still muted at best. Docking points out that sociologically the GTC is not comparable with the professional bodies in other sectors. It does not control entry to the profession, the distinctive knowledge base, the training and certification process, or aspects of self-regulation. The Teacher Training Agency does most of this. A major element of the GTC's council is appointed by government.

Nevertheless, the GTC does have one element that is common in professional bodies: a code of conduct for its members (Table 1.3). Even here, however, one has to exercise some caution. It reads like a descriptive list of well-intentioned behaviours culled from one government document or more. It is of the genre 'no sane person would disagree with this'. The statements made in it are indeed so generalised as to be wholly non-specific, if not meaningless. (What is 'professional judgement'? Who determines 'the best ways' and what are they? Who wouldn't exhibit a 'genuine concern for other people'? and so on.)

As well as the GTC, teachers have and always have had access to groups that are concerned with specific aspects of professional performance, such as the subject and phase associations (the Association for Science Education or the National Association for Primary Education, for example). Of these groups the

College of Teachers has represented generic interests and acted as a focus for individual teachers and for some of their associations. The college also has its own code of practice for members (Table 1.4). Because it is a membership organisation, this code is of course voluntary.

Codes of practice are designed to give the public assurances about the behaviour of those who exercise the particular profession concerned, but they also serve as a guide to members of the profession in question about what is expected of them. Codes should be regarded as the minimum standards, but like laws their interpretation is sometimes tested in the courts or tribunals. Even as we write there is a report in the education press about 'a teacher asked by governors to resign for acting unprofessionally in a meeting with parents' (Wright and Sharpe 2002). She was cleared of allegedly 'rolling her eyes, fidgeting and being arrogant' but judged guilty of asking two ten-year-olds to carry cookers up a flight of stairs. In a much more high-profile case a young supply teacher lost her job after inviting senior pupils to her home and allegedly having sexual relations with them.

The awareness of the chapter heading also has to be exercised over one's own behaviour: words, actions, body language. Small things can be important. One of the writers worked briefly at an all-girls establishment. The principal was interviewing for a deputy and asked which of the candidates was preferred. It was suggested that the principal might arrange for them to visit their cars, which had been left on reserved spaces. 'The one sporting the Bunny Club sticker,' it was suggested, 'might ring warning bells.'

TABLE 1.3 The General Teaching Council's code of conduct

Young people as pupils

Teachers have insight into the learning needs of young people. They use professional judgement to meet those needs and to choose the best ways of motivating pupils to achieve success. They use assessment to inform and guide their work.

Teachers have high expectations for all pupils, helping them progress regardless of their personal circumstances and different needs and backgrounds. They work to make sure that pupils develop intellectually and personally, and to safeguard pupils' general health, safety and well-being. Teachers demonstrate the characteristics they are trying to inspire in pupils, including a spirit of intellectual enquiry, tolerance, honesty, fairness, patience, a genuine concern for other people and an appreciation of different backgrounds.

Teacher colleagues

Teachers support their colleagues in achieving the highest professional standards. They are fully committed to sharing their own expertise and insights in the interests of the people they teach and are always open to learning from the effective practice of their colleagues. Teachers respect the rights of other people to equal opportunities and dignity at work. They respect confidentiality where appropriate.

Other professionals, governors and interested people

Teachers recognise that the well-being and development of pupils often depend on working in partnership with different professionals, the school governing body, support staff and other interested people within and beyond the school. They respect the skills, expertise and contributions of these colleagues and partners and are concerned to build productive working relationships with them in the interests of pupils.

Parents and carers

Teachers respond sensitively to the differences in pupils' home backgrounds and circumstances and recognise the importance of working in partnership with parents and carers to understand and support their children's learning. They endeavour to communicate effectively and promote cooperation between the home and the school for the benefit of young people.

The school in context

Teachers support the place of the school in the community and appreciate the importance of their own professional status in society. They recognise that professionalism involves using judgement over appropriate standards of personal behaviour.

Learning and development

Teachers entering the profession in England have been trained to a professional standard that has prepared them for the rigours and realities of the classroom. They understand that maintaining and developing their skills, knowledge and expertise is vital to achieving success. They take responsibility for their own continuing professional development, through the opportunities available to them, to make sure that pupils receive the best and most relevant education. Teachers continually reflect on their own practice, improve their skills and deepen their knowledge. They want to adapt their teaching appropriately to take account of new findings, ideas and techniques.

TABLE 1.4 The code of practice of the College of Teachers

Members of the College of Teachers agree to abide by the College's Code of Professional Practice by which they will:

---

1. conduct themselves at all times with integrity in the discharge of their duties according to law; and this clause overrides all others, so that where there is conflict, this clause shall prevail

2. maintain high standards of personal behaviour at all times and do nothing to bring themselves, the College or the profession into disrepute

3. take personal responsibility for the establishment and maintenance of good relations with other professional, public and private bodies

4. maintain the integrity of the profession in public and in the media

5. take no improper action which might injure or malign the reputation of other professionals

6. respect the rights, needs, aspirations and trust of the individual, regardless of gender, age, class, culture, or creed and ensure equal opportunities for all

7. respect the wishes and aspirations of parents, guardians and carers of pupils and students

8. maintain the strict confidentiality of personal information

9. ensure, as far as is possible, that individual pupils and students, and groups of pupils and students, achieve their full educational potential

10. exercise professional judgement in furthering the resolution of educational problems

11. further the development of professional skills, knowledge and attitudes in themselves and colleagues

12. ensure positive collaboration with those in educational and other institutions, authorities, examination boards and other specialists

---

The professionally aware teacher

A political animal

So we come to pull together the threads of the argument of this chapter. Teachers who aspire to doing their jobs with the highest degree of professionalism must, we have suggested:

- be aware of socio-political issues in education and in society
- operate intelligently to compensate, where appropriate, for social shortcomings
- make pupils aware – in an objective way – of these issues
- operate within the professional codes demanded of them by the democratic society that employs them.

But we have also implied that the aware teacher must be given to analysis, scrutinising the decisions that are democratically made and contributing insights to them: this is the behaviour that underpins the National Curriculum for Citizenship targeted at pupils. At the most pragmatic level this means that aware teachers must keep up to date with educational debate through the media, and take an informed interest in general socio-political issues in the same way.

Giroux and McLaren (1989) called such teachers 'transformative intellectuals':

> *One who exercises forms of intellectual and pedagogical practice which attempt to insert teaching and learning directly into the political sphere by arguing that schooling represents both a struggle for meaning and a struggle over power relations. Teachers who assume the role of transformative intellectuals treat students as critical agents, question how knowledge is produced and distributed, use dialogue, and make knowledge meaningful, critical, and ultimately emancipatory.*
>
> (Giroux and McLaren 1989 quoted in Hill and Cole 2001: 266)

This view could be seen as diametrically opposed to some government aspirations. We argue later in the book that one of the aspirations of New Labour has been to reduce teachers to technicians rather than professionals – to a view of their role more akin to painting by numbers than creating art. Indeed, the roots of this process stretch back into the Conservative administrations of prime ministers Thatcher and Major. It has been argued (Lawn 1996) that between 1920 and 1988 teacher professionalism and educational partnership with government were 'mythic' because they were modelled on colonial politics. Effectively, teachers were freed from some levels of central control in return for abandoning any attempt at political commentary. Professionalism was redefined, he suggests, in terms of not questioning the government.

This chapter provides a theoretical underpinning to much that will follow. It sets out the basic stance that education is a process of analysis and reflection – we have used the term 'awareness' as a shorthand for this – but the approach leaves open many questions:

- What are the purposes of schooling in the twenty-first century?

- What are the aspirations of education stakeholders, and how can these best be met in a time of turbulent change? (Gale and Densmore 2003).

- What are new theories of learning telling us about classroom practice? What effect will ICT and the knowledge society have in redefining learning and teaching, schools and schooling?

- What do we mean by 'lifelong learning'?

- How will we redefine the roles and professionalism of teachers in a techno-logical era?

- What effects will demographic and other changes in society have on our the-ories and practice of teaching?

- What are the real implications for teaching and of the global economy?

Our intention is to open up awareness of some of these issues in our text, but this book will not free you, as a professional, from seeking other evidence, accessing other views, and coming to your own conclusions. This is a process you can begin in the next chapter by considering the nature of pedagogy.

At the conclusion of this chapter you should have:

- Gained an insight into the nature of professionalism

- Identified some of your own beliefs and values about teaching

- Considered the practical implications that arise from socio-political decisions

- Contextualised education within some sociological data

- Become more aware of the social and political constraints on teachers

References

Crick Report (1998) *Education for Citizenship and the Teaching of Democracy in Schools: Final Report of the Advisory Group on Citizenship,* London: Qualifications and Curriculum Authority.

Crocco, M., Munro, P. and Weiler, K. (1999) *Pedagogies of Resistance,* New York: Teachers College Press.

Department for Education and Employment (DfEE) (1998) *Teaching: Meeting the Challenge of Change,* London: DfEE.

Department for Education and Science (DfES) (1965) *Circular 10/65,* London: HMSO.

Docking, J. (2000) *New Labour's Policies for Schools: Raising the Standard?*, London: David Fulton.

Eggleston, J. (2000) *Staying on at School: The Hidden Curriculum of Selection*, Warwick Papers on Education Policy no. 9, Warwick: Trentham Books.

Gale, T. and Densmore, K. (2003) *Engaging Teachers: towards a radical democratic agenda for schooling*, Buckingham: OU Press.

Giddens, A. (2000) *The Third Way and its Critics*, Cambridge: Polity Press.

Giroux, H and McLaren, P. (1989) *Critical Pedagogy, the State and Cultural Struggle*, New York: State University of New York

Gold, K. (2003) 'Poverty is an excuse', *Times Educational Supplement*, 7 March: 22.

Gratch, A. (2000) 'Becoming teacher: student teaching as identity construction', *Teaching Education*, 11(1): 119–26.

Hargreaves, A. (1997) 'The four ages of professionalism and professional learning', *Unicorn – Journal of the Australian College of Education*, 23(2): 86–114.

Hargreaves, A. (2002) 'Teaching in a box: emotional geographies of teaching' In C. Sugrue and C. Day (2002) *Developing Teachers and Teaching Practice*, London: Routledge Falmer.

Hill, D. and Cole, M. (2001) *Schooling and Equality: Fact, Concept and Policy*, London: Kogan Page.

Hirsch, D. (2002) 'Divide and you will divide again', *Times Educational Supplement*, 13 December: 19.

Hoyle, E. and John, P. (1995) *Professional Knowledge and Professional Practice*, London: Cassell.

Jerome, L. (2001) 'Teaching citizenship: from rhetoric to reality', *Education Today*, 51(1): 8–12.

Kemp. D. (1997) 'Supporting quality teaching', *Unicorn – Journal of the Australian College of Education*, 23(2) 3–10.

Kerry, T. (2000) *Surviving the Future: Changing Education in a Changing World*, Working Paper no. 40, Lincoln: Faculty of Business and Management, University of Lincoln.

Lawn, M. (1996) *Modern Times? Work, Professionalism and Citizenship in Teaching*, London: Falmer.

MacLure, M. (2001) 'Arguing for yourself: identity as an organising principle in teachers' jobs and lives', in J. Soler, A. Craft and H. Burgess, *Teacher Development: Exploring Our Own Practice*, London: PCP Open University.

Møller, J. (2002) 'Between professional autonomy and bureaucratic accountability: the self-managing school within a Norwegian context', in C. Sugrue and C. Day, *Developing Teachers and Teaching Practice*, London: Routledge Falmer.

Passmore, B. (2002) 'Heads given the power to impose fines on parents', *Times Educational Supplement*, 13 December: 1.

Plummer, G. (2000) *Failing Working Class Girls*, Stoke-on-Trent: Trentham Books.

Powell, L. (2000) 'Realising the value of self-assessment: the influence of the Business Excellence Model on teacher professionalism', *European Journal of Teacher Education*, 23(1) 37–48.

Pyke, N. (1997) 'Billions fail to add up to rising standards', *Times Educational Supplement*, 3 October: 1.

Pyke, N. (2002) 'Poor children, poor results', *Times Educational Supplement,* 11 October: 24–5.

Shaw, M. (2003) 'Alarm at results of black students', *Times Educational Supplement,* 11 March: 9.

Tomlinson, S. and Edwards, T. (2002) 'Selection in all but name', *Times Educational Supplement*, 11 October: 21.

White, P. (2002) 'Just because I am not rich, does not mean I'm entitled to less education', *Times Educational Supplement,* 13 December: 14.

Whitty, G. (2002) *Making Sense of Education Policy* London: PCP.

Wright, G. and Sharpe, B. (2002) 'GTC spares teacher sacked for arrogance towards parents', *Times Educational Supplement*, 13 December: 5.

chapter two

The incisive teacher

Principles of pedagogy

Introduction

The pedagogy debates

Pedagogy in context

In this chapter you are invited to:

- Examine the definition of pedagogy
- Understand the debate about competencies and skills
- Consider the nature and engage with the concept of reflective practitionership
- Engage with different understandings of pedagogy
- Practise your skills of reflection as applied to pedagogy

———— Introduction ————

It is unfortunate that pedagogy is such an apparently old-fashioned word because it has lost its power to attract attention or instil enthusiasm. The fact remains that it is probably the most important concept in the teacher's mental armoury. So what is it?

Pedagogy is the study of the process of teaching. In the previous chapter we examined questions about professionals and professionalism in education and teaching – the social and political underpinning. Here we look at the practice of teaching from an analytical standpoint. We will call this the science of teaching, or pedagogy.

Scientists ask what happens when or what happens if. They observe problems, set up hypotheses and design experiments to test these out, carry out those experiments under controlled conditions (where possible), record the results, draw conclusions, deduce rules or laws and operate them until better hypotheses and results come along. This is the pedagogical process, too.

The teacher begins from a problem: Sam behaves badly in class. The teacher then observes Sam and comes to a tentative hypothesis (guess) about Sam's behaviour and how to improve it (Sam is disruptive when sitting at the back with friends and needs to be moved). The teacher then puts into practice the experimental approach he/she has devised – controlled conditions are virtually impossible in classrooms (Sam is allocated a new working group near the front of the room). Results are collated (over several lessons Sam behaves acceptably and works quietly on task). Conclusions are drawn, and a new set of teaching behaviours is (hopefully) adopted. Sometimes, of course, the experiment fails and the process has to begin again. Eventually, the teacher may draw out some overall rule of procedure for dealing with Sam (Sam is disruptive if allowed to sit in the back corner with friends, and more inclined to concentrate when seated at the front of the room).

The example is simple, even simplistic. Some would argue that all the teacher has done has been to use common sense: teachers love the word 'instinct' for this kind of rapid response. But that's not quite accurate. What the teacher may have done, based on experience, is to have gone through the processes described very quickly, without consciously formulating the stages, even short-circuiting some.

REFLECTION

Have you experienced a Sam-style incident recently? What was the problem? What did you do to resolve it? Did your attempts work?

There is nothing wrong with the short-circuiting process we labelled 'instinctive behaviour'. When a novice or mentee watches a skilled practitioner/mentor at work the novice will often wonder at the apparent ease with which the role model handles situations that stretch the mentee beyond ability. But the phenomenon has attracted plenty of attention in education literature and Schon has described it with the phrase 'knowing-in-action':

> When we go about the spontaneous, intuitive performance of the actions of everyday life, we show ourselves to be knowledgeable in a special way ... Our knowing is ordinarily tacit, implicit in our patterns of action and in our feel for the stuff with which we are dealing. It seems right to say that our knowing is in our action.
>
> (Schon 1983: 49)

Good teachers make teaching and the analysis of teaching look easy – but we all know they are not. Many pedagogical problems are less simple than the one described (e.g. to what extent do boys underperform in school work compared with girls?). They need the full 'scientific' treatment over an extended period of time in order to find an answer or solution. However, there is a danger that in trying to define it we have made pedagogy sound easy and obvious, and this is misleading. There are plenty of debates about pedagogy and it is to these that we now turn.

——————— The pedagogy debates ———————

Competences or skills?

Competency-based teacher education gained credibility in the 1960s and has, like fungus, had sporadic outbreaks of growth ever since, most recently in the last 15 years. Like some fungus its presence is insidious: as a conceptual model for the process of effective teaching it is significantly flawed. It does, however, like the poisonous fly agaric toadstool, have superficial attractions.

The basic model on which competency-based teacher education works is this. It assumes that the process of effective teaching is essentially a series of actions through which the teacher goes more or less efficiently. If this process can be broken down into individual small units (competences), and the competences can then be acquired and sequenced correctly, the end product will be effective teaching. Furthermore, each competence can be learned individually and tested in the same way. A bag full of enough individual competences must therefore equal overall competence as a teacher.

This deceptively simple model has a number of advantages. If true, it means that passing on the competences is a relatively mechanistic matter that requires trainers rather than skilled educators to communicate to trainees; it robs the processes of their cognitive values. It eliminates most of what passes in classrooms for teacher judgement: it is the educational equivalent of painting by numbers. It means that the people selected to learn the competences can be those whose qualities of thinking and insight can be pitched at a lower level than on some alternative models. Politically, it has the potential to turn the science of teaching into the craft of teaching. It suggests that learning to teach can be carried out almost exclusively in classrooms by watching practitioners at work – the apprenticeship model. It has, therefore, the incidental advantage of making training cheaper. It plays down the role of intellectual engagement in the scientific process of teaching, i.e. pedagogy, and thus lowers the professionalism of those engaged in it. In turn it may make them cheaper to employ because they are no longer counted as full professionals.

None of these implied criticisms is designed to decry the value of some of the commonly used procedures and tools of competence-based teacher education.

The use of micro-teaching, the observation of experienced practitioners and the immersion of the trainee in the classroom are all valuable. But, we would argue, they are more valuable divorced from the craft-based apprenticeship model, when they are redefined as learning opportunities linked to analytical, cognitive, scientific and reflective processes (see below). The real concerns of the 'competent classroom' are more limited, as revealed in the subtitle to a recent book: 'aligning high school curriculum, standards and assessment' (Zmuda and Tomaino 2001).

So in our book we do not talk about competences. We use the more value-laden word 'skills'. How do skills differ from competences? In our view they differ in two quite critical ways. First, to have a skill suggests that the practitioner not only can 'perform the operation' implicit in the skill but that he/she understands the underlying rationale for the operation. Second, to operate at a skills level suggests that the practitioner undergoes a continuous process of reflection on the effect and effectiveness of the skills being practised.

So if one were to imagine a continuum, or set of continua, as below, then competences would be at the left side, while skills would be located toward the right:

Physical processes	_____	Intellectual processes
Ends in themselves	_____	Means to an end
Self-sufficient	_____	Reflective
Isolated actions	_____	Integrated actions
Behaviourist	_____	Constructivist

A skills-based model of teaching, developed by the Teacher Education Project in the 1980s, remains in our view a more defensible model for learning pedagogical skills than the competence models. This model (shown here as Fig. 2.1) begins from the view that a number of what might be called 'global skills' are essential to effective teaching. For example, such skills would be class management, asking effective questions, explaining clearly, or differentiating classroom tasks. These skills can, of course, be identified and they have a separate existence one from the other.

Each of these global skills implies a series of sub-skills or components: for class management these might include being vigilant, understanding the ripple effect (on-task behaviour is more prevalent wherever the teacher moves to in the room), and knowing the social dynamics of the class. Teachers or trainees can learn techniques of sub-skills like vigilance, for example, both through texts (like this one) and through watching and talking to effective practitioners.

Teacher educators can communicate these techniques and provide a basis for understanding them.

Over time, as practitioners ourselves, we can all improve the skills through experience by reflecting on and refining our own actions, and thus understanding them and their effects better. The effects of teaching (i.e. learning) are crucial. As an Ofsted survey of Key Stage 3 showed, effective learning does not necessarily result from teaching. This is a lesson that we seem to have to learn over and over again (Shaw 2003).

Furthermore, how well we operate as a teacher, our skill level, can be judged by skilled others (i.e. people who understand how to 'read' the largely invisible thought processes behind our actions and behaviour in the classroom). All of these processes go beyond the largely mechanistic competence model identified earlier.

REFLECTION

Have you improved your own skills in any area of pedagogy recently? Which area? What provoked you to improve? How did you bring about the improvement?

FIG. 2.1 A skills model for teaching

Practical teaching consists of skills

Skills can be isolated and identified

Skills can be broken down into component parts

Skills can be studied and taught

Skills can be learned

Skills can be reflected upon and refined

Skills can be evaluated and assessed

The Teacher Education Project always argued that teachers operating according to the skills model were highly aware of their behaviour and actions at all times. In using a particular tone of voice, in phrasing a question in a particular way, in standing at a specific point in the room, the teacher was consciously aware of the effect of the action. The greater and more constant this self-awareness, the deeper the understanding that went with it, the more skilled and the more effective was the teaching.

Poor teachers, by contrast, were unaware of the effect of their spoken language and their actions, the hidden messages of their body language, and so on.

There was potential or actual mismatch between the teacher's skill and the needs of the class at that moment. Self-awareness implied the ability not merely to communicate more effectively and appropriately with the class, but to be able to read the returning signals and adapt to them quickly: for example, responding to signs of incipient boredom (a yawn, a tendency for some pupils' eyes to glaze over) by a deliberate change of activity and involvement of individuals in the task.

Recent research has tended to confirm the absolute inseparability of teacher behaviours from teachers' immediate cognitive processes in the classroom. In a study by Meijer, Douwe and Verloop (2002: 164) there is an attempt to clarify 'what goes on in teachers' minds while they are teaching'. While this research concentrates mainly on the content of teaching during lessons, the findings remain seminal. Meijer et al. maintain that 'teachers' interactive cognitions are dynamic in essence' (p.169); that teachers have split-second thoughts which, while tied to the specific context of the lesson, are also reflective of their knowledge and beliefs and their 'classroom practice' (teaching skills); these thoughts are integrative in nature. If Meijer et al. are correct, then we have to acknowledge that teaching is substantially more than the hoop-jumping of the competency model, even if at the present stage of our knowledge we are not able to describe exhaustively the entire process by which it operates.

REFLECTION

What classroom 'signs' have you read recently? How did you respond to them? What was going through your mind when you did so?

Teaching as reflection

So far in the chapter variants of the verb 'reflect' have been used about the process of teaching half a dozen times times, so one could conclude that it is becoming a seminal concept of pedagogy. The research approach itself implies reflection on the process of teaching. However, as yet, no attempt has been made here to define or describe what reflection is. This omission must now be redressed.

Zeichner and Tabachnick (2001) do a useful job in reviewing the kinds of theories of reflective practice that appear in the literature of teacher education and they discern four models (Fig. 2.2). They conclude, very reasonably, that the four traditions are different in emphasis rather than mutually exclusive, but they ask: what does reflection look like in practice?

FIG. 2.2 Perspectives on reflective teaching

- *Academic perspective*: concerns itself with academic subject matter and reflection on this to produce student learning and understanding
- *Social efficiency perspective*: reflection, based on reading or research for example, that concerns itself with teaching methods and approaches
- *Developmentalist perspective*: reflection that is sensitive to and takes account of student needs, interests, learning preferences and growth or development
- *Social reconstructionalist perspective*: concerns itself with political and social dimensions of teaching and schooling, and the contribution of classroom events to social justice, democracy, equity and improvements in society

Source: Based on Zeichner and Tabachnick (2001)

Various schools of thought emerge in attempting an answer to Zeichner and Tabachnick's question about definitions of reflection. The next paragraph looks at three different approaches.

Some maintain that, since teaching is so busy an occupation (with up to a thousand interpersonal contacts per day) there is little or no time for reflection. Others suggest that 'post mortem reflection' (reflection at a quiet time after the act of teaching) is rare. Schon (1983) is consistent in arguing for a view of reflection in action: that teachers process their thoughts and change their behaviours within the time spans of lessons and even exchanges with pupils.

While our own concept of self-awareness supports Schon's view, we do not rule out the value (still less the existence) of post mortem reflection. Increasingly, such reflection – often written up as a journal or log in which classroom events are described and then subjected to scrutiny – is becoming a requirement of higher degrees in education or professional qualifications. Professional diaries, reflective logs, critical reviews and professional papers are just some of the descriptors of these outcomes of the reflective process. Such reflections are often based on critical incident theories borrowed from research paradigms, which suggest that some events and how they are handled have profound effects on the life of an institution, classroom or group. An example of an extract from a typical log of this kind is shown as Table 2.1.

TABLE 2.1   Reflection on (part of) a lesson

Class 7w Science: Migration

[This account has been shortened by the use of the ... device. In practice other portions of the lesson would be described in a bit more detail, as the opening is.]

This is a single-lesson theory period. The pupils are generally well disposed to science but are less happy with these theory sessions than practicals. Decided to open with a fairly open, questioning approach to engage attention, then focus down a bit. Began by asking the questions I had planned:

- Who knows what the word 'migration' means?
- Can you think of any examples?
- Who or what migrates?
- Why do you think this happens?
- How do the migrants decide where to go?

This bit of the lesson didn't go as well as I hoped. The class had come from PE (I should have remembered that) and there was a bit of adrenaline still flowing about incidents in one of the games. So the 'wide boy' of the class, Neil, quipped that migration was what you did out of school if you got half a chance. Laughter. Had to become disciplinarian, and this destroyed the informality a bit.

Managed to elicit eventually something along the lines of 'movements of humans or animals', and a few actual examples – birds, lemmings, nomads.

When we got down to the why? question there was a slight relapse into inappropriate humour, but we got to the point that it might be to do with consciousness of external circumstances, or to some unconscious drive. Then we were able to start looking at the much more difficult question of the mechanism that determines where migrants go ...

We went on to look at examples of creatures that migrate and started to act as 'investigators' of their behaviour ...

The pupils broke into groups to look at some long-distance migrants using data from reference books and CD-ROMS I had brought in; and then they pooled their knowledge ...

Before the end of the lesson we set up the task for next time, which is to explore what navigation systems are used, and I gave them an offprint to read for homework – a piece from the RSPB magazine on this topic ...

I think if I did this lesson again I would tackle the opening differently. I liked the open question approach and the investigation caught the pupils' interest. But I needed to get attention quicker and more assertively, especially as they always come hyped up from games. I think I would have a short but interesting print-out or newspaper cutting on the theme, and get them seated and quietly reading first – then move into the questions when everything was calm. The investigation (they like being 'investigators') would then follow on quite well: they enjoyed the Arctic tern material and they started quite a good debate (which I'll pick up for a homework task) about whether birds could navigate by the stars given that it was often cloudy.

Bain et al. (2002) studied the process of reflective log writing in teacher development. They looked at the feedback given to reflective writers by their mentors. Their conclusion was that the greatest gains to writers were achieved when the feedback concentrated on the level of reflection reached rather than on the teaching issues themselves – a case, perhaps, in support of the metacognitive process as a teaching vehicle (see Chapter 11). Their research is important in drawing out some typologies of reflective writing as follows:

- as a *record* of reflective thinking – putting your existing thoughts on paper
- as a *motivator* of reflective thinking – writing forces you to think about what happened in more detail and depth
- as an *extension* of reflective thinking – writing makes you more analytical and helps you to order your thoughts.

But reflection alone is not enough. Teachers need to be not merely reflective (i.e. to engage in a process of thinking critically and systematically about their own practice) but also reflexive (i.e. to translate the outcomes of the reflection into new forms of hopefully more effective action). Such new or experimental actions will have their roots (inevitably) in the value systems of the teacher who determines them (see Chapter 1), but will also retain the scientific approach to teaching and planning for teaching described earlier in this chapter.

We would maintain that reflection on teaching can be carried out in a number of different modes, that it may have a variety of motivations and that it should also result in either changed or at least better understood practice. This is summarised in Table 2.2.

TABLE 2.2 Reflection: a summary of modes, motivations and practice outcomes

Modes	Motivations	Practice outcomes
Reflection-in-action	To cope better with an immediate problem	Better in-class response to students
Reflection post mortem, e.g. what went wrong and why?	To improve skills long term	Improved rationale for practice
Reflection in writing, e.g. for a course of study	To fulfil requirements of external bodies, access to qualifications	Establishment of self as advanced skills practitioner
Reflection through shared practice, e.g. a discussion with colleagues in a staff meeting	To improve practice through shared professional wisdom	Security in shared practice and acceptance of areas of difficulty
Reflection for assessment, e.g. appraisal	To fulfil the requirements of the school	Professional advancement
Reflection for an audience	To satisfy personal or research-based curiosity	Published paper or lead role
Reflection for reflection's sake	Intrinsic satisfaction	Enhanced professional self-confidence

Having considered the nature of reflection and its role in helping teachers to examine and refine pedagogical skills, you might try your hand at writing a short reflective piece of your own based on a critical incident. Some notes of guidance are provided to assist you in this process (Activity 2.1).

ACTIVITY 2.1

Reflective writing

Choose a critical incident that happened to you in your classroom this week.

Write it up in a reflective way, using the notes of guidance provided below and the typology suggested by Bain et al. (2002).

What have you learned (a) from the process and (b) from the incident?

Critical incidents: notes of guidance

A key element of your writing will be to look analytically and in an evaluative way at how your incident developed. In this context, critical incidents are events (which may seem minor or cataclysmic at the time) that shape what happens next in a significant way.

Sometimes these events will be obvious (e.g. a vital component breaks at a crucial moment); sometimes it is only in hindsight or on reflection that the event will be seen to be critical (a team member drops out and another replaces him/her and happens to bring an unforeseen skill).

Identifying these critical incidents is a skill in itself, but one that improves with time.

Writing about them is a quite separate skill that involves a good deal of insight. The trick is to:

- Spot the incident

- Understand its impact on a situation

- Be able to define what has changed

- Be able to sort the negative and positive outcomes

- Be able to weigh the consequences.

Often, for the purposes of the log, it is important to describe the event (for the benefit of the reader – but quite briefly), then to interrogate it in the ways suggested above.

Critical events are open to questions like:

- Why was it important?

- What effects did it have?

- Who benefitted/was disadvantaged?

- What qualities did it bring out?

- How did it change thinking and perception?

By all accounts a very critical event was Newton's being hit on the head by a falling apple! You could think about this and use it as model for your own examples.

Understanding what is happening in classrooms

If pedagogy is the science of teaching, or even just the systematic recording of and reflection upon classroom events, then it ought to be pretty simple to understand.

Well, that's the theory. In practice, we all 'know' about classrooms and what happens in them; the trouble is we all 'know' something different. Teachers 'know' their pupils, the content and what they are trying to teach. Most school governors 'know' enough about the classrooms in their schools to make judgements about school policy, even though very few ever visit them. Politicians 'know' enough about classrooms to be able to implement all-embracing national legislation, even though that might seem to fly in the face of local, regional or specific needs and conditions. Academics, LEA managers, parents and members of the public all have their own forms of 'knowing'.

So this section tries to explore some aspects of knowing and, more importantly, understanding about pedagogy in order to gain a perspective that might be helpful to the practitioner.

Pedagogy as research

The first dimension for the understanding of pedagogy that we shall examine here is that of research. If we want to understand 'the science' of teaching, then logically we must look at the scientific (i.e. research-based) analysis of it.

At its simplest, the research approach to pedagogy suggests that teaching is a process (acts and behaviours, performed by teachers, involving students, and their learning) that can be subjected to objective scrutiny using accepted methodologies and canons of research akin to those in the other social sciences, such as psychology and sociology. The findings can be analysed, conclusions drawn, and practice improved.

This broad statement is easily defensible and widely accepted, for example, in the many research papers that appear in journals of teacher education. It is typified by the words of Carr and Kemmis (1986):

> A critical education science ... envisages a form of educational research that is conducted by those involved in education themselves. It takes a view of educational research as critical analysis of the transformation of educational values of those involved ... and the social institutional structures that provide the framework for their action.
>
> (Carr and Kemmis 1986: 14)

REFLECTION

How have you researched your own classroom practice or that of a colleague recently? What changed – actions, attitudes, values – as a result of this research?

This overall definition of pedagogy as research is useful, though there are issues to raise about it. There are at least two research traditions, and their approaches are very different. The first is sometimes referred to as 'pure' research and the other as 'applied' research.

Applied research refers, of course, to research aimed at finding pragmatic or practical answers to questions about how to teach better – the sort of thing you probably thought about in the last Reflection panel. Typically, teachers want to know what content works best, how to put across material in ways that pupils find interesting, or whether a particular approach produces improved examination results.

Much of this kind of research falls to research methods that centre around case study in general, or the particular version of case study labelled action research. The rule-of-thumb difference between these is that in case study the researcher often looks (using qualitative, quantitative, or a mixture of data) at a school, a class or an issue (teaching an aspect of curriculum, for example) as a detached observer (say, in someone else's classroom); in action research the researcher remains an active participant in the situation, involving himself in the situation and often changing the course of events (for example, experimenting with different curriculum approaches in his own class and consciously investigating the benefits and disadvantages of each).

By contrast, the 'pure' research tradition emphasises the generation of new concepts or of clarifying ways of thinking about teaching without concerning itself primarily with pragmatic outcomes. It is the cerebral process and the concern with 'ideas' that counts and not whether these make John or Jane a better teacher.

In this text we tend towards the applied research paradigm, since we are interested more in the improvement (Carr and Kemmis's *transformation*) of teaching than in speculating about its nature and conceptualisation – though of course the two processes cannot (and should not) be entirely divorced from one another. The core issue is one of perspective.

Embedded in these contrasting approaches are other debates. One of these is about the philosophical underpinning of research. The dichotomy here is between those who hold what are labelled scientific or positivist views on the one hand and those who are so-called phenomenologists on the other. Scientific approaches to research, as we have hinted above, follow in the footsteps of the social scientists in attempting, for example, to test empirically (i.e. through experimentation) the best way to achieve desired results in learning. Phenomenological approaches are described by Pring (2000), whose whole text is well worth more extended attention:

> *Since an 'educational practice' is where individuals 'make sense' (starting from their different perspectives) of experience, struggle to understand, and come to find value in different things and activities, then it cannot be grasped within general laws or theories. Educational enquiry becomes focused upon individuals, making explicit what is unique and distinctive of the 'thinking life' of each, and interpreting what is seen through the personal ideas which make each action intelligible.*
>
> (Pring 2000: 323)

Phenomenology often concentrates on what happens in specific instances or 'cases' (a single classroom, when a particular unit of curriculum is changed, in a specific school).

REFLECTION

Assume your classroom is a case, i.e. a specific instance to be studied. What do you want to know about it that would improve your functioning as a teacher within it?

This kind of research is valuable and produces viable insights to guide practice, but it is often a difficult area from which to formulate generalised behaviours. What works for you and your classroom may not work for someone else in theirs. So Pring goes on to argue that these dichotomies between scientific and phenomenological approaches are essentially false.

Another apparent dichotomy is between the value of qualitative data (open-ended observations, semi-structured questionnaire or interview data, and so on) and quantitative data (marks, scores, calculations of significance, etc.). Silverman (2000) shows that both kinds of data can work together to throw different but complementary lights on the same problem. Both approaches can be used to illuminate aspects of classroom practice.

For example, you could use test results to identify an improvement over time in your class's reading scores, but the score would not explain the reasons for the improvement. To understand why the change has come about you might have to employ qualitative data such as asking pupils, observing them when they read, interviewing the support staff about changes they had made in their approach to supporting reading, and so on.

If research ought to be underpinning pedagogy, providing both a rationale for teacher behaviour and a way of investigating improvements to practice or the effectiveness of classroom innovation, it can nevertheless fail to achieve the ideal. Often, in schools and among teachers, one can hear research and researchers vilified. At one level this is because there has been a systematic attempt by some politicians and academics to play down the significance of research (often when its outcomes fail to support a favoured dogma). But more importantly, perhaps, it is because teachers themselves are not sufficiently involved in doing research. Hancock (2001) provides a useful analysis of why this is the case, and concludes it is because of:

■ a lack of expectation that teachers should research and write about their practice

■ the demanding and busy nature of the teacher's job that leaves little time and energy for reflection and investigation

■ low teacher morale as a result of low public perception of the profession

■ the inappropriate match between research methods and ways in which teachers work in classrooms.

Good teachers, of course, investigate aspects of their teaching all the time. The prevalence of higher degree courses over recent years, however, may be changing the situation described by Hancock; and the DfES tried to promote teacher-based research through the use of Best Practice Scholarships, though in 2003 it abandoned this scheme. In the field of education leadership, as opposed to classroom teaching, Wilkins (2002: 35) argued that there was 'a degree of correlation between engagement in practitioner research, the holding of certain beliefs about education, and preferences for certain approaches' to education. He suggested the presence of a 'practitioner research community in education, which exists as a subculture'. If this is mirrored among classroom teachers, because more and more of them are researching their own classrooms, then the ambition would be to turn the sub-culture of the few into the culture of the many.

Research certainly contributes much to our understanding of pedagogy, and there is a rich tradition and history of pedagogical research in the UK even if it is not always teacher-led research: for example, by Galton et al. (1980), Kerry and Eggleston (1988) and Wragg (1993) in the primary phase, in Rutter's (1979) seminal study in the secondary field, and the work of Elliott (1993) in action-based research.

We would maintain that research and pedagogy have to go hand in hand, and that progress and development in the latter depends almost exclusively on the former.

Pedagogy as good practice

Though we have emphasised thus far an investigative approach to the understanding and achievement of pedagogical improvement, there are alternative models, of which replicating good practice is a prevalent one. This perspective has its underpinning in the belief that teachers learn more effective practice through exposure to observing or reading about good practice. This premise underpins much official literature in education. Indeed, it has become the hall-mark of the operation of Ofsted and the inspection business. It involves, typically:

- selecting out locations where an aspect of pedagogy is judged (by inspectors) to be handled well

- studying how that aspect is dealt with in the chosen locations

- identifying common elements in the practices

- distilling those elements into guidance

- recommending the guidance to other (less effective) practitioners.

This process is illustrated in a press release from Ofsted, chosen more or less at random from items being issued as we wrote (Fig. 2.3.) It could be described as an evidence-based approach (because it does use observations by competent and informed professionals). It is not, however, research, though it is often described as such. The observations are not normally carried out by specifically trained observers whose judgements have been correlated. They are often open-ended and therefore subject to changing criteria, and the instruments used (if there are any) are not normally tested for validity and reliability.

FIG. 2.3 Example of an Ofsted press release

OFSTED CONCLUDES THAT LITERACY AND NUMERACY STRATEGIES ARE COMPAT-IBLE WITH FULL PRIMARY CURRICULUM

The Ofsted report, *The Curriculum in Successful Primary Schools*, is published today. This report considers whether the primary curriculum is overloaded, given the requirements of the National Literacy and National Numeracy Strategies.

Inspectors conclude that it is possible to meet the requirements of the national curriculum and still maintain an appropriate emphasis on literacy and numeracy.

The report follows the feedback from some headteachers during the year 2000 that the National Literacy and Numeracy Strategies (NLNS) were squeezing out the rest of the curriculum.

The schools surveyed achieved success using their professional judgement to select those aspects of the national curriculum that they felt should have more emphasis. They were then able to ensure that the curriculum reflected the particular needs of their pupils and made best use of their locality.

Her Majesty's Inspectors (HMI) looked at over 30 schools which had a good quality and range of learning opportunities, and where the standards of attainment in English and mathematics achieved in the national curriculum tests in 2001 were in the top 25 per cent. These schools have achieved what others claim is not possible.

They have high standards in English, mathematics and science, while giving a strong emphasis to humanities, physical education and the arts. The richness of the curriculum in these schools, and, in particular, their achievements in the arts, con-tributed to pupils' creativity and self-confidence.

Headteachers in these schools are dedicated to school improvement, and created a strong sense of teamwork. The curriculum is viewed as the means for realising the their vision and the school's objectives. They also fully endorse the NLNS, and recognise that they were key to achieving high standards.

The report also concludes that leaving decisions about the curriculum in the hands of the schools, while still requiring them to keep within the broad framework of the national curriculum, is a workable solution to the problems of perceived over-load. The overriding factor in the schools in the survey was the greater sense of control over what to emphasise. Teachers make good use of links across subjects, creating longer blocks of time to undertake sustained work on themes covering two or more subjects.

The report states that other schools can follow the example of those in the sample and achieve these high standards, provided they are given the proper training and support. However, the report recognises that these changes cannot happen overnight. Other examples of such good practice can be found in primary schools throughout the country. The challenge is for other schools to match the level of consistency and coherence demonstrated by those in the sample.

David Bell, Her Majesty's Chief Inspector of Schools, said: 'This report shows that the national curriculum and the literacy and numeracy strategies can all be taught successfully and in ways which achieve not only high standards in English and maths but in the other curriculum subjects too.'

The report concludes that where training is provided it should:

- encourage headteachers and staff to understand that they have the freedom, within statutory requirements, to provide a curriculum that is distinctive to their own particular needs and circumstances
- consider issues of continuity in the primary curriculum, including the transition between the foundation stage and Key Stage 1, and between Key Stage 2 and Key Stage 3
- emphasise strongly the importance of the headteacher's leadership in develop-ing and improving the curriculum
- ensure that guidance and examples of ways of working reflect schools' different circumstances and the very different starting points from which any curriculum will begin
- contribute to the national initiative to reduce teachers' workloads, particularly where curriculum planning is concerned.

This press release needs little commentary, but you may find it helpful to carry out Activity 2.2.

ACTIVITY 2.2

Examining pedagogy as good practice

Read the press release set out in Fig. 2.3.

Identify the features of it that define pedagogy as replicating good practice.

How persuaded are you of the case being made by the press release?

What are the arguments both for and against this approach, as exemplified in Fig. 2.3?

What is your estimate of how likely it is that this approach alone can change practice effectively?

What possible alternatives might there be to this approach?

Pedagogy as good intention

Pedagogy as good intention shares many of the characteristics of pedagogy as good practice, but is one step further removed from the process. A definition of this approach might be that the perpetrator:

establishes a vision or intention for the outcome of teaching and infers backwards from an apparently successful result that the process of arriving at the result is necessarily exemplary.

If that sounds a little complicated, an example will clarify the matter. Because you believe that the economic future prosperity of the nation depends on good exam results, you decide that it would be a good thing if 90 per cent of pupils in a school gained five A*–C grades at GCSE level: *the intention*. You cajole staff into working towards that end: *the process*. At results time 90 per cent of pupils hit the target: *the outcome*. Therefore you conclude that the teaching in the school is exemplary: *the inference*. If this sounds familiar it is because it mirrors the history of political involvement in education since 1988.

Of course, there may be nothing wrong with the original intention (subject always to a sensitive understanding that schools and social settings are not all identical). The vision is well intentioned – the enhanced performance of pupils; though whether a public examination is the best way of achieving a measure of this is an open question. The outcome is in accord with the vision, but the process or means of arriving at that point remains open to question. Some schools will have reverted to a strongly didactic means of teaching. Other ploys will have been used, too: selecting the 'easiest' exam board or syllabus; teaching strictly to the content in a over-narrow way; promoting reliance on model answers rather than thinking skills; neglecting other important classroom activities, and so on.

Thus pedagogy is not necessarily enhanced just because the intention is benign and the desired result appears to have been reached. Indeed, inducements such as performance-related pay, which is dependent on these same tables of results, may even drive teachers further from the goals of effective pedagogy in the search for enhanced reward. Nor do teachers always judge correctly their own intentions. Fung and Chow (2002) report that among student teachers at any rate there was a widespread belief that they were pursuing a nurturing model of teaching when actually they were following apprenticeship and transmission approaches.

The Standards for Qualified Teachers (TTA 1998, 2002) have been criticised on just these kinds of ground by a variety of writers, as summarised by Docking:

■ There is no explicit account of how teaching is conceptualised.

■ The implicit requirements for teachers are more about content knowledge and craft skills to assess National Curriculum than about pedagogical excellence.

■ There is inadequate attention paid to the teaching process outside the narrow confines of one teacher–one classroom.

■ The standards represent a view of education described as 'dreary utilitarianism'. (Docking 2000: 149–50).

This kind of approach can never be adequate as the basis for a profession or for professional activity. Indeed, the whole structure of this kind of thinking may well be flawed, and the original intention itself and the philosophy underpining it have to be questioned. This at least is the view of Levin (2002) who claims:

> *The limited potential of achievement on standardised examinations to create economic success has also been verified internationally. It is obvious that one of the incentives for a nation to perform well in international comparisons of educational achievement is the assumption that such advantages will lead to more productive and competitive labour forces and economic advantage. Unfortunately the evidence does not support this assumption.*
>
> (Levin 2002: 549)

REFLECTION

What 'good intentions' can you identify in your school? Are they achieved? Why do they fail? What flawed thinking underpins them?

Pedagogy as metaphor

Our final model for examining pedagogy is rather more esoteric than the previous example, and comes from Robin Alexander. To give the flavour it will be necessary to quote from this source at some length:

> *Teaching, like music, is* **performance**. *That performance can be preceded by* **composition** *(lesson planning) and in execution is thus an* **interpretation**, *or it can be completely or partly* **improvisatory**. *The performance of teaching can be in planning* **orchestrated** *and in execution* **conducted** *– with varying degrees of competence and persuasiveness ... teaching is bounded and constrained, as is music, by* **time** *...Time in teaching comprises* **time-intended** *and* **actual time spent**, *and in each case we have* **pulse, tempo** *or* **speed** *and* **rhythm** *... A lesson can be dominated by one or more clearly discernible* **themes, melodic lines** *or indeed* **leitmotifs**, *and these can be* **harmonically** *sustained or they can be woven together in a* **contrapuntal** *relationship.*
>
> (Alexander 2001: 17)

Alexander agues that, while this may be interesting as an analogy, the picture goes far beyond that:

> *This approach to the concept of* **form** *illuminates the relationship between the structure and organisation of teaching and its meaning; that tempo takes us beyond the familiar process variables of 'time for learning', 'opportunity to learn' and 'pupil time on task'; while* **melody**, *harmony, polyphony and* **counterpoint** *help me to unravel the way the messages of teaching – whether explicit or implicit, congruent or incongruent – are developed and relate to each other over the course of a single lesson.*
>
> (Alexander 2001: 18, author's emphasis)

Alexander uses the argument to explore the issue of school effectiveness through lesson observation across a range of countries and concludes that 'school effectiveness as currently conducted manages to defy both logic and common sense by making culture peripheral to cross-cultural analysis'. He critiques preoccupation with structures and systems and regards this as reducing pedagogy from considered educational act to mindless technique.

In this approach Alexander could be construed as an extreme exponent of teaching as art rather than science. To the extent that his conclusion is congruent with that developed through the other models described here – that it dismisses the dumbing down of pedagogy to the status of a mere sequence of predetermined actions or techniques acquired in the footsteps of an experienced mentor, an imitative paradigm – it remains valid. However, the characterisation of teaching as art form is deceptively seductive. It suggests that teaching skills are inherent rather than learned or learnable; that performance may be genetic rather than acquired; and that effective lessons depend on inspiration rather than analysis to produce results. Art requires high doses of creativity and uniqueness, while – as McLaughlin (2002) rightly points out – for teachers, 'communities of practice generate knowledge and understanding that is different in kind from that produced by individuals alone'.

REFLECTION

How do 'communities of knowledge' (colleagues in your department, school, professional association, etc.) generate for you knowledge and understanding that augment your own?

———— Pedagogy in context ————

Pedagogy looks at classroom events from the perspective of teaching, but pedagogy has contexts. One of those contexts is that of learning, which we discuss in more detail in Chapter 5. These two chapters need to be seen as complementary, but for the present purpose let us take a single example of this interplay.

National Training Laboratories in Bethel, Maine, USA, have developed research resulting in a learning pyramid that demonstrates the correlation between the style of delivery (teaching) of what is learned on the one hand, and how much the learner retains (%) on the other. (This can be found at www.ntl.org.) The pyramid itself looks like this:

Lecture 5%

Reading 10%

Audio-visual 20%

Demonstration 30%

Discussion group 50%

Practice by doing 75%

Teach others/immediate use of learning 90%

Clearly, being aware of these data should condition the teacher's choice of peda-gogical approach. The use of lecture or didactic teaching would be restricted, while the immediate practice of knowledge by pupils in appropriate exercises or simulations would be heightened. So what we know (from research) about learning has an effect on the way we teach: pedagogy. Similar considerations would apply to such issues as students' preferred learning styles, and so on.

There are other contexts too: where teaching takes place; the teacher's philos-ophy of education and curriculum; the facilities and equipment available to teacher and learner; the physical conditions (such as heat, cold); the training available to staff; the culture of the school; the quality of leadership. All of these impact on the pedagogy. Awareness is a stage on the path to overcoming obstacles.

Because of the number of variables involved and the difficulties in recording and measuring the quality of teaching, wide-ranging but detailed research stud-ies of these issues are quite few and far between. At the national level, some that have come close to this kind of research are the Oracle/Galton studies in primary schools and the Rutter work in secondary locations (referred to above).

We have attached an appendix to this book which is a research study that we carried out along these lines. You should read this appendix and then proceed to carry out Activity 2.3.

ACTIVITY 2.3

Tracking the influences that help or hinder effective pedagogy

The study in the appendix to this book on pages 259–74 provides the research base for looking at pedagogy in one primary school following a school building programme.

Read the study and try to assess from the available evidence:

■ What was successful about the teaching?

■ What was unsuccessful?

■ What were the factors that contributed to lack of success?

■ Of these last, what could be changed for the better and how?

■ How would you apportion responsibility for any pedagogical shortcomings identified in the study?

■ Do any of the findings in this research surprise you? Which? Why?

■ How does this school compare with schools you are familiar with?

In carrying out Activity 2.3 you will, among other issues, be brought face to face with considering aspects of the teacher's role and the teacher's knowledge that are pursued in more depth in Chapter 3.

At the end of this chapter you should have:

■ Reached a better understanding of the notion of pedagogy

■ Discovered some of the factors that make for successful approaches to pedagogy

■ Contextualised and analysed the relationship of pedagogy to other school phenomena

■ Become familiar with reflective approaches to teaching

■ Begun to use the material to inform your own incisiveness as a teacher

———— References ————

Alexander, R. (2001) 'Pedagogy and culture: a perspective in search of a method', in J. Solar, A. Craft and H. Burgess, *Teacher Development: Exploring Our Own Practice,* London: Paul Chapman.

Bain, J., Mills, C., Ballantyne, R. and Packer, J. (2002) 'Developing reflection of practice through journal writing: impacts of variations in the focus and level of feedback', *Teachers and Teaching: Theory and Practice*, 8(2): 176–96.

Carr, W. and Kemmis, S. (1986) *Becoming Critical: Education, Knowledge and Action* Research, Brighton: Falmer Press.

Docking, J. (2000) *New Labour's Policies for Schools,* London: David Fulton.

Elliott, J. (1993) 'Professional development in a land of choice and diversity: the future challenge for action research', in D. Bridges, and T. Kerry, *Developing Teachers Professionally,* London: Routledge.

Fung, L. and Chow, L. (2002) 'Congruence of student teachers' pedagogical images and actual classroom practice', *Educational Research*, 44(3): 311–21.

Galton, M., Simon, B. and Croll, P. (1980) *Inside the Primary Classroom,* London: Routledge & Kegan Paul.

Hancock, R. (2001) 'Why are class teachers reluctant to become researchers?', in J. Solar, A. Craft and H. Burgess, *Teacher Development: Exploring Our Own Practice,* London: Paul Chapman.

Kerry, T. and Eggleston, J. (1988) *Topic Work in the Primary School,* London: Routledge.

Levin, H. (2002) 'Pedagogical challenges for educational futures in industrializing countries', *Comparative Education Review*, 45(4): 537–62.

McLaughlin, M. (2002) 'Sites and sources of teachers' learning', in C. Sugrue and D. Day, *Developing Teachers and Teaching Practice: International Research Perspectives,* London: Routledge Falmer.

Meijer, P., Douwe, B. and Verloop, N. (2002) 'Examining teachers' interactive cognitions using insights from research on teachers' practical knowledge' in C. Sugrue and D. Day, *Developing Teachers and Teaching Practice: International Research Perspectives,* London: Routledge Falmer.

Pring, R. (2000) *Philosophy of Educational Research,* London: Continuum.

Rutter, M. (1979) *Fifteen Thousand Hours,* London: Open Books.

Schon, D.A. (1983) *The Reflective Practitioner: How Professionals Think In Action,* New York: Basic Books.

Shaw, M. (2003) 'Teaching, not learning, improves', *Times Educational Supplement*, 7 March: 14.

Silverman, D. (2000) *Doing Qualitative Research: A Practical Handbook,* London: Sage.

Wilkins, R. (2002) 'Practitioner research and perceptions of school leadership', *Education Today*, 52(4): 29–36.

Wragg. E.C. (1993) *The Leverhulme Project,* London: Routledge.

Zeichner, K. and Tabachnick, B. (2001) 'Reflections on reflective teaching', in J. Solar, A. Craft and H. Burgess, *Teacher Development: Exploring Our Own Practice,* London: Paul Chapman.

Zmuda, A. and Tomaino, M. (2001) *The Competent Classroom: Aligning High School Curriculum, Standards and Assessment,* New York: Teachers' College Press.

chapter three

The educated teacher

Knowledge, understanding and professionalism

In this chapter you are invited to:

- Explore the dimensions of what it means to be 'a teacher'

- Examine the idea of what is a 'good' or 'effective' teacher

- Consider the implications of this for you as a professional

- Examine the nature of knowledge in relation to the teacher

The dimensions of being a teacher

Teaching is a complicated job that requires the synthesis of knowledge, skills, understanding and professionalism. At the simplest level, teachers can be defined by the tasks they undertake. Of course they teach, but the role, whether in a primary or secondary context, covers numerous supporting tasks. The School Teachers' Pay and Conditions Document identifies 12 professional duties that form the basis of a classroom teacher's job description, which in summary are:

- teaching

- other activities (mostly pastoral related)

- assessments and reports

- appraisal

- review, induction, further training and development

- educational methods

- discipline, health and safety

- staff meetings

- cover

- public examinations

- management

- administration.

ACTIVITY 3.1

Discovering what you do when you teach

Keep a diary for a day and jot down what you have spent your time doing in your teaching role (or observe another teacher if you are not currently teaching).

How many different tasks have you (or your observee) undertaken?

What have you (or your observee) spent most time on?

What is a good or effective teacher?

In recent years the government has invested a great deal of money in trying to define more accurately the skills and competences required to carry out the tasks of a teacher effectively or how to be 'an *effective* teacher' (this doesn't necessarily correspond directly to the idea of a *good* teacher since 'good' suggests a more subjective judgement – see below).

In June 2000 a detailed report was published by Hay McBer, based on research findings, entitled *Research into Teacher Effectiveness – A Model of Teacher Effectiveness*. This was commissioned by the then Department for Education and Employment (DfEE; now DfES).

The research identified three broad dimensions that combine and complement each other in defining effective teaching: teaching skills, professional characteristics and classroom climate.

Teaching skills

All teachers need to know their subjects, the appropriate teaching methods for their subjects and curriculum areas, and the ways pupils learn. Key aspects of these, which form the basis of Ofsted evaluation of teaching and the recommended observation schedules for performance management, are:

- Lesson flow and time-on-task

- Planning

- Pupil management/discipline

- Assessment

- High expectations

- Methods and strategies

- Time and resource management

- Homework

Professional characteristics

Ongoing patterns of behaviour that make teachers effective – how you do the job, reflecting your style and values. Five clusters of 16 characteristics were identified (Fig. 3.1).

FIG 3.1 The five clusters

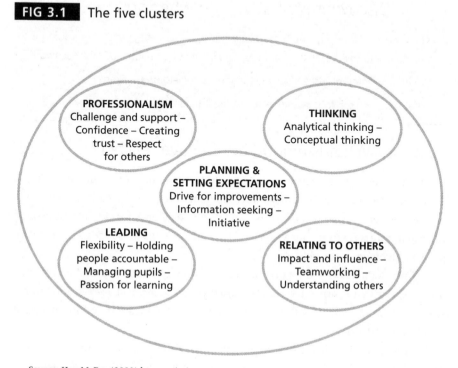

Source: Hay McBer (2000) by permission

Classroom climate

A measure was made of the collective perceptions of pupils regarding those dimensions of the classroom environment that have a direct impact on their capacity and motivation to learn. Nine key aspects of this were identified:

1 **Clarity** around the purpose of each lesson. How each lesson relates to the broader subject, as well as clarity regarding the aims and objectives of the school.

2 **Order** within the classroom, where discipline, order and civilised behaviour are maintained.

3 A clear set of **standards** as to how pupils should behave and what each pupil should do and try to achieve, with a clear focus on higher rather than minimum standards.

4 **Fairness**: the degree to which there is an absence of favouritism and a consistent link between rewards in the classroom and actual performance.

5 **Participation**: the opportunity for pupils to participate actively in the class by discussion, questioning, giving out materials, and other similar activities.

6 **Support**: feeling emotionally supported in the classroom, so that pupils are willing to try new things and learn from mistakes.

7 **Safety**: the degree to which the classroom is a safe place, where pupils are not at risk from emotional or physical bullying, or other fear-arousing factors.

8 **Interest**: the feeling that the classroom is an interesting and exciting place to be where pupils feel stimulated to learn.

9 **Environment**: the feeling that the classroom is a comfortable, well-organised, clean and attractive physical environment.

From having very little in terms of a framework for criteria and qualifications for career progression in teaching a few years ago, the government has now put into place a far-reaching structure of standards and competences. The influence of the Hay McBer dimensions permeates throughout this conceptual map (see Fig. 3.1). The influence of Hay McBer is positive in that what the authors of this report managed to do was to pull together much extant research and to synthesise it. The downside of the process was that the report was substantially retrospective. It did not break new ground, was not future-orientated and certainly did not carry out ground-breaking work into theories and methods of pedagogy or how these would impinge on schools of the future. This comment is to give a perspective to this work and does not detract from the report's worthiness overall as a statement of existing wisdom.

REFLECTION

How will schools change over the next 10 to 20 years (i.e. within your professional lifetime)? How will these changes affect our views of teaching and learning?

National standards

As a result of its current thinking, the government has put in place a set of national standards for Qualified Teacher Status (QTS). These standards have been revised recently and the latest standards appear as Teacher Training Agency (TTA) (2002). In the consultation phase of this process the standards themselves were accompanied by a handbook, which was detailed and either helpful or pre-scriptive, depending on one's point of view. The handbook was not published as part of TTA (2002), though it is a document that repays study (Teacher Training Agency (TTA) 2001). Like the Hay McBer work, these standards are worthy as broad statements of intent for today's situations and the caveat has to be borne in mind when dealing with them.

For the beginning teacher the first set of standards comprises the Standards for the Award of Qualified Teacher Status (QTS). Once QTS status has been achieved, one is then judged and evaluated against the Induction Standards. Aspiring teachers will then be looking to work towards the Threshold Standards or Fast Track Teachers' Competences and Values.

Depending on whether you aspire to middle and senior management or wish to continue in the classroom later in your career, you may then consider applying to become an Advanced Skills Teacher, although, as you have guessed, there are standards and competences for subject coordinators and for head teachers as well. Details about all of these standards are available on the internet (www.teacher-net.gov.uk is a good starting point if you want to access this type of information).

For judging established classroom teachers the Threshold Standards are the main standards and therefore represent the core competences and standards against which the profession as a whole is judged (see also Chapter 8). The major Threshold Standards are shown in Fig. 3.2.

FIG. 3.2 The Threshold Standards

Knowledge and understanding

1 Teachers should demonstrate that they have a thorough and up-to-date knowledge of the teaching of their subject and take account of wider curriculum developments which are relevant to their work.

Teaching and assessment

2 Teachers should demonstrate that they consistently and effectively plan lessons and sequences of lessons to meet pupils' individual learning needs.

3 Teachers should demonstrate that they consistently and effectively use a range of appropriate strategies for teaching and classroom management.

4 Teachers should demonstrate that they consistently and effectively use information about prior attainment to set well-grounded expectations for pupils and monitor progress to give clear and constructive feedback.

Pupil progress

5 Teachers should demonstrate that, as a result of their teaching, their pupils achieve well relative to the pupils' prior attainment, making progress as good or better than similar pupils nationally. This should be shown in marks or grades in any relevant national tests or examinations, or school-based assessment for pupils where national tests and examinations are taken.

Wider professional effectiveness

6 Teachers should demonstrate that they take responsibility for their professional development and use the outcomes to improve their teaching and pupils' learning.

7 Teachers should demonstrate that they make an active contribution to the policies and aspirations of the school.

Professional characteristics

8 Teachers should demonstrate that they are effective professionals who challenge and support all pupils to do their best through:

- inspiring trust and confidence
- building team commitment
- engaging and motivating pupils
- analytical thinking
- positive action to improve the quality of pupils' learning.

REFLECTION

To what extent do you think it is possible to encapsulate the process of teaching into a set of 'standards'? How valuable do you find individual standards in driving your understanding of your own performance?

Our view is that, although the Hay McBer dimensions and hence the standards and competency framework are soundly based and well founded in research findings, they are not a simple 'tick list' of skills that are easily quantified. In practice these 'standards' could be judged and interpreted differently according to the individuals involved and the context within which the teacher operates. However, it is useful to begin to consider what you think these standards look like in action (Activity 3.2). (The texts by Kerry on questioning, explaining, setting learning objectives, task setting, and differentiating – referred to in Chapter 5 – do log these key skills against the national standards and the Hay McBer report, as well as commentating on what else is required of master teachers.)

ACTIVITY 3.2

Finding evidence for teaching and standards

Look at each of the standards (Fig. 3.2) and jot down ideas on the kind of evidence you think would prove a teacher is meeting these standards.

Now go back and think about the standards in relation to your own practice (or that of a teacher whom you have observed closely).

Which are areas of strength for you?

Which areas do you feel less confident about?

How could you improve these areas?

While later in the book (Chapter 10) we discuss teachers as managers, there is also a relatively new formal opportunity that provides a potentially interesting way for master teachers to keep their feet firmly in the classroom, while maximising and developing the role of expert teacher. In the past, highly talented teachers could only really enhance their status and pay through taking on managerial roles and responsibilities. However, not all excellent teachers make excellent managers – nor indeed do they want this type of role. In fact management tasks often actually impinge upon and take over the time and energy needed to secure the highest quality of classroom teaching. The role of Advanced Skills Teacher (AST) has been brought in by the government as a way of utilising the skills of *excellent* teachers to disseminate effective practice and use their skills and expertise with other teachers to raise standards. The creation of AST posts is agreed between individual schools and their local education authority (for fuller details see www.teachernet.gov.uk/professionaldevelopment/opportunities/ast/info).

The key word in this discussion is *excellent* – although such a qualitative judgement is hard to define and, as we indicate, depends on the way teachers synthesise all the key skills, knowledge and understanding to effect quality learning. The criteria for the assessment of an Advanced Skills Teacher still covers most of the same key aspects as those for an NQT and for Threshold Standards. It adds, however, the requirement to demonstrate that ASTs have the ability to advise and support other teachers effectively. The achievement of the requisite national standards to the AST level are assessed by an external assessor using the following evidence:

- classroom observation (at least two lessons)
- an interview

- a discussion with the candidate's head teacher and any other staff familiar with the candidate's work

- a review of documentary evidence including the completed application form and a portfolio.

The guidance given on the teachernet website in relation to the assessment standards is shown in Fig. 3.3:

FIG. 3.3 Advanced Teaching Skills

What is the assessor looking for?

The assessor will want to satisfy himself or herself that candidates meet the standards for Advanced Skills Teachers (ASTs). These are:

1 Excellent results/outcomes

As a result of aspiring ASTs' teaching, pupils show consistent improvement in relation to prior and expected attainment; are highly motivated, enthusiastic and respond positively to challenge and high expectations; exhibit consistently high standards of discipline and behaviour; show a consistent record of parental involvement and satisfaction.

2 Excellent subject and/or specialist knowledge

Aspiring ASTs must keep up to date in their subjects and/or specialism(s); have a full understanding of connections and progressions in the subject and use this in their teaching to ensure pupils make good progress; quickly understand pupils' perceptions and misconceptions from their questions and responses; understand ICT in the teaching of their subject or specialism(s).

3 Excellent ability to plan

Aspiring ASTs must prepare lessons and sequences of lessons with clear objectives to ensure successful learning by all pupils; set consistently high expectations for pupils in their class and homework; plan their teaching to ensure it builds on the current and previous achievement of pupils.

4 Excellent ability to teach, manage pupils and maintain discipline

Aspiring ASTs must understand and use the most effective teaching methods to achieve the teaching objectives in hand; display flair and creativity in engaging, enthusing and challenging groups of pupils; use questioning and explanation skilfully to secure maximum progress; develop pupils' literacy, numeracy and ICT skills as appropriate within their phase and context; are able to provide positive and targeted support for pupils who have special educational needs, are very able, are from ethnic minorities, lack confidence, have behavioural difficulties or are disaffected; maintain respect and discipline and are consistent and fair.

5 **Excellent ability to assess and evaluate**

Aspiring ASTs must use assessment as part of their teaching to diagnose pupils' needs, set realistic and challenging targets for improvement and plan future teaching; improve their teaching through evaluating their own practice in relation to pupils' progress, school targets and inspection evidence.

6 **Excellent ability to advise and support other teachers**

Aspiring ASTs must provide clear feedback, good support and sound advice to others; are able to provide examples of coaching and training to help others become more effective in their teaching; can help others to evaluate the impact of their teaching on raising pupils' achievements; are able to analyse teaching and understand how improvements can be made; have highly developed interpersonal skills which allow them to be effective in schools and situations other than their own; provide a role model for pupils and other staff through their personal and professional conduct; know how to plan and prioritise their own time and activity effectively; are highly respected and able to motivate others.

Advanced Skills Teachers still spend 80 per cent of their time in working with their designated class/classes. The other 20 per cent of their time is expected to be spent on outreach work in such areas as:

- leading professional learning groups
- advising other teachers in classroom organisation and teaching methods
- providing model lessons
- spreading good practice based on educational research
- producing high-quality teaching materials
- advising on professional development
- establishing professional learning teams in schools
- helping to support performance management of other teachers
- supporting teachers experiencing difficulties
- helping with the induction and mentoring of newly qualified teachers
- participating in initial teacher training
- supporting support staff.

Advanced Skills Teachers are paid on a separate pay scale from class teachers, and the working time requirements are disapplied (as they are for head teachers and deputies).

What areas would you need to improve or develop to be in a position to apply for Advanced Skills Teacher status? What advantages would you see in this move for your own career?

The transformatory dimension

What it takes to transcend being merely 'satisfactory'

The transformatory dimension in teaching, the element that moves a teacher from competent to 'effective', is that of *professionalism*. We make no apology for continually raising this issue (see Chapter 1). It represents the *active intent* to synthesise the knowledge, skills and understanding in particular ways that transform the learning experience for individual pupils in a class. It involves making *professional judgement* about choosing from the range of knowledge and skills a teacher has, at a particular time, in a particular place, with a particular pupil/class to achieve the best learning outcome for that situation.

Underpinning all professional judgement is necessarily a value system of what is good teaching and what outcomes are being sought. One of the most powerful determinants of this can be our own prior experience. When you decided you wanted to become a teacher you probably had an image in your mind of what you thought teaching would be like and how you would want to be perceived as a teacher (Activity 3.3). This was probably based on your experience of teachers through your own school career and what you liked or disliked about them.

ACTIVITY 3.3

Thinking about teachers and their values

Jot down the key traits and behaviours you value in a teacher.

How do these traits and behaviours relate to the Hay McBer dimensions and the Threshold and AST Standards?

Is there a dimension that seems to predominate?

Are there any key issues that, in your opinion, are omitted?

The way we can temper or question the subjectivity of our underpinning value judgements about teaching is through our knowledge and understanding of pedagogy (see Chapter 2). What all attempts to define the 'good' teacher clearly establish is the complexity of the role. The tasks undertaken by a teacher are multi-faceted enough and the intellectual demand of synthesising the content and pedagogy is of a high level, but the main factor that makes teaching so challenging (but ultimately satisfying) is the interpersonal nature of the role. This is where the power lies and it is where the idea of professionalism is most important.

Teaching asks us to give a great deal of our personal self. However, by being aware of our personal and professional values, traits and approaches we can maintain a professional distance that ensures we make a positive impact on all pupils, rather than just those with whom we find it personally easier to relate.

We think this is where the idea of the 'effective teacher' is most useful – in that, although teachers may be 'good' teachers for some pupils, it is possible to be an effective teacher for all our pupils. But teachers do directly influence the pupils in their care over a considerable period of time. This responsibility should never be forgotten or underestimated. An experience one of us had might illustrate the point. This was how the story was told:

> Having taught in secondary schools for some years, I moved to a new job 150 miles away. I had been (I thought) well liked by pupils, and successful in encouraging learning. One specific student, however, an older boy, had had major problems at home, and had confided in me. It is always hard to know what, if any, value such care has for the pupil. However, after I had been in the new job a while, my wife and I came back home one Saturday after a shopping trip to see a Jaguar sitting on the drive. Not having any rich friends, we thought at first we had burglars. Two young men emerged from the car. One was the troubled pupil of some time ago, the other – it emerged – his older brother. 'We've just come to see if you're settling in OK,' they said.

The perceptions of year 8 pupils that were used to front the Hay McBer report really highlight the effective nature of quality teaching:

A good teacher . . .

is kind
is generous
listens to you
encourages you
has faith in you

keeps confidences
likes teaching children
likes teaching their subject
takes time to explain things
helps you when you're stuck
tells you how you are doing
allows you to have your say
doesn't give up on you
cares for your opinion
makes you feel clever
treats people equally
stands up for you
makes allowances
tells the truth
is forgiving.

Of course, pupils are not the only stakeholders. A teacher's competence will also be judged by the head teacher, colleagues, parents, governors and, of course, Ofsted. However, getting it right with the pupils will or should hold the greatest sway with all other stakeholders. Thus the Teacher Training Agency based a recruitment campaign around the idea that people never forget a good teacher. The truth is they remember those who inspired them or those they hated. Teachers cannot base their career on aiming to be memorable – and one can never please all the people all of the time. However, it is worth considering the positive traits that are identified repeatedly in the teachers whom people admire (Activity 3.4).

ACTIVITY 3.4

Considering 'best' teachers

Look at two or three of the *Times Educational Supplement*'s 'My Best Teacher' features, or ask non-teaching friends about the best teacher they ever had (and their worst!).

What are the key traits identified in each article or account?

What are the similarities/differences across the articles or accounts?

How do they compare to your values (see Activity 3.2)?

Knowledge and the professional

Earlier (Chapters 1 and 2) we discussed at some length the concept of professionalism applied to teaching. In this chapter we have looked at professional expertise – what it means to be a teacher. However, before we leave this topic, it is important to raise some important theoretical issues and to consider their significance for master teachers.

How does professional knowledge work?

Eraut (2001) outlines some of the theories about how professionals acquire knowledge and go about their tasks. Though much of the material he surveys concerns the medical field, important principles apply. He points out that in making clinical judgements (and the same could be claimed for educational judgements) there is a balance between intuitive thinking on the one hand and analytical thinking on the other.

Both clinicians and teachers meet problems that they have to deal with 'on their feet'. One argument is that, in meeting these problems, the teacher (in our case) learns from experience. He or she meets situations, discovers (maybe by trial and error) how to deal with them, adds to the armoury of experience, and uses that armoury to tackle future problems. We have discussed aspects of intuition elsewhere in this text (Chapter 2).

However, teachers also acquire through study, training and professional reading a bank of information about how things happen in classrooms – theories and structures. They may use this theoretical knowledge in an analytical way, comparing and contrasting their situations with things previously known or learned. In practice, it is quite probable that we all do both of these things in some kind of mix that may be dependent on time, opportunity and circumstance. Thus, if a pupil disrupts the lesson by being late, the teacher will deal with the situation intuitively – maybe by settling the pupil quickly to work so as not to disrupt others, maximising the flow of the lesson itself, deliberately not making a public issue of the event. If the pupil is repeatedly late, or lateness spreads to other pupils, then a more analytical approach may be called for: investigating the reluctance to come on time; seeking out reasons for the pupil's behaviour; adjusting the approach of the lesson to make the beginnings more interesting; introducing systems of reward for punctuality; experimenting with various approaches to find one that is effective (Activity 3.5).

ACTIVITY 3.5

Assessing critical incidents in teaching

Look back over your last week's teaching. Isolate one or two critical incidents that have happened to you during the week.

How did you deal with them?

What kind of thinking did you use?

What part did intuitive behaviour play? In what ways did you analyse the situation more carefully?

Try to become more aware of your thinking processes as you react to classroom situations.

Eraut also makes an important point about the relationship between knowledge and the ways in which data are presented or expressed. Thus, the kinds of statistical data provided to schools in the PANDA report (see Chapter 7) are likely to be subjected to analytical thought, while the kinds of planning that teachers often do and that result in the spider graph and similar models come closer to the intuitive end of a continuum of knowing.

What is important for master teachers is less to explore in depth these complicated theories about how learning operates, and more to be able to recognise the modes of thinking they are bringing to problems and to test their appropriateness. Thus, the intuitive approach may well be appropriate for one of the thousand-plus social interactions a teacher has with pupils in a normal school day, but a more analytical approach may be better as a means to planning an improved curriculum.

Who owns knowledge?

Paechter et al. (2001) consider the traditional view: that in a classroom the teacher's knowledge counts, and that of the student does not. This view leads to the concept that what the teacher does is to deposit knowledge into the student – a view prevalent in many government documents, and above all during the late 1980s and throughout the 1990s. Some would see this model as underpinning the current National Curriculum even in its revised forms. But knowledge is power – so this model makes teachers powerful and students powerless. Furthermore, it is a model that helps to distance 'school knowledge' from other knowledge. Sometimes this other knowledge is seen as irrelevant, even valueless.

One living example of this was George, a young man of school-leaving age who had failed to master anything but the most rudimentary reading and writing and very little else of school knowledge. His ambition was to be a painter – emulsioning walls rather than creating expensive images of sunflowers, that is. But George was one of the shrewdest judges of character we have ever met. Whether in TV soap life or real life, he 'saw through' people and assessed their strengths and weaknesses. In the 'real' (as opposed to the school) world this was an important skill. It would not feature too comfortably on a GCSE record, however.

This model of school knowledge also contributes to the view that some areas of knowledge are valuable and others not – that physics is a significant subject and being able to craft a chair is not. As Paechter et al. express it:

> *According to this characterisation, school knowledge represents a narrow selection from wider possibilities.*
>
> (Paechter et al. 2001: 169)

What is or is not valuable school knowledge is also subject to the whims of fashion. Thus in the 1960s vocational education was prevalent in secondary schools, but in the 1980s it was not. Now in 2003 the curriculum is being subjected to a move back to vocationalism. Similarly, in the 1960s in primary schools learning by discovery was de rigeur; by the 1980s it had become frowned upon. Since about 2001 primary schools are beginning to rediscover this as a learning method. These movements have much to do with shifting philosophies and values, but for master teachers it is important to understand the processes of change and weigh the values detached from fashion, fad or dogma.

We believe that any true definition of lifelong learning has to value all learning and all knowledge. Knowledge serves different purposes: some of it vocational, some practical, some engaging the theoretical mind, some the aesthetic, and so on. Knowledge is not compartmented; its value is often in the links between, not in the separation of, its insights.

Owning knowledge gives the learner power (whether an adult such as a teacher, or a pupil in school). Knowledge is challenging. Some schools and some teachers find that idea threatening. We, however, suggest there are better descriptors – liberating, enabling, fulfilling. In the same way, we believe that teachers should be knowledgeable. They should be in tune with current affairs; inquisitive about what happens in the world around them; in touch with new developments in their own specialisms; and replete with informed interest in a broad range of other subjects. They should see every situation as a learning situation, and grab at chances to mature and increase their own experiences across the range of human activity.

How 'knowledgeable' are you in the sense we have just described? Are your experience of life and your own thirst for knowledge adequate to fire and enthuse young minds, and to act as an example to them?

What are the constraints on knowledge imposed by society?

Knowledge is not free from a context in society and community values. For teachers there are two very important constraining factors that influence the way in which knowledge is received in schools. These are social class and gender. Since an earlier chapter dealt at some length with the former, here we shall concentrate on the latter.

Traditionally, some subjects have been the domain of boys, for example physics. Others have been the domain of girls: history, perhaps, and biology. Furthermore, the curriculum was once constructed so that boys and girls went off to different lessons. Boys went to metalwork, girls to home economics. One might argue that all that has now changed. In place of these craft subjects we have unisex technology; girls and boys have equal access across the curriculum.

In theory, this is all true. There may still linger, though, an underlying cultural legacy about which things girls ought to study and which are suitable for boys. The issue is more subtle than that; teaching may convey hidden messages. A fine mathematics lesson taught by a first-class honours female graduate who had been an officer in the Royal Navy might seem to epitomise good practice – until, that is, you are let into the secret that the pupils sat in two blocks on either side of the central gangway between desks. Boys sat on one side, girls on the other – from choice. The teacher taught from the boys' side and addressed more than 80 per cent of the questions to boys.

What are your hidden prejudices and covert (or merely unconscious) behaviours?

There is the further argument that boys and girls learn differently; that the move towards course work has favoured girls' ways of thinking and their self-disciplined approach to learning. Thus there has been an ongoing and still continuing debate about why boys underperform in schools, and above all at Key Stages 3 and 4. This issue is summed up in Kerry (2001). Much of this controversy is jejune, in our view. A recent 'debate' in the *Times Educational Supplement* (2002) carried the emotive heading: 'Females are good at passing exams and using coloured pencils, but does real understanding of topics elude them?' Conversely, there is a constant pressure to defend boys' abilities. Thus Henry (2002) states:

> Results from the 7,000 entries show that boys perform better at the very highest level, even in traditionally 'feminine' subjects such as English. Girls outclassed boys only in critical thinking and French.
>
> (Henry 2002: 1)

This is not the moment to argue the case, but at one school we know and that we would rate as exemplary, the results for boys and girls are consistently similar year on year. Fig. 3.4 shows a typical performance graph for this school for boys and girls at GCSE level.

FIG. 3.4 Comparison of boy and girl performance at GCSE level at All Saints

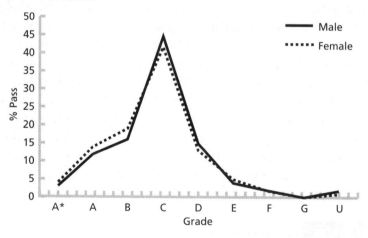

Conclusion

Being a teacher is a complicated role that carries considerable responsibility in terms of the impact (both positive and negative) it has on the pupils we teach:

- It requires us to know what to teach.

- It requires us to have a range of skills so that we can carry out the tasks involved in teaching.

- It requires us to understand the ways we can synthesise our knowledge, understanding and skills to connect with our pupils to achieve the best learning outcome.

- It requires us to make the right professional choices.

In the busy life of a teacher it is easy to become bogged down in dealing with the everyday tasks and demands, but to be an effective teacher we need to be self-aware and ask questions of ourselves to make sure we are being true professionals. Sometimes what appear to be simple questions or clear-cut issues turn out to be quite other. The issue of professional knowledge is like that. Once again in this chapter we have discovered that being a master teacher is less about jumping through hoops or following a template and more about becoming a critical thinker prepared to challenge accepted wisdom.

In Chapter 4 we pursue this theme by examining the teacher's effective roles, specifically relationships with pupils and what makes these effective.

At the end of this chapter you should have:

- Considered the implications of the government's standards and government-sponsored reports on what it means to be a teacher

- Looked at the Advanced Skills Teacher route as a means to professional development

- Reflected on the kinds of knowledge that teachers need in order to be effective

- Explored some dimensions of effective teaching

———— References ————

Eraut, M. (2001) 'Theories of professional expertise', in C. Paechter, M. Preedy, D. Scott, and J. Soler, *Knowledge, Power and Learning*, London: PCP Open University.

Hay McBer (2000) *Research into Teacher Effectiveness*, London: Report for the DfEE, June.

Henry, J. (2002) 'Boys outshine girls at highest level', *Times Educational Supplement*, 23 August: 1.

Kerry, T. (2001) 'A review of some recent issues in the education of the more able', *Gifted Education International*, 15(2): 195–206.

Paechter, C., Preedy, M., Scott, D. and Soler, J. (2001) *Knowledge, Power and Learning*, London: PCP Open University.

Teacher Training Agency (TTA) (2001) *Standards for the Award of Qualified Teacher Status,* London: TTA.

Teacher Training Agency (TTA) (2002) *Qualifying to Teach,* London: TTA.

Times Educational Supplement (2002) 'Are girls harder to teach than boys?', *Times Educational Supplement,* 16 August: 13.

chapter four

The effective teacher

School ethos and class management

In this chapter you are invited to:

- Consider how you can identify the key imperatives and values in your school
- Think about how you, as an individual, can support, influence and develop the ethos
- Understand your class within the context of the overall school ethos
- Analyse strategies for supporting differing pupil profiles/needs

—— Identifying a school's ethos ——

A powerful indicator of what matters in a school is the first impression one gains upon visiting it because, of course, this will mirror some of what is experienced by pupils, parents and other visitors. Although the first impression can be influenced by whether you are nervously looking around as a potential candidate for a job or seeing it for the first time on an interview day, it should give you an initial 'flavour' of the school. This will then be reinforced or overturned by your ongoing daily experience (Activity 4.1).

ACTIVITY 4.1

Investigating first impressions

Think back to when you first visited your current school.

What were your first impressions – of the premises, the teachers, the pupils, the support staff?

How would you describe the atmosphere?

How do you think the school has changed since your first impressions were formed? (You might discreetly ask a new parent what attracted them to your school, if you are unable to disengage yourself from the fact that you have been in your school for a long time.)

How have your initial impressions of the nature of the school changed or developed?

All schools have a mission statement and/or aims. This is another source of evidence about what matters in a school. However, one must be slightly wary, as written intent is often very different from reality. Mission statements and aims of intent have sometimes been formulated very thoroughly, with input from all stakeholders, and are subject to regular review. But it is unfortunately just as likely to be the case that they are bland statements that are merely for show or are carried forward year on year. So how can you distinguish which category your school's mission falls into (Activity 4.2)?

ACTIVITY 4.2

Examining the school's mission

Obtain a copy of the school mission statement/aims.

Look at each aspect and note down what you see in your everyday experience of the school that supports the stated aim, but also note anything that (in your opinion) undermines it.

Is there a key aspect of the school's values/way of doing things that you think is not represented in the aims?

How do your professional values (see Chapter 3) relate to the stated school aims? Is there any conflict?

The most powerful written document in terms of representing and moving forward a school on its stated aims and priorities should be its school development plan (SDP). School development planning and strategic visioning have been areas of rapid development in recent years. However, again one has to be slightly wary as it cannot be assumed that development planning is a well-organised process in your school. If it is, it should give a very strong indication of what matters to the school community. The review of past priorities, targets and performance should give a strong indication of where the school is at. Current priorities should show the areas that the school wants to strengthen. Budgeting and resourcing should be directed to supporting these areas (Activity 4.3).

ACTIVITY 4.3

Analysing the school development plan

Obtain a copy of your school development plan (or one from a school you know well).

From the document, can you tell who was involved in drawing up the plan?

You have looked at the mission statement/aims in Activity 4.2. Can you see a direct link between these and the identified priorities in the SDP?

What are the key areas identified?

Do they cover any of the following: development of teaching and learning; curriculum development; staffing; resourcing; premises; participation of stakeholders?

Is the SDP used as an active working document in staff meetings?

As a class teacher, what do you experience that supports the priorities in action?

Are there any priorities that you are surprised that are there?

Are there any priorities that you think should be there that aren't?

The other major component of a school community is obviously the pupils. The way they behave and respond to the framework, opportunities and constraints of their school is obviously an important part of the ethos of a school. Although a sound, well-based framework of rules, rewards, sanctions and approaches should provide a strong guide to the pupil community, different socio-economic contexts can lead to a school framework having to accommodate and respond to differing pupil needs.

There has to be an understanding of key factors and values represented in the pupil community if the school framework is to serve successfully and support the needs of their most important stakeholder. All schools have children who demonstrate challenging behaviour to a greater or lesser degree. (This is a separate issue, which is discussed later.) However, there can be wider trends and tendencies that are important for a school to identify and accommodate or challenge as appropriate to the school aims (Activity 4.4).

ACTIVITY 4.4

Analysing pupils' attitudes and behaviour

Think about the attitude and behaviour of pupils in your school.

Are there any characteristics that come to mind about general behaviour and attitudes? What examples can you give as a basis for your perceptions?

Are there general trends that support and demonstrate the aims of the school in action? Are positive traits celebrated and reinforced?

Are there any general trends (there are isolated incidents in all schools) in behaviour and response of pupils that are undermining the overall aims of the school? If there are any such trends, what if any actions are being taken to counter these problems?

Active participation in your school's ethos

The above reflective tasks should have challenged you to think in depth about the ethos of your own school and the key issue of the relationship between aims and actions. From the micro-level of one school we move to consider ethos and climate in schools generally.

The dimensions of school climate (which sets the scene for classroom climate) have been identified by various writers. Before examining these, it is worth pointing out that, in a minority of instances, one can discover 'good' classroom climate in schools that have a poor overall ethos and, more commonly, poor classrooms in schools with 'good' overall ethos. Where these things occur it is usually because individual teachers' skills mismatch, for better or worse, with those overall in the organisation. But what are these dimensions of climate? The following list gives a flavour:

1. *School facilities and plant*: internal and external plant in good order, maintained, tidy and looked after; examples of students' work on display and celebrated.

2. *Environment*: free from physical or psychological danger; the kind of place where pupils feel free to express their views, ask questions and make errors from which they can learn.

3. *High expectations by teachers and head*: these expectations are focused on all members of the school community, not just students; expectations include confidence by teachers that students will live up to the standards required. Some researchers claim that heads set the tone on this dimension by their behaviours.

4. *Staff and support staff relationships*: marked by the quality of the attitudes of respect and professional trust among the adults in the school.

5. *Democratic or collegial processes within the school*: students are set an example of shared decision-making, and have decision-making opportunities them-

selves; attitudes of trust prevail; communication systems are effective; collaborative activities may predominate.

6 *High levels of student participation*: students contribute in lessons and in democratic activities such as debates and school councils; provision of opportunities for consultation with staff about issues such as uniform and rules; pupils act as leaders and monitors.

7 *Teaching skills*: discussed throughout this book, but here their role in helping to set the tone of a school is acknowledged. Good teaching removes negative factors such as boredom and substitutes positive ones such as enthusiasm.

8 *Staff–student relations*: these are encapsulated in participation, for example in extracurricular activities; they show in the quality of conversation between peers, and between students and staff; good behaviour provides a context in which good relations can be sustained.

9 *Effective use of rewards and praise*: the good performance of students is recognised in all fields of achievement, not just the academic, often publicly, and praised. Other students are not resentful or antagonistic to high levels of achievement; there may be formal systems of reward for good work or attendance.

10 *Student morale*: because good school climate fosters an atmosphere of personal worth, students have high self-image; they respond to expectations by carrying out what is required of them, such as working diligently and completing tasks.

11 *Minimisation of negative peer influences*: good school climate lowers the negative effect of negative peer cultures and promotes positive ones such as 'cool to learn'.

12 *Home–school relations*: where good relations and systems of communication exist between home and school, the ethos of the school is improved through respect.

From the list it will be seen that climate is subtle and multi-faceted.

REFLECTION

What kind of climate operates in your classroom? In your school? Are there mismatches? What are they? Why do they exist? Can they be overcome? How?

Some writers have emphasised the correlations between school climate and socio-economic context. There can be little doubt that ghetto schools do often occur in deprived areas, but the reason for the correlation may include factors such as the difficulty of obtaining staff of adequate calibre to produce good climate in such schools, poor histories of home–school relations and low community expectations. These factors do not of themselves rule out that a well-managed school may produce good climate in difficult circumstances. Schools in relatively favoured neighbourhoods may have no acceptable ethos at all. Only a few weeks ago one of us stood at a bus stop on the route from a local comprehensive school, which has a good academic reputation in the area and is oversubscribed. When it came, the bus was full of students from this school who spat on the heads of people in the queue and intimidated pensioners who boarded.

This last may be explained by Corrie (1995), who alerts us to the possibility that schools can produce pseudo-cultures based on false impressions and skin-deep practices relating to such factors as collaboration. Indeed, such a situation may accommodate all parties, serving 'to protect the head teacher from challenge and the teachers from change' (Corrie 1995: 1).

Classroom climate as an outcome of school climate

Classroom climate must inevitably be conditioned by school climate. The skill of the teacher is to marry the two by being familiar with the declared aspirations of the school, and by acting consistently with them both in public and within the privacy of the classroom walls. In the case of a school with a less than ideal climate, a more concerted effort is required in order to establish the kinds of norms that we have listed above, but this time solely within the teacher's own classroom.

What is surprising is how often students respond positively to this. They actually appreciate a calm atmosphere of order and mutual respect. On one occasion we were asked to conduct professional development in a failing school. A precondition we imposed was to spend a day shadowing a pupil to make our own assessment. The climate in the school was indeed quite chaotic. At lunch we sat among pupils and talked informally. One older boy summed up the dichotomy beautifully:

> This would be a good school [he said] if students were to be quiet and listen, and just get on in an orderly way.

He was right, and most the pupils were yearning for this to happen. In that instance, the head had simply given up and couldn't engineer the necessary changes.

Managing the classroom

The expression 'classroom management' is used in this text not to include the management of pupils' behaviour (see below) but to embrace a cluster of skills that make the classroom operate smoothly. These skills also underpin aspects of classroom climate (also see below), but are the context within which 'climate' or 'ethos' operates rather than being part of the climate itself. The dimensions of classroom management are diverse and wide-ranging, and are probably best summarised by Table 4.1. Turner-Bisset (2001: 93) makes the point that experience of a wide range of classroom management systems may contribute to teachers' overall skills because models of classroom management imply models of learning and teaching. This may well be true; at the most basic level, the teacher can move flexibly between the three main teaching modes (whole-class teaching, group activity and individualised learning) only in a classroom context that is flexible enough to allow for these. Table 4.1, however, provides a rather more rounded and detailed picture of this area of skill.

Creating the climate of the classroom

There is general agreement among educators that school climate is important, and thus that classroom climate should mirror and reflect it. There is little systematic attempt to define it or its parameters. In the literature it appears under a bewildering variety of terms: atmosphere, tone, feeling, milieu, culture. Sackney (2000) draws on other writers to produce a composite definition of it:

> *A relatively enduring quality of the internal environment of the school that is experienced by the members (students, teachers, administrators, secretaries, consultants and custodians); influences their behaviour; and can be described in terms of the values, norms, and beliefs of a particular set of attributes of the school ... [affecting the] educational environment of the entire school*
>
> (Sackney 2000: 3)

TABLE 4.1 Dimensions of classroom management: some questions

Plant

Is the classroom clean? Tidy? Well-organised, with set places for items that need to be accessed during lessons? Reasonably equipped? Can confidential material be locked away? Can pupils get access to items they need without disturbing the teacher or peers? Are the walls and noticeboards used effectively to support learning? Do students take responsibility for maintenance of order and tidiness? Is the furniture appropriate for the tasks undertaken? Is furniture the right size for the age of pupils? Is safety well-managed and understood? Do pupils treat the space with respect? Is it organised to be flexible in use? Is the space set out so that there are no 'dead areas' where pupils can hide from the teacher's notice? Is it secure? Are there ground rules for its use, e.g. about eating and drinking? Is the space properly aired between and during lessons? What impression would the room make on visitors, such as governors or tutors from other institutions? Are the space and procedures reviewed regularly, and are adjustments made to working practice?

People

Apart from you and the pupils, who uses the space? Teaching assistants, LSAs, trainees on child care or initial teacher training courses, volunteer helpers? Are you informed fully about each person's job description, and the expectations the school has of them? What procedures are there in place for managing their day-to-day work? How are their individual contributions coordinated? What systems have you put in place for overseeing their preparation? Monitoring their actual performance? Providing them with feedback? With whom do you liaise about these helpers, or report on them, and how is the process managed? What effect does their presence have on the children's learning? How do the children view these assistants – are their attitudes positive towards them? How is the general welfare of pupils in the classroom looked after, e.g. are there effective systems in place for safeguarding property, keeping completed work from damage, and so on? What are the school policies about parental access to classrooms?

Resources

How do you provide and store learning resources? Are they readily available to pupils within and beyond lessons? Where necessary (e.g. a class library) are there systems in place for cataloguing, issuing, checking stock? In the case of computers and other hardware, what are the procedures for security? For maintenance? For use by pupils? For maximising their potential? For updating software? Do you set an example by your own use? Homework clubs or after-school use of resource centres and libraries are a resource: how do you encourage pupils to use facilities like these?

Finances

If you control any school finances, do you know the exact boundary of your budget? For how many pupils does it have to provide? Over how long a period? What are the ordering and accounting procedures required in order to spend?

Can goods be ordered from any source or only through approved sources? Are there discount schemes you could utilise? How do you decide about priorities for spending? Whom do you consult – other staff, pupils, the head, assistants, parents, no one? Do you work effectively with the bursar/finance officer? Can you carry money over for more major purchases in a new financial year? How do you keep your running total? How do you judge the quality and effectiveness of the things you buy?

Personal time

Can you organise yourself? Do you arrive on time to school, lessons? Do you help pupils to organise time: for example, by finishing lessons promptly, by practising exercises against the clock, by marking homework within a reasonable/agreed period? Are you one of those teachers who is always running to catch up? Do you plan your days as far as possible? Use a diary or Filofax system? Make lists of jobs, prioritise them and cross them off as you do them? Do you get your own work (e.g. reports on children) in on time? Control your workload by making sensible decisions about the tasks children do (e.g. not setting seven classes long pieces of work that need marking on the same day)? Do you make time for planning and preparation? Do you rota in key tasks such as meeting with assistants? Do you monitor progress through the curriculum so that work is covered properly? Do you use strategies such as handouts to augment work that cannot be covered in detail in class? How effectively do you use homework tasks for pupils – are they just reinforcement or do they advance learning? How do you use breaks and lunchtimes? Can you balance involvement with extracurricular activity with some personal time?

Achieving effective behaviour management

Every teacher remembers the first time he/she was left alone with a class for a full lesson: the naked fear of whether one would survive the pitfalls of behaviour management. Behaviour management is one of the most fundamental of all the skills that a teacher must possess, indeed, without which a teacher cannot operate. But the literature of behaviour management, even the most recent, is littered with anecdotal approaches and tips for teachers rather than with any rationale for how and why teachers should operate in this area. Good of their kind, but typical of the genre, are Bryson (1999), Robertson (1997) and Wragg (1993). (Incidentally, we part company with Robertson on the issue of touching pupils: touch as a means of control should be avoided wherever possible.)

However sound the advice of such manuals, for the present purposes what is more appropriate is to establish some kind of theoretical underpinning for teachers' actions when managing pupil behaviour. A very specific approach of this kind can be found in Merrett and Wheldall (1990) and the companion volume Wheldall and Merrett (1990), which promote what is called 'positive teaching'. In Table 4.2 we attempt just this task of providing a more theoretical approach. The table sets out some of the purposes behind behaviour management and tries to establish why they are requisite. It then looks at some typical steps that teachers take to bring about these desired behaviours. The table is illustrative rather than exhaustive and you will certainly be able to add to each of its columns and to the lists within them.

In the process you should be aware of the extent to which you are conditioned by your deeply held convictions about children. For example, if you believe that people are inherently evil, or that some have incurable genetic tendencies to be so and have to be steered away from their 'natural' weaknesses, it will affect the way you approach the cells in the table. If you believe in essential goodness, which is corrupted by environmental and socioeconomic factors, you will approach the issues differently.

Other common scapegoats for bad behaviour are gender (boys are worse behaved than girls, goes the message), or parents (because they have lost control over their children's behaviour), or television (too much violence), or computers (too much access to anti-social games). While intelligent attempts to find causes for poor behaviour may help in the quest for strategies that obviate it, the real issue is straightforward enough. Behaviour management is necessary because schooling is social act and individuals cannot act without a degree of responsibility for the common good. Teachers have to ensure that the purposes of the school are achieved within a safe and secure environment. They have to act impartially in achieving these outcomes. Master teachers are not reactive to developing behaviour problems. They are proactive in providing circumstances in which they are minimised and forearmed with strategies for dealing with them should they arise.

TABLE 4.2 The purposes and desired outcomes of class management

Purpose	Desired outcome	Possible means
To what end?	To achieve the outcomes of the task that has been planned, organised and defined by the teacher towards the furtherance of some aspect of learning.	Keeping work interesting. Varying the nature of the work. Keeping pupils busy. Setting realistic time-scales. Enforcing deadlines.

Purpose	Desired outcome	Possible means
In what context?	In the classroom, in any other part of the school, for homework, as private study.	Maintaining quiet in study areas. Requiring the keeping of a homework diary. Setting rules about noise and movement around the school.
To promote what purposes?	To further learning, to progress towards targets and predetermined attainment, to achieve greater efficiency as a learner, to promote self-worth and integrity, to achieve greater cohesion within the student group.	Using praise selectively to reinforce positive behaviour. Use of personal tutorials to commentate on progress. Encouraging collaborative working. Encourage turns and sharing.
To support what value system?	To promote the climate and ethos of the school as it is defined; to underpin personal responsibility; to encourage the codes that will action citizenship in adult life; to further moral and/or religious ideals held by the school.	Celebrating successes in academic and non-academic achievements. Rewarding (e.g. with public praise) behaviour that promotes the desired values (e.g. charity work). Making best use of personal and social education lessons. Involving pupils in owning school rules.
Against what ideological/ philosophical background?	To further the completion of a task; the self-fulfilment of the individual; or the purposes of the group.	Providing incentives and privileges. Giving responsibilities to students. Making use of peer approval.

All the learned strategies in the world, however, will not help with behaviour management unless the 'chemistry' between you and the pupils is right. Listen to the many studies about what students want from teachers and they always come out with the same list, give or take a few items:

■ fairness

■ honesty

■ willingness to listen

■ a sense of humour

■ interesting

■ well-organised

■ consistent

■ caring

■ willing to spend time

■ responsive to individuals

■ approachable

■ flexible

■ open.

These, and personality factors, are the great intangibles of behaviour management.

REFLECTION

To what extent and in what ways do you fit into the categories of preferred behaviour listed by pupils (above)?

Relations with pupils – finding the right tone

In one sense class management is the formal dimension of relations with pupils and students. But a prerequisite of good class management is to find the right tone and balance in the relations that operate between teachers and pupils, and between pupils themselves. In this section we look systematically at some of these issues and how they work for individuals and classes.

Individual classes, individual psychologies

Every experienced teacher knows that classes develop their own collective personalities or identities. So it is important to make an early assessment of the class(es) with which one is working. One class, for example, might be very conformist and quiet; another may be bubbly and boisterous. The first will need the teacher to draw out their enthusiasms, while the second will need a teacher who can channel these. Master teachers understand these differences and can adapt their approach accordingly or – if the solution is difficult – will know how to seek support and advice.

Though classes do tend towards these group personalities, the master teacher will also be sensitive to those pupils who do not conform to the group norms. They may need particular help, guidance or support. Extreme cases might involve bullying, but usually situations are not as critical as this.

Knowing who they are

The process of creating good personal relations cannot begin until the teacher knows all the pupils. For primary teachers, the chances are that they will know names on the first day; secondary teachers who take a whole series of classes may take longer. Part of the skill of being a teacher is to know names quickly.

Beyond the knowledge of names is the ability to quickly read the signs about individuals – who is timorous, who is extrovert, who escapes to the back corner to make trouble, and who dominates the life of the group? Knowing these things – emotional intelligence at the teacher's own level – is part of the master teacher's skill. The basic aim here is to connect at some level with every child in the class. If the only way through to Jamie is to learn about fishing, then you have to find out about fishing! We are back to one of our pieces of basic advice: a good teacher is interested and interesting.

Prior knowledge

Of course, teachers don't necessarily start with blank pieces of paper. Pupils will come with records (see Chapter 3) and one of the perennial problems in education has been the failure of teachers to come to grips with information that is passed between colleagues or between schools. In some cases, written records might be augmented by handover teachers meeting the new staff face to face. Master teachers carry out their homework, as well as retaining an independence of view, leaving room to be surprised by pupils in positive ways.

Personal prejudices and preferred teaching styles

It is also necessary to be aware of one's own preconceptions. This is an issue we have addressed throughout the book. In a very long history of relations with children we have met only a very small number (less than a handful) who did not appear to have any redeeming features. If you don't like children as a generality, then teaching is the wrong job for you. The master teacher finds something to like in every child.

Caring and respect

Out of the process of finding likeable features comes the attitude of caring that we placed, because of its importance, in the preface to the book as a fundamental of teaching as a profession. This caring becomes mutual, and loyalty builds out of it. One comes to see children as people, not pupils.

Mutual planning

In terms of learning, this mutuality picks up another theme of the book: redefining the ownership of learning. Learning should be a shared process, not something inflicted by a powerful teacher on to a powerless pupil. At the heart of theory of social constructivism is that of metacognition (see Chapter 11). Together these two theories underpin the view that learning is a social – and thus mutual – process.

Working together, tutorials, contracts and target-setting

The way in which mutual learning works is seen in the systems that schools and teachers put in place in order to promote it. In Chapter 5 we discuss at some length the importance of sharing the learning objectives of lessons, and how these can then drive a shared understanding of the desired outcomes. This process may take place within individual lessons, but will also be formalised on a medium-term basis into systems of personal tutorials, learning contracts and target-setting for individual pupils according to their needs and abilities. These systems can become ends in themselves and thus counter-productive: the systems take over the purpose. In Chapter 7 we discuss the nature of this process in the context of assessment. Master teachers will make a judgement about whether a 'tutorial' should consist, for an individual student, of a few seconds, feedback during the lesson, a longer chat at a prearranged time to review progress, or a formal interview that might even involve a parent.

Individualising learning

For learning to be meaningful it has to be targeted correctly. We revisit this theme in Chapters 5 and 7. Here, it is only necessary to remind the reader that the best education will result when the needs of individuals are met specifically and learning is tailored to actual need. This does not mean that teachers will be producing an individual plan for every pupil or student, but they will be making a subtle judgement that the emphasis of a task may need to be changed from one child to another.

Nurturing and in loco parentis

From what we have said so far it will have become clear that the relationship between teachers and pupils is close and intimate: but there are dangers in this. Legally, teachers are in loco parentis, but they are not parents. There is no need to overplay the obsession of the press with paedophiles, but – and it is a very significant but – all teachers have to be aware of the dangers of physical contact. Male teachers in particular have to avoid this kind of contact, which is hard when a child is injured or very emotional, or when teenagers try out their sexuality on teachers. Unfortunately, the dangers inherent in this, for men especially, have contributed to lowering the numbers of males recruited into the profession, and especially as teachers of young children. Above all, professional judgement needs to be exercised and in close liaison with professional awareness.

REFLECTION

To what extent do the points made in this section of the chapter accord with (a) your personal values for education; (b) the school context in which you work; (c) the aspirations you have for your own classroom?

———— Drawing together the threads ————

This book has emphasised the issue of values and teachers' understanding of their own values. The subject of class management too often degenerates into class control. What we have tried to communicate here is that effective class managers achieve through actualising their values into positive relationships. But class management, while being a crucial teaching skill, is not the only one. In Chapter 5 we move on to look at some other important skills for master teachers.

At the end of this chapter you should have:

■ Thought about what factors create school climate and ethos

■ Analysed the relationships between school and classroom climate

■ Considered the role of class management and discipline as factors in creating positive school and classroom climates

■ Understood the importance of relationships between teachers and pupils in contributing to positive school and classroom ethos

■ Drawn together some views about the effectiveness of yourself and your school in this area of operation

References

Bryson, J. (1999) *Effective Classroom Management*, London: Hodder & Stoughton.

Corrie, L. (1995) 'The structure and culture of staff collaboration: managing meaning and opening doors', *Educational Review*, 47(1): 89–99.

Merrett, F. and Wheldall, K. (1990) *Positive Teaching in the Primary School*, London: PCP.

Robertson, J. (1997) *Effective Classroom Control*, 3rd edn, London: Hodder & Stoughton.

Sackney, L. (2000) *Enhancing School Learning Climate: Theory, Research and Practice*, Report no. 180, University of Saskatchewan: SSTA Research Centre.

Turner-Bisset, R. (2001) *Expert Teaching*, London: David Fulton.

Wheldall, K. and Merrett, F. (1990) *Positive Teaching in the Secondary School*, London: PCP.

Wragg, E. (1993) *Class Management*, London: Routledge.

chapter five

The thinking teacher

A review of teaching skills

In this chapter you are invited to:

- Consider your philosophy and approach to teaching
- Understand that pedagogy is the essential element of school-based education
- Review a range of essential teaching skills and the debates surrounding them
- Reflect on the needs of pupils through issues such as learning styles

Introduction

Educational reform and debate over the last decade or so have encouraged both the public and professionals to lose sight of fundamental truths: schools are about learning, and at the heart of the learning process are the skills of pedagogy. Amid the welter of discussion about standards, governance, financial control, examination results, performance-related pay, inspection data and the rest it is easy to lose sight of the anchor process of education: the interaction between teacher and learner, its quality and effectiveness. If the pedagogy of the Plowden era of the 1960s and 1970s can be criticised as idealistic, education in the 1980s, 1990s and beyond must be pilloried as mechanistic. X per cent of the budget should be spend on this; governors should have written policies on that; schools should achieve these targets; heads must qualify in those ways; teachers must be evaluated against this predetermined scale of Ofsted values; pupils must all reach required standards. Here is a hoop – jump through it. But the problem with hoops is that they are like doughnuts; it's easy to fall neatly through the hole in the middle and miss the essential cake, and the occasional jam, that surrounds it.

The 1960s and 1970s were concerned with process and with understanding those processes; the 1980s and beyond concentrated on outcomes. Two ends of a telescope, but in reality both are important. Good processes produce good outcomes. There is no harm in assessing outcomes provided one understands the processes that produce them.

This chapter looks at the essential skills – the pedagogical skills – that underpin the educative process. It does not attempt to impart individual teaching skills, but to challenge the reader – who will be experienced in teaching skills already – to think more deeply about them. The essence of the chapter came out of a reference given by a head for one of his staff. 'Miss Smith,' it said, 'is concerned with the essential Why? questions of education, not just the How? questions.' Miss Smith was a thinker. So what made Miss Smith tick? Let's begin with a Why? question.

_____ Why do teachers act as they do in lessons? _____

Long ago, we came to the conclusion that effective teachers are highly self-conscious in the way that they behave in lessons. This insight emanated from research undertaken by the Teacher Education Project (1976–80). At the time we called this process self-analytical. By this descriptor we meant that as teachers went through the act of teaching they were examining and modifying their own behaviour in the light of feedback from pupils. Whether the teachers were controlling behaviour, imparting information, or probing for insight, they were aware of their own tone of voice, gestures, body language, spoken language, techniques (questioning, explaining) and so on, and aware also of the effects these were having on the learning process.

Other workers have described this phenomenon in other ways. Schon (1983) and Pollard and Tann (1993) speak about reflective practice, though this descriptor might imply that the process takes place beyond the lesson only, after an interval of time. Meijer, Douwe and Verloop (2002) describe the process as 'interactive cognitions'. This phrase really just means something like 'how teachers think as they teach'. This thinking will be determined by factors such as:

- the knowledge of the topic that the teacher has
- previous experience of dealing with similar situations
- the teacher's knowledge of pedagogical theory and practice
- the teacher's beliefs and values.

You can put these theories to the test in a small way by carrying out Activity 5.1.

ACTIVITY 5.1

Self-aware teaching

Choose a segment of a lesson you are planning to teach, perhaps the first 15 minutes with a class with which you feel comfortable.

(Ideally, you should get a colleague or technician to videotape the part of the lesson you intend to use for this exercise, though this is not essential. If you do have the session videotaped you should pre-warn the pupils so that they are not distracted by the camera.)

Teach the entire lesson. Later, when you have time but as soon as practical, try to reconstruct the lesson in your mind. Write down the reconstruction. You may find it helpful to use a grid like the one shown below. The boxes are filled in as examples only. You can amend the format to suit your lesson.

Lesson content broken into 'episodes'	What you did	What you were thinking	The effect on pupils
Pupils filed in.	Exchanged remarks with individuals as they settled.	I was trying to set a pleasant tone for the lesson. I know this class well and they respond in a friendly way and don't take advantage.	Pupils quickly sat down and got out notebooks and pens, as is normal.
Jason asked: 'What are we doing today?'	I said we were starting a new topic, but first they had to answer a short quiz to guess the topic.	Jason is very enthusiastic but tends to take over. I wanted to keep control of the theme at this point.	The pupils gave a mixed reaction: some thought I meant a test and groaned (but good-naturedly); others were intrigued.
Started the quiz.	I gave out some quiz cards with instructions not to turn them over and read them.	I was hoping I had pitched the quiz right so that no one got the answer instantly. I know this class likes a bit of challenge and mystery though they can get noisy.	The pupils were curious and showed interest.

Lesson content broken into 'episodes'	What you did	What you were thinking	The effect on pupils
Asked them to try to solve the quiz with consulting their neighbours.	Walked through the rows partly to discourage pupils from comparing notes and partly to gain feedback on answers.	I wanted them to struggle a bit with the answers so that we could go on and discuss the thought processes by which they had tried to solve the puzzle.	Pupils were involved, but important not to go on too long so those who could not solve the puzzle did not get bored.
Asked who thought they had answers.	Picked someone I knew had the wrong solution in order to raise some discussion, but someone not vulnerable to criticism.	I wanted to expose the thinking processes the pupils had gone through, but I knew I would need to be sensitive to Jo's wrong answer.	In the discussion the pupils got quite excited and tended to talk over one another (so I had to remind them of the class rules).

Now use the completed grid to think about:

■ how you used your knowledge of the topic to manipulate the lesson

■ the actions you took in the light of your previous experience of dealing with similar situations

■ the things you did as a result of your knowledge of pedagogical theory and practice

■ the beliefs and values you were trying to convey during the lesson.

(If you made a video of the lesson segment, now is the time to compare your reconstructed lesson from the grid with what actually happened. How accurate was your assessment?)

How self-aware were you? Did you find being self-aware easy? If not, why not? What did you learn from the process?

The purpose of this chapter, as we stated at the beginning, is not to give you a potted version of received wisdom about teaching skills. There are plenty of manuals that aim to do this and we shall refer to some of them. Rather, since our readers will be experienced and able teachers already, the intention is to get you to reflect on areas of your own teaching skill and how they might be revisited and developed. Activity 5.1 has set the scene for this process by emphasising that effective teachers are self-aware teachers; and that self-awareness is in itself a teaching skill. In the remainder of the chapter we look at important areas of classroom activity with a view to heightening your awareness of these and your ability to critique your performance in them.

Reviewing teachers' prior knowledge – subject, curriculum and pedagogy

As experienced teachers we do not come to our classes empty-handed, but bring with us a whole welter of knowledge, experience and understanding. Indeed, Jenlink (2001) describes the master teacher of our text as a 'scholar-practitioner'. The first of these 'knowledges' to which we would draw attention is subject knowledge, be it a specialist knowledge in a secondary school or a generalist knowledge in the primary sector. Fundamental to the teaching process are three things: a teacher/mediator, one or more learners, and something to be taught and learned – knowledge.

Herein lies the first debate. It is about the emphasis put on the supremacy of each of these three elements. In writing this chapter I picked the first seven titles (books and journals) about teaching, all written by teacher educators, off my bookshelf. Not one of the authors made subject knowledge a central theme, and the topic did not even appear in some of the indexes. By contrast, the first two government documents selected (Ofsted 2001, Teacher Training Agency (TTA) 2002) put knowledge at the heart of the process. That simple consultative act summarises the trichotomy that exists in the education world. We can construe education in one of three ways:

1 Education is knowledge-centred.

2 Education is teacher-centred.

3 Education is child-centred.

With which of these three statements do you empathise most? If you have selected one you may just have fallen into a trap. They are interdependent; at any given moment one may take some precedence, but none can exist alone. It is not about either/or, it is about balance and appropriateness to the purpose. Knowledge – knowing facts, things and events – is important of itself, but not as important as knowing where facts exist, how to access things, and how to evaluate events. Putting the child's needs, readiness, experiences and maturity at the centre of the learning process is fundamental, but not at the total expense of adult guidance, judgement and discretion. The hardest of the three philosophies (for that is what they are) and the most difficult to sustain in theory is the teacher-centred. Yet the practice of classrooms has, historically, been thus. Teachers traditionally dominate the talk, the decisions, the ground rules of school life.

This book takes a particular stance on subject knowledge. It suggests that teachers need to value their knowledge expertise because only then will they fulfil the criterion of being able to convey enthusiasm for knowledge to pupils. But the prerequisite of valuing their knowledge is that teachers sustain and develop it, that they are learners at their own level in their own areas. The teacher who is not a student of the subject(s) taught is not an adequate teacher. Being a continuing student is one of the marks of being a master teacher.

But teachers need more than updated subject knowledge and a keenness for what they teach. They need to contextualise that knowledge into creating a curriculum. In reality, what we call a National Curriculum is not; it is an agreed syllabus. The National Curriculum documents set out the content and topics to be covered; only rarely do the documents stray into the wider realms of curriculum.

Curriculum goes beyond information. First, it takes in the distinctive nature of subject disciplines – how historians treat evidence to interpret events, for example; how scientists push back the boundaries of knowledge; or the ways in which morality develops over time in world religions. Curriculum thus recognises that the world of 'information' is a limited world unless that knowledge is related to its contexts. Curriculum makes connections. It explores the boundaries of knowledge as they cross over the penumbras between disciplines. The scientist can only fully appreciate the theory of evolution if he/she also understands the social, religious and historical penumbras that charged that theory with such potential intellectual dynamite that they forced Darwin to keep news

REFLECTION

How do you integrate knowledge across subject boundaries within your classroom and within your school?

of it under wraps for years.

Eisner (1996) puts the argument about integration rather differently, using a different vocabulary, but towards the same ends and with much persuasion. He suggests that knowledge consists of 'forms of representation':

> *Those sensory qualities used in the culture to generate the symbolic forms we call art, music, dance, poetry, literary text, mathematics, science, and the like ... Secondly, I have argued that each form of representation is potentially subject to different* **modes of treatment***. Language, for example, can be treated in both literal and literary ways. The literal emphasizes a conventional mode of treatment, while the literary emphasizes an expressive mode ... Knowing the ways in which forms of representation can be treated means knowing the potentialities they possess for the representation of meaning. Fostering our understanding of these potentialities ... ought to be ... essential features of the programs we provide in schools. I also indicated that each form of representation can be variably located on a* **syntactical structure** *that extends from the rule-governed to the figurative.*
>
> (Eisner 1996: 88)

Eisner argues for presenting students and pupils with a wide range of learning experiences based on his model, to the ends that both schools and our culture and society are enriched. He concludes:

> *Educational equity is not likely without a range of opportunities that are wide enough to satisfy the diversity of talents of those who come to school and who share our future with us. As we seek genuinely to reform ... schools we will need to release ourselves from the grips of traditional stereotypes about what schools should be, how teaching is to proceed, what appropriate curriculum content entails, and how evaluation should occur.*
>
> (Eisner 1996: 89)

Esteve puts the issue differently again, but the message is the same:

> *Most of our teachers do not present academic material as a means of understanding the world around us, but as a series of separate pieces of information via which students learn facts, classification, definitions and law that are subsequently incapable of being used.*
>
> (Esteve 2000: 12)

Burton, Middlewood and Blatchford (2001) set out four models of curriculum and curriculum control or ownership. Similar models are set out in Table 5.1. In practice, schools and teachers operate on all four continua to a greater or lesser extent. What this section does is to challenge you to identify the dimensions of your own practice and that of the context in which you work.

Use the continua in Table 5.1 to interrogate the nature of your own curriculum.

TABLE 5.1 Dimensions of curriculum construction

Student-centred	<<<<<	>>>>>	Subject-centred
Process-related	<<<<<	>>>>>	Content-related
School/classroom-led	<<<<<	>>>>>	Government-led
Flexible	<<<<<	>>>>>	Target-based

Having looked in this section at knowledge and curriculum, we turn our attention now to pedagogy itself – the sacred art of the teacher, the science of how teaching and learning work. This has been discussed at length in Chapter 2 and we shall not revisit the same ground. However, attention is drawn here to a tantalising piece of research, albeit with a small sample and that of initial trainees. You may recall that in the introduction it was suggested that a key characteristic of teachers was care. We used the word in a broad sense: care for pupils, care for professionalism, and care for classroom process. Ethell and McMeniman (2002) discovered that for beginning teachers the key concept in judging teachers was care in a narrow sense (the affective domain). As time progressed they began to realise that subject and pedagogical knowledge were also significant. One beginning teacher, Mary, stood out in this respect:

> Mary was unique among the participants in that, through her written personal history, she articulated an awareness of the complexity of learning to teach and awareness that teaching involved both propositional and procedural knowledge.
>
> (Ethell and McMeniman 2002: 226)

This whole debate, distant as it may seem from the practical realities of day-to-day classrooms, is in fact fundamental not only to master teachers in order to further their understanding, but to teachers generally and the teaching profession. Cochrane-Smith (2000) discusses it in terms of what she calls the 'knowledge question' and the 'learning question'.

The knowledge question deals with what teachers should know. It has three broad answers. The first is the formal knowledge of the kind they get from university and other courses. The second is about experiential knowledge grounded in successful practice. The third is the knowledge that is generated by teachers enquiring into their own classrooms, and interrogating these processes when conducted by others.

The learning question features 'practitioner enquiry about problems of practice, collaboration with other professionals, and a concept of learning over time' (Cochrane-Smith 2000: 16–17) but rejects the notion of mere 'training' by focusing on growth and development. Likewise Dimmock (2000) is careful to distinguish between so-called 'best practice' and 'informed practice', since the former is limited by the belief that there is only one right way to proceed in every case.

But Cochrane-Smith points out that, while the knowledge and learning questions are often answered in statements that use remarkably similar language, below the surface are deep tensions. She concludes:

> If we frame knowledge and learning questions as a matter of prospective and experienced teachers learning to apply formal knowledge and demonstrate 'best practices', we ignore more than three decades of research on the social and psychological construction of knowledge and on the enormous significance of cultural differences, culturally relevant pedagogy, and culturally relevant assessment ... We also de-emphasise the importance of the construction of local knowledge in and by school communities and deemphasise the role of teachers as intellectuals and change agents.
>
> (Cochrane-Smith 2000: 18)

Stones put the issue in more direct language, but similarly and as a general standpoint for this chapter we would want to reinforce his view:

> Since teachers cannot predict all possible situations with which their pupils are likely to be faced, the pedagogical skills that teachers need should be appropriate to the development in pupils of abilities of general application. Thus the skills should not be concerned with pupils acquiring highly specific competencies, nor should they treat in a superficial way the acquisition of general capabilities.
>
> (Stones 1984: 50)

How much of the knowledge, understanding and skills that are communicated in your classes could genuinely be described as 'transferable' in the sense of Stones' quotation above?

Setting the cognitive tone

As well as the classroom climate and the behavioural management of classrooms (which were dealt with in Chapter 4), master teachers have to establish an intellectual climate, a view of how children think and the levels of cognition to which they should aspire. The case is put by one of the present authors in Kerry (2002a):

> *Learning ... involves processes beyond the mindless stimulus-response of trotting out 'correct' answers. It demands that students think. However, thinking is a dangerous process. For one thing one can think 'wrong' answers. An important part of thinking is speculation, and this may lead to the 'step in the dark' which proves to be incorrect. How will the teacher react to this? Sadly, there does appear to be a view of teaching and learning which suggests that* **learning right answers** *is more important than thinking out – despite a few false starts –* **insightful answers** *for one's self ... Regurgitation is a low level exercise: the real skill is learning to break new ground. But breaking new ground may meet a hostile response from a teacher anxious about getting on and getting things 'implanted' in students' minds, especially in a climate of assessment. For a student to be willing to engage in a genuinely cognitive process he or she has to feel totally secure that the teacher will react positively, even to well-thought-out errors.*
>
> (Kerry 2002a: 26)

Intellect has to be valued and that can only happen in a cognitive climate that is open to ideas and debate. While we shall not labour this point (you can pursue it further in the quoted text), it is one of the great pillars on which effective teaching stands.

What do you do as a teacher to encourage insightful answers from your pupils?

Identifying learning objectives

The rehearsal of learning objectives has become the essential mantra of the teaching profession since the rise of Ofsted in the early 1990s. They should not be confused with targets (Department for Education and Science (DfES) 2002), which are the guiding principles of New Labour. Targets are the standards that teachers, politicians, parents or the community expect pupils to attain. Learning objectives are (in the short term) the intentions for lessons, (and in the longer term) for projects, courses, syllabuses. It has been argued (Kerry 2002a) that they come in five domains, as is shown in Table 5.2.

Learning objectives are essential simply because they are the items that provide the compass bearings for the direction of learning; they are integral to planning. Master teachers share the learning objectives with their pupils so that both parties can assess whether the learning journey is on the right track and whether it is on target to reach its destination.

TABLE 5.2 The five domains of learning objectives

Knowledge	At the end of the lesson what do I want students to know that they did not know before?
Understanding	At the end of the lesson what do I want students to understand that they did not understand before?
Skills	At the end of the lesson what do I want students to do that they could not do before?
Attitudes	At the end of the lesson what do I want students to feel about the subject matter that they did not feel before?
Social/affective	How do I want them to be able to work (e.g. collaboratively, with mutual respect)?

Differentiating

While the overall learning objectives for a lesson may be clear, not all pupils have equal ability; achievement will come at different cognitive levels. Differentiating work for pupils with different abilities and aptitudes (especially within the same class) is one of the skills of master teachers. Yet, important though it is, guidance on this topic is frugal in the literature. It does not even appear in the index of texts such as Turner-Bisset (2001). A search for differentiation in classrooms reveals a predominance of differentiation by outcome; i.e. all pupils are set the same work and what distinguishes them is how they perform on it. This approach is limited and inadequate as a sole solution. Differentiation has to be built in at the lesson-planning stage, which means that effective teachers need a range of strategies on which they can call. This might be an opportune moment to review your own approaches through the Reflection and Activity 5.2.

REFLECTION

Discovering what you do when you teach

Keep a diary for a day and jot down what you have spent your time doing in your teaching role (or observe another teacher if you are not currently teaching).

How many different tasks have you (or your observee) undertaken?

What have you (or your observee) spent most time on?

ACTIVITY 5.2

Considering differentiation strategies in your teaching

Begin by reviewing your last week's work. What strategies, other than by outcome, did you use to differentiate work for pupils of different aptitudes and abilities?

Now look at the boxed list. Over time, find opportunities to try out each of the suggestions. When you have tried each one, record its major strengths and weaknesses.

Method of differentiation	Strengths	Weaknesses
Using graduated worksheets		
Making available resource packs of additional information		
Asking open questions more often		
Using individual learning contracts		
Challenging pupils' assumptions		
Increasing the use of support assistants		
Encouraging pupils to self-pace		
Removing unnecessary repetition		
Using homework time for an extended project		

Method of differentiation	Strengths	Weaknesses
Promoting self-marking or self-criticism of work by pupils		
Allowing a variety of responses to tasks: e.g. pictures, cartoons, video		
Asking cognitively demanding questions		
Setting tasks with no single correct solution		
Using role play		
Setting tasks with increased cognitive demand		

Finally, if you want to see how other teachers responded, you can read the outcomes in Kerry (2002a: 95–7).

Task-setting

Of course, differentiation implies that teachers will be setting pupils tasks to complete – something that teachers do all the time, and a teaching skill integral to the effective performance of all teachers. Again, one might expect a significant bulk of literature about setting classroom tasks, but there isn't one. The national standards for teachers (Teacher Training Agency (TTA) 2002) are amazingly coy on the issue, perhaps assuming that it is so fundamental a skill that little mention needs to be made of it and no guidance is required. However, research by Bennett and Desforges (1984) indicates clearly that many classroom tasks are ill-directed (i.e. they are too hard or too easy). Classroom studies by Kerry (in Wragg 1984) showed that tasks could be cognitively of a higher order or a low order, and that they were predominantly the latter. Master teachers set tasks that overcome these problems, aware that a diet of low-level operations is stultifying for many pupils, even those with special learning needs. They eschew the low-order tasks (copying, regurgitation, unnecessary memorisation, endless practice) except for essential revision and seek out the higher order, as shown in Table 5.3. They create a variety of tasks within a lesson to aid the process of differentiation.

TABLE 5.3 Higher-order* tasks reviewed

Task type	Example
Imaginative	Write your impressions of being caught up in a devastating flood
Evidence collection, problem-solving, deducing, reasoning	Devise an experiment to test which colour feeder (if any) birds prefer
Application	How does this circuit board work?
Analysis	Why do you think the outcome of the battle was such a disaster?
Synthesis	Using what you know about the Roman history and about the terrain, devise a better site for Hadrian's Wall and justify your suggestion
Evaluation	Review a Harry Potter book and say why it appeals to children and young people

* This categorisation is based on an adaptation of the work of Bloom (1956)

——— Explaining ———

One thing you can bet on: teachers talk. Most of that talk is some form of explanation – explaining information, or explaining what to do (i.e. giving instructions). Explanations lend themselves to analysis on criteria of effectiveness, and the master teacher will perform well on these criteria. Kerry (2002b) set out one such set of criteria for effective explanations and this is included here as Table 5.4.

This table does not exhaust the parameters of effective explanations. Good teachers will be aware (just as they are when setting tasks) of the cognitive levels of the explanation. Explanations can be low-level, dealing with facts alone or bodies of information – the Romans first came to England under the command of Julius Caesar; they can be at higher levels, either the conceptual level (which provides reasons, explanations and general principles); or at the abstract level. At the conceptual level the teacher might explain the propaganda value of Caesar's British expedition. At the abstract level he/she may analyse the nature of the Pax Romana.

Good explainers take account of audience. Effective explanations may be enhanced by the use of visual materials that aid understanding. Explanations are part of classroom language, and their role and effectiveness are part of the whole language policy for the class and the school.

The principles of good explaining need to be perpetuated in other contexts: in devising written worksheets or in preparing IT-based or e-learning materials. Next to effective behaviour management, the skill of explaining is probably the most vital for the teacher's day-to-day effectiveness.

TABLE 5.4 Criteria for judging the effectiveness of explanations

Criterion	Example
Dynamic introduction	A striking turn of phrase, dynamic picture, sound effect
Defining new terms and key concepts	'Migration is a mass movement by some creatures in response to a stimulus or the seasons'
Linking to concrete experience	'You remember we saw the swallows massing on the phone lines in October…'
Using positive and negative examples	'But you don't see house sparrows doing the same thing…'
Building in tasks	'Now, go through the field guide and find me half a dozen migrants, and half a dozen species that don't migrate…'
Introducing and using technical language	'The urge to migrate seems to be in part genetic, which means…'
Developing rules and principles	'Much migration is in response to the need to sustain good feeding…'
Using connectives to enhance meaning	'While it is true that robins may have a partial migration pattern, nevertheless their movements are not like those of swallows…'
Exploiting linguistic ploys	'Now I want to emphasise this point…'
Using repetition and emphasis	'In every case – and I mean every case…'
Using appropriate pace	The teacher will keep a check on whether the pupils are following the explanation, and slow down or pause if need be, or speed up if there is evidence of it being too easy
Numbering points	'Let's recap on this: first, we said … and second that…'

Using humour	'You could say swallows were like wealthy film stars – one home from which to work (breed), and a warm pad in a foreign country to avoid the winter…'
Linking to other knowledge	'Can you think of any examples of human migration?'
Providing for feedback	'Jamie, just recap for us …'

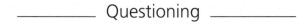

Questioning

As teaching skills, questioning and explaining complement one another: many explanations are punctuated by questions in order to elicit feedback (and thus check understanding), but equally questioning is a skill in its own right and with its own rationale as Kerry (2002b) records:

> *Enquiry lies at the heart of the education process; and enquiry takes place through the formulation of questions, problems and hypotheses which require answers and solutions.*
>
> (Kerry 2002b: 65)

The Teacher Training Agency (TTA) (2001) draft handbook requires of teachers:

> *A repertoire of questioning techniques, which are inclusive and which encourage pupils to contribute, to expand on topics, to reflect, to evaluate, and to share relevant personal insights and experiences.*
>
> (TTA 2001: para 3.2.1)

The basic criteria for establishing successful questioning by teachers in their classrooms are set out in Kerry (2002b) and are summarised in this list:

- Encourage pupils to talk – and to talk constructively and on-task.
- Establish the ground rules – such as not interrupting each other.
- Create a learning ethos – one that encourages high-level cognition and problem-solving.
- Keep students curious – don't give away every answer.

- Make investigation a central teaching method in your classroom.
- Make sure that students themselves own the problem.
- Encourage students to make the intuitive leap.
- Value everyone's contribution – even incorrect or partial answers.
- Monitor the learning in progress.
- Continually raise the cognitive stakes.

Higher-order questions reflect the higher-order tasks discussed earlier in this chapter. They ask pupils to imagine, reason and use evidence, analyse, apply, synthesise and evaluate. Research has suggested that less than 10 per cent of questions in classrooms are at a higher order of operation. Dillon (1988) usefully points out that students can and should ask questions as well as act as targets for them. Students' questions are equally sparse in the analysis of lesson transcripts. Dillon also points out that teachers wait too short a time for answers, claiming that 'students are habitually given less than one second' to come up with answers (Dilton 1988: 102) – a situation understandable with novice teachers who are afraid of the potential of silences for misbehaviour, but an error that should not creep into the work of master teachers.

It is helpful then to think of questions not as isolated events so much as sequences that build up from small beginnings into endings that have cognitive significance. This is one mark of master teaching.

—————— Assessing, recording and reporting ——————

It is important, in this review of teaching skills, not to play down the skills of assessing, recording and reporting. However, as they are covered in some detail in Chapter 7 the reader should pick up their story at that point.

—————— Learning on your feet ——————

Like other worthwhile forms of knowledge, teaching skills are not things to be 'implanted' on the apprenticeship model, as we have seen; nor can they be simply plucked out of books or from the internet. They are a subtle mixture of theoretical understanding, applied and action research, experience and practice that can be honed and extended for a professional life time. Be grateful: teaching would be boring were it otherwise!

Woods (2002) sums up things well in the following list of factors in what he calls 'creative teaching':

- the magic, thrill, excitement, enthusiasm, joy of teaching and learning
- the charismatic qualities of educators
- the democratisation of the teaching–learning process
- the creation of (positive) classroom atmospheres
- emotional connections between teachers and pupils
- a mix of discourses and styles
- uncommon accomplishment.

He goes on to assert:

> *Teachers [use] their skills of invention and innovation to find 'ways through' to pupil learning, to orchestrate conflictual elements in the teacher role, to resolve satisfactorily the many dilemmas thrown up in the classroom from moment to moment, to improvise and employ all moments of the day to optimize learning, and, not least, to cope with the many pressures and constraints.*
>
> (Woods 2002: 75)

REFLECTION

What are the skills of 'invention and innovation' that you use to 'find your way through' to pupils' learning?

How teachers convey these messages about the nature and cognitive demand of learning to pupils leads us to the next section.

Example and image

In this section we want only to tell a short story to illustrate the point that skilled teachers have to lead learning from the front, by signalling its place in their lives and their enthusiasms. So the story is this:

> *Celtic Park secondary school (Kerry and Kerry 2001), as part of its drive to recruit pupils from feeder primaries, put on a day for able year 5 pupils. They were to come and have an enjoyable and demanding learning experience. This would fire their enthusiasm for attending Celtic Park at transfer time. So the lesson took place and groups of youngsters, who had been accompanied by various*

adults, settled down to the tasks. One task was to write a poem on a given theme. As the children worked on, with great enthusiasm, we noticed one adult (as it turned out, a head teacher) sitting quietly in a corner, writing. Curious, we stole a look over his shoulder. He was doing the task as set to the pupils. Afterwards he showed us the result: he had drafted and improved the poem and it was pretty good. 'I often sit down and do tasks alongside the children,' he said. 'How else would they know they were important?'

Learning styles and meeting pupils' needs

To round off our review of teaching skills for master teachers we look at an underlying philosophy: that learning and teaching need to be tailored to the needs of pupils and that means learning and teaching styles have to be adapted to their needs. There are a number of ways of approaching this issue. At its simplest, and from the teacher's perspective, one might say that many different teaching methods/styles are available to the teacher. These include such activities as telling a story, explanation, questioning, completing a task such as a written exercise, formal debate, informal discussion, carrying out an experiment, doing a project, taking part in a quiz, role play, drama, composition, or a mock examination – there are plenty more. Individual pupils will prefer some teaching methods to others. The skill of the teacher is to keep the classroom experience high on variety so that all pupils get something of what they most like and not too much of what they dislike. This is a reasonable pragmatic approach that many effective teachers adopt.

But there are other approaches. Alexander (2001: 15) makes a good point about the organisation of the school timetable. He emphasises that one can alter the nature of learning and the variety of activities that can be attempted by having flexible lesson lengths. We have experience of a secondary school in which all learning was divided into one of three curriculum blocks: humanities, science and mathematics, and leisure. Teachers taught in teams and pupils were assigned to tutorial groups but often taught together. The blocking of subjects meant that the timetable could have a combination of slots: whole-day, half-day, double and single lessons. Blocking combined with team teaching also meant that work could be interdisciplinary. This flexibility provided precisely the flexibility Alexander describes.

A further factor in the learning styles controversy picks up the theme of the legitimacy of the child-centredness philosophy. Much ink has been spilled in this debate, especially with respect to the Plowden (1967) report into primary education which sparked it. Kerry (2001) defends the Plowden position and enumerates the good things to which it has led (Table 5.5). He refutes the position taken by Simon (1999) who grossly overstates his case as a way of rejecting the message:

> By focussing on the individual child (at the heart of the education process lies the child) ... the Plowden Committee created a situation from which it was impossible to derive an effective pedagogy ... If each child is unique, and each requires a specific pedagogical approach appropriate to him or her and to no other, the construction of an all-embracing pedagogy, or general principles of teaching becomes an impossibility ... Teachers who attempt to implement these prescripts ... lead from behind.
>
> (Simon 1999: 42)

The fact is that the child-centred approach requires of teachers a high level of skill to achieve, and promotes factors that are not easily measured. Thus it does not appeal to mechanistic teachers or to politicians looking for a quick fix though their most recent publication tries to re-invent it (DfES 2003). It reflects, in an exemplary way, the parameters of 'care' as we defined this characteristic of master teachers earlier in the text.

TABLE 5.5 The benefits of the Plowden philosophy

Is it possible to return to that self-evident truth [at the heart of the educational process lies the child] as a guiding principle in education, and if so what would it mean?

It is possible to give only a brief glimpse at the potential for rediscovering child-centredness in education, but here are just a few of the possible results of that process:

1 A curriculum framework (as opposed to a tightly defined content-based curriculum) that provides:

- an entitlement for all
- scope for the most able to be creative
- opportunities for those with learning difficulties to have their specific needs met more flexibly.

2 A recognition that there are some basic skills that need to be acquired for successful learning at any age or stage.

3 A technology-based curriculum that plays more than lip service to anytime–anywhere learning, i.e. one that values learning rather than attendance.

4 A redefinition of the nature and role of schools as community learning centres in which everybody, adult or child, pursues vocational and non-vocational learning on a lifelong model.

5 A recognition that many people 'teach' and that the teaching function may be attributed to different groups of people, in different ways, at different times.

6 An acceptance that reaching the goals of one's learning is individually important, rather than an obsession with summative assessment and institutional league tables.

7 The replacement of a culture of failure and blame in education by a recognition of the importance of success as a motivator, and success born out of inherent interest in learning.

8 A recognition that knowledge and advances in knowledge require the realisation that while knowledge is composed of disciplines, these are only contributory factors in an integrated understanding of complicated problems.

9 An acknowledgement that higher levels of cognition are reached more often and more meaningfully in knowledge that is integrated rather than compartmentalised.

10 A rediscovery and recognition of teachers' professionalism and the valuing of this by society and especially parents and pupils.

Source: Kerry (2001: 24–5)

Theoretical models of learning styles try to identify types of learner. Thus Honey and Momford (1986):

Reflectors	–	learn through feeling and experience
Theorists	–	learn by watching and value ideas
Pragmatists	–	learn through thinking and problem-solving
Activists	–	learn by doing.

Alternatively, Galton and Simon (1980) suggested the following self-explanatory category system:

- attention seekers
- intermittent workers
- solitary workers
- quiet collaborators.

Triggs and Pollard (1998: 109) emphasise the multiple dimensions of learning as they impinge on learning style. For their model these are the variables that interact:

- relationships: of self and others with family, peers and teachers

- a sense of identity: intellectual and physical

- the learner's own material: linguistic and cultural resources

- learning challenges: experiences and relationships on which to draw

- learning stances and strategies: self-confidence, motivation

- opportunity to learn in social settings

- quality of teaching and assistance in learning

- informal learning outcomes: self-esteem, social status

- formal learning outcomes: attainment.

REFLECTION

Which of these categorisations of learning styles strike chords in your own experience? How consciously do you set out to meet a variety of needs, and what more could you do?

If, as is claimed (Winkley 1997) 'the essential difference between the school of the 1990s and of the 21st century is our emphatic determination to adjust organ-isational procedures ... to suit the needs of individuals', then we have indeed regrasped the Plowden philosophy and projected it on to both primary and sec-ondary students. It certainly provides the best hope there is around. The alternative recalls a passage from Ciaran Carson's autobiographical book *The Star Factory,* with which our own education empathised too much:

> *We were constantly interrogated, since much of our routine of learning was by rote. Rote did not end with primary school alphabets and tables, for it entered into full plethora in grammar school. We learned lists of Latin (and) French words, together with their proper conjugations and declensions, their voices, tenses and moods; we sang names, dates, places, populations; we got poems, songs and recitations off by heart ... All subjects had a greater or lesser liturgical exactitude. There were correct answers to everything.*
>
> (Carson 1988: 213–13)

One way in which this bleak picture has changed is through the use of learning technologies in schools – to which topic we turn our attention in the next chapter.

At the end of this chapter you should have:

■ Reviewed the major teaching skills required of master teachers and all teachers

■ Related these teaching skills to issues in the debate about pedagogy

■ Thought through some issues of learning style as they apply to your situation

■ Become more self-aware in your teaching

■ Taken on board a range of thinking about the theoretical underpinning of teaching skills

---

References

Alexander, R. (2001) 'Pedagogy and culture: a perspective in search of a method', in J. Soler, A. Craft, and H. Burgess, *Teacher Development: Exploring Our Own Practice,* London: PCP Open University.

Bennett, N. and Desforges, C. (1984) *The Quality of Pupils' Learning Experiences,* New Jersey: Lawrence Earlbaum.

Bloom, B. (1956) *Taxonomy of Educational Objectives,* London: Longman.

Burton, N., Middlewood, D. and Blatchford, R. (2001) *Managing the Curriculum,* London: PCP.

Carson, C. (1988) *The Star Factory,* London: Granton.

Cochrane-Smith, M. (2000) 'The future of teacher education: framing the questions that matter', *Teaching Education,* 11(1): 13–24.

Department for Education and Skills (DfES) (2002) *Education and Skills – Delivering Results: A Strategy to 2006,* London: DfES.

Department for Education and Skills (2003) *Excellence and Enjoyment,* London: DfES.

Dillon, J. (1988) *Questioning and Teaching: A Manual of Practice,* London: Croom Helm.

Dimmock, C. (2000) *Designing the Learning-Centered School,* London: Falmer.

Eisner, E. (1996) *Cognition and Curriculum Reconsidered,* 2nd edn, London: PCP.

Esteve, J. (2000) 'Culture in the school: assessment and the content of education', *European Journal of Teacher Education,* 23(1): 5–18.

Ethell, R. and McMeniman, M. (2002) 'A critical first step in learning to teach', in C. Sugrue, and C. Day, *Developing Teachers and Teaching Practice,* London: Routledge Falmer.

Galton, M. and Simon, B. (1980) *Progress and Performance in the Primary Classroom,* London: Routledge.

Honey, P. and Momford, P. (1986) *A Manual of Learning Styles,* Maidenhead: Peter Honey.

Jenlink P. (2001) 'Scholar-practitioner leadership: a critical analysis of preparation and practice', paper presented at the annual meeting of the American Educational Research Centre, Seattle, WA, April.

Kerry, T. (2001) *Plowden: Mirage, Myth or Flag of Convenience? Towards a More Humane View of Managing the Curriculum for the 21stC,* Working Paper no. 43, Lincoln: University of Lincoln.

Kerry, T. (2002a) *Learning Objectives, Task Setting and Differentiation,* Cheltenham: Nelson Thornes.

Kerry, T. (2002b) *Explaining and Questioning,* Cheltenham: Nelson Thornes.

Kerry, T. and Kerry, C. (2001) 'The Celtic Park challenge of excellence' , *Education Today,* 51(2): 10–15.

Meijer, P., Douwe, B. and Verloop, N. (2002) 'Examining teachers' interactive cognitions using insights from research on teachers' practical knowledge', in C. Sugrue and C. Day, *Developing Teachers and Teaching Practice,* London: Routledge Falmer.

Ofsted (2001) 'Inspecting modern foreign languages', London: Office of Her Majesty's Chief Inspector.

Plowden, Lady B. (1967) *Children and their Primary Schools,* London: HMSO.

Pollard, A. and Tann, S. (1993) *Reflective Teaching in the Primary School,* London: Cassell.

Schon, D. (1983) *The Reflective Practitioner: How Professionals Think in Action,* New York: Basic Books.

Simon, B. (1999) 'Why no pedagogy in England?', in J. Leach and B. Moon, *Learners and Pedagogy,* London: PCP Open University.

Stones, E. (1984) *Supervision in Teacher Education,* London: Methuen.

Teacher Training Agency (TTA) (2001) *Standards for the Award of Qualified Teacher Status,* London: TTA.

Teacher Training Agency (TTA) (2002) *Requirements for Initial Teacher Training,* London: TTA.

Triggs, P. and Pollard, A. (1998) 'Pupil experience and a curriculum for life-long learning', in C. Richards and P. Taylor, *How Shall We School our Children? Primary Education and Its Future,* London: Falmer.

Turner-Bisset, R. (2001) *Expert Teaching: Knowledge and Pedagogy to Lead the Profession,* London: David Fulton.

Winkley, D. (1997) 'A vision: the twenty-first-century primary school', in C. Cullingord (ed.), *The Politics of Primary Education,* Buckingham: Open University Press.

Woods, P. (2002) 'Teaching and learning in the new millenium', in C. Sugrue and C. Day, *Developing Teachers and Teaching Practice,* London: Routledge Falmer.

Wragg, E. (1984) *Classroom Teaching Skills*, London: Croom Helm.

chapter six

The innovative teacher

The ICT revolution and its implications for learning

What are ICT and globalisation?

What implications does ICT have for knowledge and learning?

What evidence is there that ICT is beneficial to learning?

What effects does ICT have on teachers and their roles?

Is it all benefit?

Nerd or dunce – where are you on the spectrum?

State of the art or out of the ark?

Deciding why, how and when to use ICT

In this chapter you are invited to:

- Consider the implications of ICT and globalisation for a view of learning
- Understand the implications for teachers and teaching of the ICT revolution
- Translate these theoretical constructs into teaching skills and strategies
- Prepare to make your own transition to the 'new' learning world

In this chapter we look initially at the theoretical underpinning of learning in the new world of information and communications technology (ICT), globalisation and internationalism. Then we move on to examine some of the practical issues that affect teachers and their skills in individual classrooms.

___ What are ICT and globalisation? ___

ICT is frequently employed as shorthand for 'using a computer' (often simply as a word processor), but this denies its revolutionary aspect. ICT embodies within itself storehouses of knowledge of beyond encyclopaedic proportions. It provides the user with the option to access that knowledge in selective and self-chosen ways and at any time. It moves out the boundaries of communication from local to global and it constructs knowledge according to new and more flexible rules where interconnections between information are not only possible but also in the user's control. Users are not merely recipients but, potentially, creators. Users are not merely teachers but learners.

Globalisation has two directions of meaning. First, it recognises that, via the use of electronic communication, people everywhere are potentially in touch with one another. Second, there is the deeper implication that people – that is, cultures, politics, norms, values, economies, financial systems, etc. – are more interdependent as a result. Spender (1998) puts this starkly:

> *The new technologies, however, have revolutionised society, changing forever work, relationships, understandings, leisure, communication – and learning – all in the space of a generation … ours. We were born into, and reared in, one culture – with its basis in print, a scientific approach, manufacturing, and a gold/paper currency system. We are having to operate in another culture – digital – which is characterised by being relative, and based on intellectual property … In varying forms, we are all suffering from cultural shock. We are reeling from the constant need to rethink, re-evaluate and think differently – having to change how we make sense of the world, what our values are, what our work, authority, expertise, and identity have been.*
>
> (Spender 1998: 3)

What implications does ICT have for knowledge and learning?

ICT gives youngsters an opportunity to learn more flexibly, and schools a chance to utilise that flexibility to offer a more varied service to learners. Developments such as video-conferencing and the use of computers allow an unprecedented set of opportunities for learners (Kerry 2000):

- The very best lessons on a given topic from any source, anywhere can be made available for access at any time.
- Access to learning no longer requires attendance at a given place or at a given time.
- The role of the teacher becomes a more 'on-demand' affair, and the delivery of the expertise may itself be at a distance, for example by e-mail.

These changes affect the essence of what we understand by schooling and question most of the 'givens' of education as we know it. Here are just a few of the other revolutions that such a use of ICT has the power to deliver:

- a breed of super-teachers producing the best lessons for global transmission
- the demise of the school building
- the end of the traditional years of schooling – because learning can be lifelong in the most genuine sense

- learning as a self-paced activity

- learning that can be assessed at any time the student chooses, sweeping away the constraints of annual examinations

- choices for learners – about how, when, what and why they learn

- unprecedented change in the nature of the profession of teaching and its associated structures such as the Local Education Authorities and even Ofsted itself (Lonsdale and Parsons 1998).

For the present purpose of this section, the key focus of change is that to the concept of learning. There are four standpoints that need to be investigated:

- that the curriculum has to be redefined

- that the nature of learning has to be redefined

- that the ownership of learning has to be reallocated

- that the nature of assessment has to be redefined.

The curriculum has to be redefined

Let us paint a simplistic picture. Pre-1988 teachers were controllers of the curriculum: in the best schools they devised and planned curriculum across all subjects with a steer and oversight from the head teacher. While this process provided rich experiences in good schools, it could lead to impoverished and repetitive work in poor schools; and what was lacking across the board was any level of entitlement for all pupils. The picture was clearer in secondary schools when pupils began to work towards public examinations. After the 1988 Act heads and teachers lost control of the curriculum to government, which established a National Curriculum. This was intended as a way of ensuring a basic entitlement for all pupils, but was not well thought through, so that it turned out to be more of a syllabus, and constant revisions were necessary even to the present time. Sometimes, as in the case of literacy and numeracy, there was pressure not only to cover specific ground but to do so in specific ways. This curriculum is enforced through school governance by non-teachers and by inspection. While this curriculum continued, ICT began to develop alongside it, with schools having increased access to technology and its powerful potential. Thus the question for the future remains: how can curriculum be determined and ring-fenced in a knowledge society and global context?

This is the dilemma we currently face. At one level we can hypothesise that schools will use e-learning sources in place of, or as well as, printed ones. We can suggest that able teachers, supported by excellent ICT support staff, will produce their own e-learning materials; that they will teach using interactive white boards; that the school will establish an intranet. All this has happened here and there. We could go further: the government will promote a national grid for learning, to make available everything from lesson notes to policy or propaganda. But when we have said all this we are a long way short.

The real curriculum dilemma is that when learners are free to learn anything, any time, anywhere, at their own pace, the control of curriculum as we have known it is dead in the water.

The nature of learning has to be redefined

As with curriculum, so with the learning process. Bowring-Carr and West-Burnham (1997) put it like this:

> IT has loosened us from the limitations of time and space ... School is no longer the main place to go for information. It may be the place to go for encouragement, guidance, coaching, socialisation, fun, sport, theatre and a whole slew of community activities, but the prime task of imparting, checking, and testing the retention of information need no longer be a main activity carried out in a school as we know it today.
>
> (Bowring-Carr and West-Burnham 1997: 58)

Hough (2000) describes progress made in an institution which:

> has developed a practical state of the art application that captures the intellectual knowledge of the organisation and moves the school from a 'community of learners' to a 'critical learning community'. It supports ... the new virtual classroom and creates the positive shift from an instructivist model of teaching to a constructivist model of learning, in which the learning process is controlled and built by the learner ... The technology-enhanced learning environment continues to build upon learnings and now embraces the significant partnership of learning culture, continuous improvement and learning community. Information technology provides a sound basis as the school aims to recreate itself as a knowledge ecology.
>
> (Hough 2000: 16)

But Hough's description leads us to the third issue.

The ownership of learning has to be reallocated

Hough again puts this graphically:

> Access to technology has changed the role of the teacher and the purpose of the classroom for ever. Technology-aware teachers are now attempting to transform information into learning scaffolds that students can use to apply to new learning situations ... but for the first time, suggests Salomon (1997: 6) 'education has to chase technology down the classroom aisles and through the Internet channels to tailor old pedagogical rationales to new possibilities'.
>
> (Hough 2000: 9)

The nature of assessment has to be redefined

In this new learning climate many aspects of 'old thinking' have to go by the board. High on this list is our current cumbersome approach to assessment. The 'old' learning of the age of print is dominated by written examinations, controlled by examination boards, working to traditional timetables (with assessment opportunities available just once or twice a year), and on preconceived notions of critical moments (for example, that most students will take GCSE examinations in year 11). In the world of 'new' learning all this is a nonsense.

Lifelong learners, according to Candy, Crebert and O'Leary (1994), will develop enquiring minds and critical spirits. They will continue learning literally over a lifetime. They will develop a sense of the interconnectedness of knowledge across traditional boundaries. They will learn to interrogate information in a variety of forms, and to use and manage what they learn; they will develop skills of self-confidence and self-organisation to promote their own learning. They will operate within their preferred learning styles to proceed to deep learning, i.e. learning that results in changes in the ways that the learner behaves and sees the world.

These learners, of any age, will require – where relevant and appropriate – assessment on demand. Assessment, like learning, will have to be available on-line. It will not be confined to predetermined times and seasons, nor to particular ages. The able learner will be able to choose assessment after a short period, the slower worker after whatever time lapse is appropriate. Like learning, assessment opportunities will be available any time, anywhere (Newman 2000). This again gives the learner, not the teacher, ownership of the learning process.

——————— What evidence is there that ICT is ———————
beneficial to learning?

While all this may sound grand and futuristic, are we able to say with any degree of certainty that ICT has a beneficial effect on learning? There are surprisingly few systematic studies that try to address this issue; of these one of the best is by Taylor (2000). What is good about this work is that it actually comes to grips with the question of whether, when using ICT, students operate at higher orders of thinking. Taylor carried out a study of a large number of lessons in a comprehensive school in the Midlands. He devised a system (based on an 11-point Bloomian-style scale, Bloom 1956) to estimate the cognitive levels at which pupils engaged in these lessons were working. In those lessons where pupils were using laptop computers Taylor suggests that his observations indicate that 56.5 per cent contained thinking at level 6 or above on the scale. In lessons where no laptop work was involved, his observations suggest this figure fell to 19.7 per cent – a drop of 36.8 per cent.

Thus Taylor's inital conclusion is that the use of laptops does appear to promote higher order thinking. These investigations are on-going and so the conclusions that can be drawn from them are tentative; but if proven over time they suggest a masssive swing to higher level thinking as a result of the use of ICT.

Even more positively, Taylor thinks that use of laptops leads to increased motivation to learn among both boys and girls. Thus, motivation by girl students in non-laptop lessons was rated as 81.4 per cent; but in laptop lessons this rose to 92 per cent. For boys, high motivation was estimated in non laptop lessons for 67.5 per cent of time, but in laptop lessons this rose 75.9 per cent.

Taylor also made measurements of the duration for which students stayed at level 6 thinking and above during laptop and non-laptop lessons. When laptops were not used students stayed at level 6 for 12.5 per cent of the time; but in laptop lessons this figure rose to 40.3 per cent of learning time. These figures certainly suggest that ICT can enhance the cognitive value of learning and sustain that higher-order learning for longer.

The other consistent finding is that offering boys the chance to learn using ICT keeps them focused on learning in a way that classroom studies do not (Bleach 1998), thus helping to close the widely reported performance gap between girls and boys. Increased interest in systems of on-line assessment (Hackett 1999; Newman 2000) to obviate resistance to traditional pen-and-paper-testing provides powerful motives for increased ICT in the classrooms of the future.

What effects does ICT have on teachers and their roles?

Gillmon (1998) predicted that teachers in the developing world of ICT would need the skills for:

- everyday data analysis and management
- multi-media resource compilation
- on-line communication with external agencies, parents and pupils.

Professional development would need to help teachers to learn how to:

- develop students' skills in information retrieval and analysis
- assess pupils' progress in acquiring skills related to the information age
- analyse data and evaluate resource materials.

Scrimshaw (2001) argues the case for the computer as a means for extending the curriculum, placing much emphasis on software as the agent for learning. Though he admits other possibilities, this view of itself is somewhat limiting. First, the technology can be used to go well beyond this brief. Second, as Kennedy (1999) argues, schools and teaching need to be redefined in the light of the power of technology:

> [They will] take on new ICT infrastructure that will fundamentally alter the teaching/learning process. They will equip young people for employability in the knowledge economy and engagement with the values and institutions of society, ensuring that they become informed and active citizens. They will be community resources for life-long learning, providing internet access to the community, social services for students and their families, and the focus of community building and support activities.
>
> (Kennedy 1999: 12)

Most writers agree that teaching will move away from the didactic towards models that embrace coaching, tutoring, supporting and facilitating.

Is it all benefit?

Sceptical readers might interject at this point that our chapter has painted a rather glowing picture – a picture of change, certainly, and change can be threatening –

but a picture of progress, of excitement and of challenge. They might say that this is not true to their experience. Well, such sceptics might be right, and it is incumbent on us to balance the picture with at least some of the problems that surround ICT and its implementation in classrooms.

First, there is the issue that by no means all schools are as advanced in introducing the hardware (let alone the software). This is due to lack of resources. If a school can afford only two computers per classroom, then ICT can hardly be the centre of children's learning experiences, whatever the declared intention of National Curriculum. Add to this the fact that technology moves on at breakneck speed, so that today's new purchases are obsolete in three years' time, then the corollary is that these schools will never catch up. The truth of this is irrefutable and only massive injections of cash from fiscal sources will solve the problem. So the future has to be one of favoured and unfavoured schools – unequal opportunity.

Second, in a society where laptops are increasingly the tool for school students, and access to the internet or intranet a necessity for homework, some pupils will inevitably be disadvantaged. The children of poor families will miss out, and the children of more affluent families will benefit. This is also true – another form of unequal opportunity.

Third, the increased use of laptops has brought opposition from an unexpected direction – fears about children's posture and health as a result of lugging overloaded schoolbags over long distances and carrying them around all day.

Fourth, there are social penalties for ICT development: increased isolation of the learner, diminution of social skills, and increased vulnerability to exploitation by groups, from advertisers to paedophiles.

These problems do not even begin to move into the wider picture of the role of ICT in controlling the health or otherwise of the global economy, the opportunities for social control or the dangers caused by global terrorism. All of these issues will impinge on teachers, learners and society in general. However, in the balance between benefit and cost it is suggested that schools, teachers and pupils have much to gain from the technological developments of the last few years.

Furthermore, we recognise the efforts that government has made in recent years to equip teachers with laptops and to provide some training in the use and potential of ICT. But it is still not enough to realise the best elements of the vision. So in what follows there is the tacit recognition also that teachers will be operating at different levels of progress in different school contexts.

Nerd or dunce – where are you on the spectrum?

Awareness of the ideological implications and potential impact of ICT on teaching and learning is important in helping teachers to consider and develop responses to the opportunities and challenges it represents. However, regardless of how one responds to the issues raised above, the fact is we already live in a technological age and there are some basic skills that we need now or can predict we will need in the very near future. These needs remain valid regardless of the baseline of technological capacity of a particular school.

All teachers have been required to engage in a basic level of training within recent years either through the New Opportunities Funding (NOF) training initiative or as part of their initial teacher training. However, depending on how regularly and in what circumstances ICT is used, there is still a wide range of competency and confidence levels among teachers. From a personal point of view the first thing to consider is where you are now in terms of your own ICT utilisation and skills. Regardless of the age phase of your pupils, it is now essential to be a confident and competent personal user of ICT (Activity 6.1). The following is a brief overview of key skills and competence areas in ICT:

- word processing
- basic spreadsheets and charting
- databases
- paint or graphics packages
- installation and running of software from disc, CD-ROM, etc.
- PowerPoint presentations
- accessing and searching the internet
- e-mailing, including attaching files
- using a basic digital camera and uploading photographs
- using a video camera
- adjusting basic controls and setups on computers and printers you use regularly
- managing your desktop and 'defragging' (getting rid of unnecessary files and data to keep your computer running efficiently)
- knowing where you can get support for basic troubleshooting/problem-solving.

Being able to use TVs, video recorders/players, CD players, tape recorders, overhead projectors, photocopiers, laminators, etc. we will assume as given.

Taking stock of ICT skills

Look at the skills/competence areas above and ask yourself the following questions:

How frequently do I use this aspect of ICT: (a) in the classroom? (b) in supporting my work as a teacher? (c) in my home/leisure time?

Which aspects do I feel confident in?

What aspects of this do I feel uncertain about?

Which areas have I never used?

There is a lot of overlap in the knowledge needed of basic commands, control keys, keyboard skills, and so on, across these skill areas. There is a plethora of software and hardware on the market. You cannot be an expert in everything, but proficiency in the above areas should ensure you have enough transferable and flexible skills (and most importantly the confidence) to come to grips with most new software and hardware demands – with appropriate support and minimal training. You might just note that some pupils may be more proficient than you at some of the IT skills. That is inevitable, but it is not an issue in the sense that whatever the pupils' skills you are the one who guides the learning process.

State of the art or out of the ark?

What have you got access to in your school context?

As indicated above, although the government is investing considerable sums to achieve a basic minimum entitlement in all schools, the relevant difference in provision can be massive. First of all you need to make sure you know what is available in your school (and what isn't) (Activity 6.2).

Carrying out an ICT audit

Hardware audit

How many computers does your school have?

How are they organised (as a suite, across classrooms, are they moveable, laptops, are they networked)?

What subsidiary equipment is there – digital cameras, scanners, sensor equipment, floor robots, control equipment, electronic whiteboards, multimedia projectors, etc.?

How do you get access to their usage – timetabling, booking, casual agreement, first come first served?

Is there any hardware in your school that you do not know how to use and need training on?

Is there any particular piece of hardware lacking in your school that you think you should have access to? You do need to be able to justify the educational imperative for this.

Software audit

What is the basic suite of software available across all computers in your school?

Are there any aspects of the basic package that you feel uncertain about utilising and need further training on?

What CD-ROMs or online materials do you have available to support the subject areas or age phases you teach?

How well do they support and enhance the key learning objectives you want to address through ICT?

Are you familiar and confident with the software you currently use as part of your core learning tasks?

Are there any gaps in the software that you think would help you to support key learning objectives better?

REFLECTION

Are there any ICT resources that are available to you but that you are not using in your teaching? Why don't you use them? Is the decision based on sound teaching choices or lack of confidence with the ICT that is available?

At the time of writing, all schools are required to have some form of strategic plan for ICT development in order to access the National Grid for Learning (NGfL) moneys that are aimed at maintaining the impetus of ICT resourcing and development in schools. This includes considering the training needs of staff. All schools currently have access to additional funding for digital content as well. As a teacher, you need to be actively involved in working with the ICT coordinator, head teacher or whoever is leading the developments in your school, so that they know what support you need and about any requirement for additional resourcing. It really is part of your master teaching role to take the initiative here.

_____ Deciding why, how and when to use ICT _____

There is an old general adage that it's not what you've got, but what you do with it that matters. This is an extremely good maxim in relation to ICT in schools. The key issue for teachers is having the knowledge and understanding to utilise ICT effectively to support learning. This really returns us yet again to the issue of pedagogy – the understanding of the Why? questions of teaching. Master teachers extend their pedagogical framework and awareness to embrace the potential of ICT as a learning tool while understanding its wider impact on 'curriculum' (see below).

It is important to consider what ICT is good at doing. Some broad areas where ICT is particularly powerful are:

- manipulating, editing and presenting information (text, images, sound) to a very high standard
- 24-hour access to information/data on a wide (mind-blowing) range of subjects and issues
- ability to interrogate databases
- simplifying/standardising/speeding up routine procedures
- facilitating, quick, cheap, global communication
- modelling and simulation of real-life situations.

In terms of educational usage, Table 6.1 sets out some examples of how these strengths might be used in educational situations. Analyse your own ICT usage (Activity 6.3).

TABLE 6.1 The power of computers

Research on subject topics	Up-to-date data about a range of businesses
Exemplifying concepts, ideas, materials and actions	Seeing a volcanic eruption live
Simulation of otherwise inaccessible experiences and activities	Walking through a Roman city or an Egyptian tomb
Editing	Amending a text to address the audience appropriately
Analysing and creating visual material with a sense of audience	Creating a cover for a CD-ROM or music CD
Visual creativity	Creating an original graphic piece for an internet-based art display
Creativity with sound	Creating a composition that can be played remotely
Using large files of data	Calculating means of accumulated weather data from different sites
Reasoning and inference	Answering questions about the data displayed on scientific explorations of space
Communicating	Talking to other people in a school in France or Spain in the target language
Writing with a sense of purpose and a sense of audience	Writing an article about a moral issue for an internet-based magazine
Questioning and trying things out	Talking to an expert on-line
Modelling events and actions, causes and effects	Reconstructing or prioritising causes and effects of a war
Data capture	Remotely capturing temperature or river flow data
Rehearsing routine tasks	Practising and testing spellings

Source: most examples are taken from a presentation by D. Passey, Senior Research Fellow, Department of Education Research, Lancaster University

ACTIVITY 6.3

Analysing your own recent ICT usage

Think about your usage of ICT over the last half-term.

How have you used ICT to support learning?

Look at the strengths of ICT identified above and the examples of how it might be used.

Which aspects are reflected in your planned usage of ICT to support learning?

Are there any identified aspects that you did not use ICT for, but that you covered in a different way? Do you think the learning could have been more effective if you had used ICT?

Are there any powerful aspects of ICT that you never or rarely utilise to facilitate learning? Why? Is it linked to lack of resources, lack of training, or lack of confidence, or because you think there is a better way?

Teachers – in danger of imminent extinction?

This could be a tabloid headline, but the question certainly is: if children can learn what they want, when they want to – what will teachers do?

To answer the question one has to look at the other side of the equation. The other side (some might say the more important side) of the coin is knowing what ICT is not good at. There are many layers to this answer and how we engage with this is the really fundamental issue in the shaping of education for the future.

On a practical level, ICT can be problematic in that the technology is still not always reliable. In primary schools in particular, technological support is often patchy and the software and hardware can fail – so bear this in mind in planning and have a back-up activity or strategy to carry things over until the problem can be solved.

In terms of the actual limitations of ICT, its main lack is the fact that it does not use all of the human senses (yet). It is still largely two-dimensional and the internet is still largely text-based (which still supports the predominance of the need for developing the '3 Rs' for pupils). It obviously does not replace the need for pupils physically to do things.

A consideration in secondary schools is the recent move back in curriculum terms to vocationalism, and the possible view that ICT as a subject in its own right may provide employment opportunities for pupils. While there is truth in this, one should not assume that this is the main purpose of the subject area.

We need to return to the issues considered at the beginning of this chapter – how we define education, curriculum, learning, and teaching determines the attitudes to and use of ICT. A view of education as primarily to impart knowledge leads to the hypothesis that ICT may make schools obsolete. However, if schools are about empowering learners to participate, engage, question, collaborate, debate, create, then ICT is just a powerful tool to support and promote the process, not to replace it.

Indeed, the technological age is developing at least as many problems as it solves and our pupils need to learn to engage with these issues. One of the biggest problems technology is creating is in terms of moral dilemmas and choices. Above all other implications for education is the need for pupils to be taught the higher-level skills to challenge and interrogate the images and information with which they are bombarded. Much technology actually encourages passive voyeurism and positive action is needed by educators to combat this.

So our conclusions are again positive in terms of teaching roles. What technological development should actually mean for education is that teachers are not in danger of extinction; indeed, quite the opposite. Teachers with high levels of skill and understanding are even more essential than ever before. What is changing is what should be taught and how we teach it, which are the key issues at the heart of this whole book.

To illustrate this thinking, we may choose to show a video of a lecture from a top specialist on a particular subject (see above). But to realise in full the potential learning that this stimulates, we then need a highly trained professional – the master teacher – to plan a learning situation in which pupils can explore and assimilate the imparted information and then actually use and apply what they have learnt to other situations, at the pace and in the style most appropriate to the individual child at that point in time. With or without technology it all comes back to the same issue: becoming a master teacher. This is the theme of this book and we pursue it further in the next chapter.

At the end of this chapter you should have:

■ Considered the impact of ICT on teachers, students and the process of teaching

■ Reviewed your own attitudes towards and skills in ICT use

■ Engaged with the debate about the changes that ICT will bring about in the learning process

■ Recognised the impact for good that ICT can have on pupils' cognition

■ Put ICT in context as one – albeit fast-developing – arm of education

References

Bleach, K. (1998) *Raising Boys' Achievement in Schools,* Stoke-on-Trent: Trentham.

Bloom, B. (1956) *Taxonomy of Educational Objectives,* London: Longman

Bowring-Carr, C. and West-Burnham, J. (1997) *Effective Learning in Schools,* London: Pitman.

Candy, P., Crebert, G. and O'Leary, J. (1994) *Developing Lifelong Learners through Under-graduate Education,* Canberra: Australian Government Publishing Service, National Board of Employment, Education & Training.

Gillmon, E. (1998) *Building Teachers' ICT Skills,* London: Technology Colleges Trust.

Hackett, G. (1999) 'Tests for brightest pupils to be on-line', *Times Educational Supplement,* 26 November: 1.

Hough, M. (2000) *Technology and Change: Sustaining or Disrupting Leadership in Education,* Monograph no. 26, Canberra: Australian Council for Educational Administration.

Kennedy, K. (1999) *Schools for Tomorrow,* Monograph no. 89, Victoria: Incorporated Association of Registered Teachers of Victoria.

Kerry, T. (2000) *Surviving the Future: Changing Education for a Changing World,* Working Paper no. 40, Lincoln: Lincoln University.

Lonsdale, P. and Parsons, C. (1998) 'Inspections and the school improvement hoax', in P. Earley, (1998) *School Improvement After Inspection? School and LEA Responses,* London: PCP

Newman, G. (2000) 'An assessment tool for 2000 plus', *Education Today,* 50(3): 29–34.

Salomon, G. (1997) Novel constructivist learning environments and novel technologies: some issues to be concerned with, keynote presentation, EARLI Conference, Athens.

Scrimshaw, P. (2001) 'Computers and the teacher's role', in C. Paechter, M. Preedy, D. Scott and J. Soler, (eds), *Knowledge, Power and Learning,* London: PCP Open University.

Spender, D. (1998) 'Global directions and developments in learning technologies', Seminar Series Paper no. 80, Victoria: Incorporated Association of Registered Teachers of Victoria.

Taylor, G. (2000) 'Does ICT really improve learning?', *Education Today,* 50(4): 23–30.

chapter seven

The organised teacher

Performance analysis, assessment and planning

In this chapter you are invited to:

- Explore what constitutes assessment

- Develop your understanding of the implications of performance analysis on you as an individual class teacher

- Find out about key statistical indicators that are used to judge the performance of your school/pupils

- Consider how performance analysis relates to assessment for learning

- Explore the characteristics of effective assessment and planning that inform effective teaching and learning (without taking over your life – or indeed how do you actually get a life outside the job?)

What is assessment, what is its purpose and who is it for?

Assessment is an essential element of teaching (see Chapter 5), but in some of its guises it is a very controversial area. It is also an element of teaching, according to the statistics in Ofsted annual reports, that is often a weaker element in teachers' performance (Her Majesty's Chief Inspector of Schools 2002). It can also be an extremely emotive area for teachers because of the range of activity that the term 'assessment' incorporates and the purposes to which assessment data are put. Thus, Ross (2001) warns:

> The mechanisms for assessing curriculum often reveal as much about the motivations and ideologies of the educationally powerful as they do about the efficacy of the learning that has taken place.
>
> (Ross 2001: 125)

This is a rather chilling sentence, but it sums up the political and professional divide we discussed at the beginning of the book. The external or public view of assessment is inexorably linked to the formal examination framework. For many teachers, assessment has become all too closely linked in their minds to politically generated percentage targets and with copious record-keeping.

We aim to lay to rest some of the shibboleths and tensions with which assessment can be viewed and to persuade the reader that understanding and using assessment appropriately is truly the basis of effective teaching and learning. Bowring-Carr and West-Burnham (1997: 75) are right to warn that assessment needs to be carried out in a variety of ways and equally correct to emphasise that some assessment methods can restrict learning and narrow its focus if used unintelligently (p. 66). We aim to avoid both pitfalls.

The dictionary definition of assessment is 'estimating the value'. In order to estimate a value, it follows that there must be a 'measure' against which to assess. The problem comes in deciding what the measures are and whether they actually relate to that which we 'value' – fitness for purpose. Of course, anything based on values always generates controversy and debate, as we have seen in an earlier chapter (Kerry 2001).

What actually constitutes 'assessment' is a spectrum of activities carried out to define a pupil's achievement or performance against an identified objective or planned outcome. Although there is some overlap, there are two main dimensions to assessment: formative and summative.

Formative assessment

This is the ongoing assessment that teachers use to plan next steps in teaching and learning. Teachers use questioning, observation of how a pupil responds, marking of completed work, short tests, etc. to establish what a child understands and can do in relation to planned objectives.

Summative assessment

The purpose of summative assessment is to sum up/give a snapshot of what has been achieved at the end of a given period of time or unit of work. This end might be established through a written test or practical task, interview, review and moderation of completed work, and review of formative assessment judgements/scores.

Teacher's task

It has to be remembered that a primary teacher has to assess not just one but around 30 pupils across the full range of curriculum subject areas, not to mention monitoring pastoral needs. In secondary schools, teachers are assessing over a narrower subject spectrum, but are dealing with many classes, across a wide age range. Furthermore, parents ask more searching questions now about pupils' performance and expect to be given assessment data (Crozier 2000: 5) so teachers need to be more fluent in justifying assessment outcomes (Activity 7.1).

What also makes assessment such a complicated and potentially emotive area is that it varies according to who it is for and what each person needs to know or thinks they want to know, for example:

- yourself as a teacher
- pupil
- pupil's next teacher
- parent
- head teacher
- governors
- LEA
- government.

ACTIVITY 7.1

Assessment and its stakeholders

Jot down your thoughts on the following questions in relation to the above list of stakeholders in the assessment process and its outcomes:

1 What does each of these people *need* to know?

2 What else might they be interested in knowing or think they would like to know?

3 Which form of assessment/activity would provide them with the information they need?

The public and external focus on summative assessment, especially in terms of the formal framework of public examinations (GCSEs, A Levels etc.) and the more recently conceived Standard Assessment Tests/Tasks (SATs) (Education

Reform Act 1988), is frequently criticised by teachers and educationalists as narrowing the curriculum and inhibiting effective teaching to address the higher-level skills and attitudes necessitated by a technologically developed society, i.e. problem-solving ability, personal effectiveness, thinking skills, willingness to accept change, ability to interrogate the plethora of information around them (Broadfoot 1995).

This criticism is due to the high-stakes nature of success in such testing, especially in relation to subsequent life chances for individuals, in relation to school accountability, and in terms of measuring the effectiveness of national initiatives and political aspirations for the education system. The key imperative for shaping such assessment has historically and necessarily been focused on measuring individual performance in tests that appear to be fair, objective and reliable.

Against this though it is interesting to note that when the National Curriculum was initiated, the system of assessment for primary school pupils was based on educational best practice rather than pencil-and-paper formal assessment, which through teacher observation of tasks/pupils' engagement with processes questioning was more suited to assessing a range of skills. In practice, this proved totally unworkable in terms of teacher time.

Indeed the new Foundation Profile, which is currently being introduced for reception pupils, is based on recording assessments of individual pupils against some 90 statements. How workable this will be and whether the time taken is justified in relation to learning gains remain to be seen. The issue of balance is a very important proviso in relation to effective assessment. Although it is essential, the methods, time and resources it takes need to be balanced against the time taken and appropriate in relation to the teaching and learning gains it brings about.

A further issue that adds to the emotive and controversial nature of formal assessment is that, in an age that espouses 'political correctness' and the vision of equality of opportunity, statistics of educational performance all too often highlight inequalities, as Peter Mortimore identified:

> It has been found, in many countries and at many different times, that if the method of assessment is competitive, a correlation is found between success and social advantage. Not surprisingly, pupils whose conditions of life enable them to be well-fed and well-housed, and for their parents to be well-informed and confident about dealing with the system, tend to do well. Pupils with the opposite characteristics tend, on the whole, to do much less well; although exceptional, talented and well-motivated pupils will buck this trend. The result of this phenomenon is that assessment frequently tests the background of pupils rather than the quality of their education.
>
> (Mortimore 1992)

The fact that free school meals have until relatively recently been used as the main benchmarking tool for performance analysis further bears out the fact that educational performance cannot be seen in isolation from socio-economic context (Kerry 2000). The following statement was made in the 2002 National Summary Data Report for Primary Schools, and in effect acknowledges this link by trying to deny it:

> Although research evidence shows correlations between school tests and examination outcomes and the socio-economic characteristics of their pupils, the latter should not be taken as determinant of schools' educational outcomes, nor of pupils' attainment on entry to a school. Social deprivation should not lead schools to accept low levels of attainment or to set unacceptably low expectations of their pupils.

This links closely to the problem of the publication of raw data as a measure of school effectiveness and quality in the so-called 'league tables', in itself an unfortunate label. Raw data can misrepresent the quality of schools, and this has been a major concern in relation to parental choice. However, again we have to balance the myth against the reality. Some parents do trawl inspection reports and league tables and 'choose' their child's school. But this is not a new phenomenon generated purely by the league tables, as all geographical areas have always had unofficial league tables of schools based on reputation, location, type of intake, etc.

In reality the fact is that 'choice' of schools is actually very limited, due to limitations on places and such issues as transport (unless one can afford to pay). The main concern for schools and educationists is that they should all provide high-quality provision that is relevant and appropriate for their community. And although it may not be politically correct to say so, what is appropriate for one community area may not be relevant and appropriate in a different context.

ICT has been a major influence on the increased impact of performance analysis for schools/classes/individuals, due to the way it facilitates copious statistical analysis 'at the press of a button'. Number crunching has almost become a new religion, offering the promise of objective 'truths' and measurable accountability. Monitoring and target-setting based upon statistical analysis have been and look likely to continue to remain the main 'weapons' and driving forces of government-led initiatives in education. Indeed, since education is so important to the individual's life chances and wider social and economic well-being, it is right that schools should be held accountable.

Understanding and working with performance analysis

'But what have such issues got to do with me, as an individual teacher in the classroom?' you might ask. 'Isn't that down to the head teacher and governors to worry about? I just want to get on with what matters: teaching and learning.'

Whatever the rights and wrongs of it, the evidence from the statistical data is an important factor in determining targeting of funding, targeting of inspection and support (pressure or freedom), school status and earned autonomy. Such data can even determine whether or not you and your colleagues receive a financial bonus (through such initiatives as School Achievement Awards). Further, on an individual teacher level, it is a statutory requirement to have pupil performance as evidence and a target in your Performance Management and Threshold applications (see Chapter 8). Just because one does not like a system does not give the right to unilaterally withdraw from it; that is a truth that all teachers have to face, indeed that all professionals have to face.

Thus, it is essential to develop a better understanding of the key statistical data being used and particularly to know how to challenge supposed 'truths' in certain circumstances. Contrary to the old adage, figures do not speak for themselves. Master teachers need to understand and be able to open them up to interpretation. So what is the use of spending all this time, effort and energy on performance analysis and testing if it is so controversial and only affirms the socio-economic status quo?

Although the measuring devices may be less than perfect at times, we do need standards and values against which to assess and to question. The use of statistics in education has proven value. For example, having a more systematic testing structure at the transfer between primary and secondary education starkly emphasised the number of children who were failing to achieve basic levels of literacy and numeracy, which are now even more essential skills in our technological, information-driven world.

Such scrutiny and comparison have also supported the targeting of funding and support to need. The intransigence of performance in secondary education at Key Stage 3 can also be seen to be pushing forward the drive and debate to diversify and develop the secondary curriculum to better meet the needs of the majority of its pupils.

Taken as one indicator within the overall evaluation of school effectiveness, in the context of other 'assessments' that are now pursued much more systematically through school self-evaluation, LEA moderation processes and Ofsted, statistical data lead schools to ask:

- Is that good enough?
- Could we do better?
- How do we do better?

It cannot be argued logically that such questions are unimportant. Performance analysis also challenges us to better understand our schools and the impact of our strategies and to articulate and acknowledge the job we have to do within our school context compared with others.

Nationalised levels and standards, it can be argued, are leading to more collaborative moderation and working among teachers, which is producing more consistency in formulating and understanding marking criteria, progression and expectations. If in the process teachers are required to analyse what they do and develop their discourse to explain it, this will be a significant bonus.

The figures available to heads and teachers in schools provide a relatively reliable and normative framework against which to track individual pupil performance and progress in institutions. Even if we disagree with the exact criteria of formal assessment, the fact is that they do generally work as a sorting tool. For example, at primary level, if children are unable to achieve a secure level 2 in reading (the average level of expectation at that age), this statistical finding does correlate very closely with teacher assessment of unsatisfactory development of reading fluency and confidence. Since poor reading impedes so many other aspects of education, to highlight this judgement is a significant thing to do.

REFLECTION

What is your personal philosophy of assessment: its aims, purposes, audiences and outcomes?

The fact is that in teaching, alongside other public services, notably health and policing, the demand for accountability will rightly continue and with it national statistics and measures as an element of this. As professionals, teachers need to make sure they can understand and interpret the statistics that are being used to judge their pupils, themselves and their school. Above all, they need to be able to take a critical stance in interpreting data supplied by the government.

— Performance and Assessment Data (PANDA) report —

Like the animal, it has teeth; people might think it looks black and white, but in reality it is often grey. So the key document that is used to assess school performance is the PANDA. This is generated by Ofsted and distributed to individual schools, the LEA and inspectors (when a school is due to be inspected). It is distributed annually, usually in October/November of each year. This document is not available to the general public, although aspects of it may be reported via the Ofsted report, which is a public document. The sections of the report are broadly as follows:

1 *Basic characteristics of the school*: number on roll; free school meals; English as an additional language; special educational needs. These figures are given for the past five years and are compared with the national average.

2 *Inspection judgements*: the composite judgements from the school's last Ofsted report in relation to standards of attainment, quality of education, school climate and management and efficiency are given and compared with national judgements and free-school-meals benchmark groups.

3 *Attainment summary*: gives a broad overview of test and examination results of pupils in comparison with the national average, free-school-meals benchmark groups, and for some phases based on prior attainment.

4 *Attainment*: this section makes up the bulk of the report and focuses predominantly on the most recent results. The results are analysed as follows:

- comparison with national averages in terms of:
  - levels
  - average points
  - gender
  - trends over time
- comparison with national benchmarks based on free school meals and prior attainment (where available) in terms of:
  - levels
  - average points

5 *Additional information*: this section looks at:

- attendance compared with national figures
- contextual information, based on census information for wards geographically close to your school in relation to:
  - % of adults with higher education
  - % of children in high-social-class households
  - % of minority ethnic children
  - % of children in overcrowded households.

The gradings used within the PANDA report are shown as Fig. 7.1.

FIG. 7.1 Gradings used in the PANDA report

Interpretations of grades

In the majority of cases, interpretations in the PANDA report fall into one of the following seven categories. Below is an explanation of the categories. In every case, the average is measured as the median for all schools nationally or all schools within the stated benchmark group:

A* This means that pupils' results at the school are *very high* in comparison with the national average or, where appropriate, the average for schools in similar contexts. The school's results are within the range of the top five per cent of schools across the country.

A This means that pupils' results at the school are *well above* the national average or, where appropriate, the average for schools in similar contexts. The school's results are within the range of the top quarter of schools across the country but not the top five per cent.

B This means that pupils' results at the school are *above* the national average or, where appropriate, the average for schools in similar contexts. The school's results are within the range of the top 40 per cent of schools across the country but not the top quarter.

C This means that pupils' results at the schools are *broadly in line* with the national average or, where appropriate, the average for schools in similar contexts. Differences from the national average or the average for schools in similar contexts are unlikely to be statistically significant.

D This means that pupils' results at the school are *below* the national average or, where appropriate, the average for schools in similar contexts. The school's results are within the range of the bottom 40 per cent of schools across the country but not within the bottom quarter.

E This means that pupils' results at the school are *well below* the national average or, where appropriate, the average for schools in similar contexts. The school's results are within the range of the bottom quarter of schools across the country but not within the lowest five per cent of schools.

E* This means that pupils' results at the school are *very low* in comparison with the national average or, where appropriate, the average for schools in similar contexts. The school's results are within the range of the lowest five per cent of schools across the country.

Definition of some benchmarking terms used within the PANDA

The grades shown above (A*–E*) are derived by using National Benchmark tables, which split national results into quartiles.

Upper quartile: the upper quartile for any particular assessment is the score or level for which 25 per cent of the results are higher than this value.

Median: the median for any particular assessment is the score or level for which exactly half of the results achieved are higher than this value and the other half of results achieved are lower.

Lower quartile: the lower quartile for any particular assessment is the score or level for which 25 per cent of the results are lower than this value.

Average points

For the purpose of statistical analysis, the SATs levels are given a numerical value, e.g. level 2a = 17, level 3 = 21, etc. It is important to know that the numerical basis is then used as a basic tool for target-setting. Four points per year is considered challenging progress, while three points per year is considered normal progress.

Target-setting

There is a national framework of target-setting that is based around performance analysis. This emanates from the broad political targets set at government level. These targets are then analysed and distributed down to requirements and benchmarks for LEAs, based upon the past performance and the socio-economic profile of their overall area of responsibility. LEAs then pass these down as indicators for individual schools, based upon the past performance and socio-economic profile of the individual school catchment. (This system is being modified as we write.) In turn, these imperatives may influence targets set for you as an individual teacher (underpinned, negotiated and informed by analysis of individual pupils in a cohort). Certain targets for each key educational phase (except, at the moment, Key Stage 1) are required to be published in reports to parents.

The teacher of the formal assessment year is not the only person who is affected. Tracking of pupils, predictions of likely results and profiling of classes to indicate likely problems and support requirements mean that target-setting for all teaching years is influenced. It is imperative that master teachers and all teachers understand the trends and indications of performance in their school. Particularly in a big school, the head teacher and senior managers may have very little individual knowledge of pupils in terms of their personalities, motivations, home issues and so on. Unless as an individual you understand the statistics underpinning standard expectations and challenging targets and can engage with this debate (and can prove with evidence that some individuals will not achieve the indicated progress, or even that some should exceed it), you may find yourself given inappropriate progress targets. You yourself have to be able to engage in the discourse of formal assessment.

_____ National Summary Data (NSDP) report _____

The National Summary Data (NSDP) report is a document that gives further national statistics to support school self-evaluation, and is to be used as an annex to the PANDA. It gives further information on terminology and calculation of attainment and progress in the PANDA. More detailed information is given on attendance figures in different school groups. It looks at comparisons of length of taught week. It looks at expenditure patterns in schools. It also gives more information about the background information to school characteristics and inspection judgements reported in the PANDA (Activity 7.2).

ACTIVITY 7.2

Investigating PANDAs

Ask your head teacher if you can have a copy of your most recent school PANDA and the supporting NSDP. (In most schools the head teacher will already have discussed aspects of it and shared the main issues in relation to school development planning.) Make sure you are aware of what statutory targets are required to be set within your teaching phase and the one above and below your main teaching groups.

Browse the total report.

- What overall trends does it indicate for your school?
- How do these trends relate to the reality of your experience?
- How well does your school compare with national attainment?
- How well does your school compare with benchmark groups?
- Are the gradings fair, given what you actually know of your school and the cohorts involved?
- How do the data relate to your experience of the attainment/strengths/weaknesses of the pupils in your classes?
- How is this analysis followed through in priorities and areas for development in your school?

The problem with such aggregated school data, particularly for small schools, is that cohorts in any given year, even in relatively affluent socio-economic areas, can fluctuate. This may distort the data. For example, in a small primary school, a cohort of 20 pupils would be worth five per cent each in terms of the data. If you happened to have a high level of pupils with special educational needs in that cohort, or a high-scoring pupil happened to be absent from the tests, your percentages could look very poor. Statistics state facts, not reasons. In reality, your teaching standards probably did not drop. Indeed, as a teacher you may have actually been more effective with this group than a prior high-achieving cohort.

Those that achieved level 3 may have done very well given their baseline. This is precisely the type of knowledge and understanding one has to bring to bear as part of the performance analysis – the ability to interpret, not merely accept, the figures that emanate from these measures.

The 'average points score' measure is slightly more equitable in that it does not include absences and gives credit for below level 4 scores.

The PANDA gives a statistical table, which indicates percentage changes that would need to occur in order for a valid judgement to be made about variation in results between two successive years (Fig. 7.2). Unfortunately, when results are published in the performance tables and newspapers, this sort of information isn't in people's minds and the figures are more likely to be viewed erroneously.

FIG. 7.2 PANDA data interpretation

Cohort size for each year	Percentage change
20	18
30	15
40	13
60	10
80	9
100	8
150	7
200	6

———— Autumn package (AP) ————

This is available online (www.standards.dfes.gov.uk/performance/ap/). The Autumn Package (AP) allows schools to plot their own data against national comparisons, much of which is then printed in the PANDA. However, it does allow an individual school to analyse data earlier than the arrival of the PANDA. The fact that the PANDA does not allow for any information about re-marking to be incorporated means that, where this has been an issue for schools, they will need to plot their data via the Autumn Package to get a true picture. In effect, the PANDA is technically part of the Autumn Package, but published later.

The Autumn Package has a very useful section that is not published in the PANDA – national value-added information using pupil-level results. This is probably the most useful performance analysis tool for the individual class teacher, in that it allows one to chart individual pupil performance against prior attainment. Therefore, the teacher can look at a picture of the class performance from KS1 to KS2, for example, to see how pupils did overall; whether there were a few individuals who performed better or worse than other similar pupils; and whether there are any trends between the different subject areas, etc. This can be a useful guide, for teachers who may inherit a new class, to have ahead of that time, as it gives an overall picture/profile of performance to indicate broad needs in basic skills. Graphs based on prior attainment can also help you consider potential progress and set targets for individual pupils based on their prior attainment. Such graphs can also flag up relative teaching weaknesses between subject areas or, where a school has more than one class of a particular year group, differences in teaching (Activity 7.3).

ACTIVITY 7.3

Interpreting data

Look at the two charts (Figs 7.3 and 7.4) below (based on a fictitious class of year 6 pupils). Now consider these questions to decide how you would interpret the data:

- How are the majority of individuals performing in relation to expectations based on their prior attainment?

- Are there any individuals who have performed outside the normal expectations based on prior attainment?

- Are there any trends that you would want to interrogate further: i.e. comparison between broad performance in subject areas; comparison between SEN pupils, average and high academic achievers; gender differences?

- What could be the underlying issues indicated by broad trends in relation to teaching for this cohort?

- What could cause individuals to perform outside the national norm (either above or below) and their cohort group?

- If you were the year 7 maths or English teacher taking on these pupils next, what assumptions would you start to draw about the further needs for this group?

- If you were judging the performance of a year 6 teacher based on these results, what areas might you want to question and target for development?

FIG. 7.3 Reading: value-added line

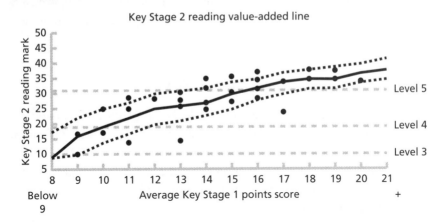

FIG. 7.4 Mathematics: value-added line

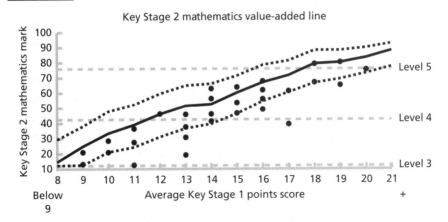

___ Other statistical analysis and assessment tools ___

Local education authorities (LEAs)

LEAs will generally have their own raft of reports and statistics that they will generate for their schools, to utilise in monitoring and evaluation and as a shared focus to underpin the negotiation and agreement of annual statutory school performance targets.

Many LEAs are setting up statistics that compare an individual school with other 'similar' schools within the authority. The 'similarity' can be informed by such figures as school roll, special educational needs figures, deprivation index figures and pupil stability.

Deprivation indices

Deprivation index figures are referred to in the PANDA although, as indicated, they can be out of date. However, they are often used by schools that are in authorities with an historic poor take-up of free school meals, which means the socio-economic circumstances of their pupils can be heavily misrepresented in benchmarking. The website www.statistics.gov.uk/neighbourhood will give you access to information about your area.

QCA optional assessments

These are available for some of the interim years between statutory assessments. The majority of schools use them to develop children's familiarisation with the formalised testing formats and as one ongoing indicator of progress to monitor teaching and learning and to identify areas for development within the school. It has to be remembered that most schools will have a systematic period of preparation for the statutory tests, which is not the case for optional assessments. Therefore, this has to be borne in mind in tracking, particularly in the year following the statutory testing of a cohort as a drop or 'flattening-out' of progress may relate to the difference in preparation and revision.

Standardised assessment of specific skills or underlying ability

There is a range of other assessments that are regularly used by schools. At secondary transfer, even in non-11-plus areas, some schools may use verbal or non-verbal reasoning papers or CATs to gain some measure of underlying potential. Many schools use group reading tests to monitor reading age. All schools and LEAs will have access to testing packages that they may use to support identification and targeting of SEN (Acitivity 7.4).

ACTIVITY 7.4

Finding out about formal assessments

Find out what formal assessments are used over and above statutory assessments within your own school context.

What can they can tell you about groups or individuals within your class?

Consider to what purpose the results are being put in your school and the relative impact this has on school priorities and you as an individual teacher.

———— Assessment and planning for teaching ———— and learning

You might wonder why we have put assessment before planning in this chapter, since it is often planning that tends to dominate teacher time out of the classroom. However, as I am sure you have gathered from preceding chapters, the processes of reflection upon knowledge synthesised with empirical experience, self-awareness, evaluation, and planned action for ever-improving learning/teaching are central to our view of 'master teaching'. Without some level of 'assessment' of the needs of the class/group you are teaching, you cannot plan – even if it is the first day of teaching them or you are a supply teacher just taking them for one day (see also Kerry 2002).

REFLECTION

Before you teach a new group/class for the first time, what is the bare minimum of information you need to plan a session?

It is important to acknowledge the different strata of assessment levels (and thus the corresponding planning strata – as assessment and planning are part of a continuum/cycle) that funnel down to the individual. As indicated by Gipps (1994):

> *We need to start from what children have in common as members of the human species in order to establish the general principles of teaching, and then determine what modifications are needed to meet individuals' needs.*
>
> (Gipps 1994: 27)

The dimensions of what we need to know in order to teach effectively include the following.

Broad-level knowledge

What age group is the class? Based on your professional/subject knowledge and in relation to the whole school framework for continuity and progression, what would be your broad expectation of their current knowledge, understanding and interest level? What teaching and learning strategies are broadly relevant to this?

Class-level adaptation

What is the broad profile of the class, i.e. prior attainment (based on teacher assessment, statutory assessment), other assessment indicators, percentage of SEN and gender balance?

What implications does the overall class profile have for pitching of whole-class stimuli and introductory activities?

Group-level adaptation

What will be the optimum grouping for working, dependent upon learning objective and task type (ability, friendship, gender, learning style, mixed ability with different roles anticipated)?

Where will the teacher input/available classroom assistance and focus need to be in relation to the learning objective and task type at different points in the lesson?

Individual-level adaptation

Most individualisation is not appropriately written into and addressed in planning in advance. An exception to this may be in meeting the very specific needs of pupils such as those with special educational needs or a child whom you know is generally or specifically gifted and therefore outside the 'group level'.

Most individualisation is achieved through assessment in action during the learning session. It is those high-level skills that you bring to bear in ensuring you connect with each individual child regularly and frequently:

- bringing together your ongoing assessment of each individual in terms of their attainment, attitudes, motivation, interests, and so on
- using this knowledge to individualise and target questioning; amount of response time given; appropriate intervention to solve a problem in their access to a learning objective; appropriate challenge and support; praise; demonstrating you know the individual and that you care about them as an individual.

Teaching and managing learning is a creative and dynamic process. Quality assessment, followed by planned action, is the glue that holds it together.

Keeping a record

Record-keeping is the real crux for many teachers in terms of workload issues and is still a difficult area of time management in which to strike a balance. Just how much detail do you need to record in your assessment and planning? Then there is the further and sometimes conflicting issue of what you have to record and how you have to record it in the context of your particular school.

Different schools can have very different expectations in terms of detail required and rigidity of proforma usage, etc. Guidelines from the DfES on managing workload are encouraging head teachers to accept annotations/notes on scheme plans and such like to avoid what commonly occurred in the past – copying out information from one place to another. Of course, this is where ICT really comes into its own. The increasing and changing use of support staff is also a significant factor in workload terms. One can take information easily from a range of sources, transfer it from one area to another and even adapt and tailor it to your requirements. This can result in quite detailed and professional planning with minimum effort. Some teachers plan in copious detail, some record in very short notation. Larger schools tend to be more rigid about 'house style'.

Although, in the end, it is the quality of teaching and learning that is the key indicator of effectiveness, we do have to be professional about recording levels. We have to accept that our recorded planning and assessment, although predominantly for ourselves and informing our next teaching step, also have additional functions:

- for school monitoring and evaluation to check curriculum framework coverage, variety of teaching strategies, range of activities, continuity and progression, individual progress, etc.

- to indicate your requirements and intentions to teaching assistants or other support staff

- to inform a supply teacher, or other teachers who may take your class at short notice, of the key areas, aspects and tasks to be covered

- as evidence of your professional strategy and intentions for inspectors or observers (although you mostly know of these occasions in advance and may well give more detail than usual)

- to inform the child's next teacher

- to be able to report effectively and accurately to parents.

From the point of view of what needs to be recorded, we are going to start in this section from the perspective of planning. This is because, in terms of balance, the quality and level of information we record for planning is more fundamental than the recording of assessment. This statement may seem to be at odds with the assertions we made earlier in the chapter that assessment has to precede planning. A key issue is that assessment is a thinking process not merely an outcome. It is a thinking process that is mediated and evinced through what we plan. As indicated above, assessment and planning, rather than being distinct entities, are in reality more a continuum of reflection that underpins effective teaching.

If we return to the strata of assessment above it will be useful to think about key requirements of recording in terms of these layers:

- broad-level/class-level
- long-term
- medium-term.

The long-term key learning objectives and content are likely to be a 'given', established through a whole-school curriculum framework or subject syllabus.

It is in medium-term planning where you will translate the broad needs to those more specifically of the actual class you will be teaching. Using what you know of the age, characteristics, attainment, etc. (i.e. the available assessment) medium-term plans need to identify:

- key learning objectives you aim to address (see Chapter 5)
- overall themes and activities through which the learning objectives will be achieved
- chronology and order of the key steps/activity for the block of work
- main resource requirements.

The recording of assessment that feeds into this level of planning comprises mostly the *summative elements* and *performance data* (see above). Teachers do need to keep a record that indicates the learning outcomes from key blocks of work for individuals. This does not necessarily mean pages of detailed notes per pupil, but rather an overall normative indicator of outcomes on a class grid should be acceptable or a score sheet – a broad brush-stroke. A comments column might be appropriate in any recording proforma, but comments should be needed only where the learning outcome or performance of a pupil is unusually different from broad expected levels or was influenced by exceptional circumstances.

Class level/group level – short-term planning (weekly/sessional)

Building from medium-term planning outlines, the short-term planning should break down the key aims into smaller steps and give more detail in relation to issues such as the following:

- key aspects of each session, e.g. introduction, stimuli/demonstration/event to generate interest, pupil tasks, likely plenary focus

- resources needed

- key questions

- differentiated objectives within overarching objective

- deployment of available staff and other resources.

Recording of assessment at this level should normally constitute brief notation of intentions. One might need an additional column within the plan that indicates any class or group response, or a problem that is outside the expectation of what was planned/anticipated. This may require a change to the next planned step or approach. You also need to note any particularly successful or unsuccessful aspects of your teaching to inform future similar sessions. This is also the point at which you may record issues relating to individualisation of work; again use initials and short notes/key phrases, words, abbreviations, colour-coding or any other means that has an impact for you personally.

What is stressed here is that you need to develop efficient 'shorthand' that enables you to note what you need to remember to inform future planning and teaching. Detailed prose is inefficient and relevant only to end-of-year reports (which again can be effectively supported by appropriate use of ICT).

You may choose to keep a more detailed reflective log or diary to support and focus an area of your teaching you wish to develop (see Chapter 11), but this would be short term strategy.

――――――― Individual level ―――――――

Individual education plans, notation of planning, marking and pupil feedback

Individual education plans (IEPs) may be required for individuals who are at extremes of a class's overall profile. Generally these are associated with special educational needs pupils, i.e. those with learning difficulties, but they should sometimes be considered for pupils with special learning needs because of high ability. Normally these IEPs will be separate planning documents that then need to feed into class plans – again through a brief note or code related to the pupil's initials that flags up your awareness and intent (keep it short, focused and manageable). Such documents will usually be written and developed collaboratively with other professionals in or beyond school (support staff or the school's educational psychologist) and ideally in partnership with parents and pupils.

As indicated above, if individuals need very specific intervention that may require follow-up in the future, a note should be made within your plans. If the intervention you gave, based on your assessment at the moment, was effective then you may choose not to note it. If it was a new strategy and you want to ensure you use it again for others, then a note may act as a memory jogger. As always, you as the professional must make choices.

Marking and pupil feedback are essential points of contact and mediation between the teacher and the individual. Again, this is another area of time management that is very difficult to balance in the day-to-day pressure of the classroom. The full marking of key pieces of work can be extremely time consuming and energy-sapping. Developing an effective coding system that is shared with pupils is one way of managing this. Prioritising aspects of work for fuller analysis and marking/feedback is also important. For example it may not be a valid use of time for a teacher to spend two hours marking a weekly spelling test list or tables test, but giving feedback on the essay that pulls together several weeks' learning may be more learning-efficient. The message is to consider professional effectiveness at all times.

REFLECTION

What aspects of your present recording strategy are learning-effective? Which ones are not and should be modified or discarded?

Building in verbal feedback during the process of teaching is very important. Verbal feedback is extremely powerful – a positive assessment comment can motivate and raise a pupil's self-esteem like nothing else (conversely a negative personal comment can be extremely damaging). However, individual conferencing is extremely time-consuming and has implications for what the rest of the class are doing. Again, it is about using your professional judgement about balance and need over time and will relate strongly to your educational values and aims (see Chapter 1).

Most of your individualisation work does not need to be formally recorded. The fact that it is happening (or not) will come through very strongly in any observation of teaching in terms of how well pitched your lessons are to your pupils and the quality of your relationship with the pupils.

As a short-term strategy for an individual pupil who is presenting problems or concerns, you might choose to keep an observation log on him or her. This is very time-consuming but may be the only effective way to improve this individual's learning through your greater understanding of the problem. Lovey (2002: 82) gives an example of recording for individual pupils with special needs.

───── Checklist for balance and prioritisation ─────

Retaining energy and oomph

Planning, recording, assessing and reporting are heavy burdens on the teacher's time, but all of them are key processes for master teachers (Activity 7.5). As this chapter draws to its close, therefore, we have tried to provide some advice and guidelines that will hopefully help you to keep a balance in the time management of these activities.

1 Don't reinvent the wheel. Use available schemes or pre-produced materials and sheets, or extant exemplar materials for routine tasks. Focus your energy on planning key educational events and experiences in relation to major objectives rather than on routine tasks. The motivation and energy this generates from the pupils will increase your enthusiasm and energy levels.

2 Use notes, abbreviations, key phrases; photocopy any published notes you are using and annotate.

3 Get a computer and use cut-and-paste.

4 Set yourself a reasonable time target for planning and assessment and stick to it. If you are tired, you will be irritable and boring as a teacher.

5 Make sure you leave time for yourself and hobbies. Quite apart from your personal entitlement to 'a life', the best ideas often come up when you are doing something totally unconnected with the job.

6 If your school requirements are unnecessarily bureaucratic and unresponsive to different teacher styles, raise the issue with the head teacher or your line manager. Make sure you have some positive suggestions and models for improving the situation though, rather than just having an unsubstantiated, unprofessional moan.

ACTIVITY 7.5

Assessing planning

Consider the planning and assessment you record in light of the strata and levels identified above.

■ How *effective* is your current assessment and planning?

■ How *efficient* is your current assessment and planning?

Undertake a time audit over a period of two weeks of marking, other assessment recording and planning.

Are there any areas in which you could save time, while still retaining the essential elements?

Conclusion

Assessment for learning and formal summative assessment do not have to be diametrically opposed. Teachers, especially master teachers and school leaders, have to develop the confidence and expertise to interpret and acknowledge the role of formal assessment as a monitoring tool for areas of basic skills and knowledge, while at the same time promoting the value of more holistic and qualitative assessment. The way the school's, one's own and externally moderated evaluation systems are being developed does acknowledge that formal assessment is only one of many important measures of quality of educational provision and attainment – though in the rhetoric of pro and anti camps this fact is sometimes obscured.

What we assess in schools has to relate to what society thinks education is for, and there are two broad strands to this (Mortimore 1992):

■ an instrumental activity designed to achieve specifiable and uncontroversial educational goals

■ an ethical activity guided by values … which are open to continual debate and refinement.

Both perspectives are essential in schools – education should not be an either/or. Indeed, the impact of technological development and the burgeoning of the 'knowledge economy' mean there are basic skills that children need to develop even just to access what is around them. But importantly, they then need to develop the higher-level skills to be able to engage with ethical activity, since our technological age bombards them with text, images and sound bites purposefully geared at manipulating them (see Chapter 6). Teachers' planning and assessment have to reflect and balance these key imperatives.

We also have to accept the political realities: that a formal testing framework, despite the fact that criteria and performance indicators may develop and change in the future, is here to stay. We need to understand the role, benefits and insights of this approach alongside the more formative assessment in the classroom, the latter being able to adapt and respond to the higher-level and affective aspects of learning which we know are essential but not easily quantifiable.

However, we need, above all, to develop efficient and effective record-keeping that indicates our professional understanding and intent, but leaves us with the energy and enthusiasm to inspire our pupils and to have a life outside the classroom. For master teachers, being organised means effecting good time management in order to plan, assess, record and report on pupils effectively to all the stakeholders in the education process. These processes are part of the business of accountability that forms the theme of the next chapter.

At the end of this chapter you should have:

- Considered the purposes of assessment, planning, reporting and recording

- Reviewed your own systems for these four operations

- Become aware of the need for master teachers to be able to understand, manipulate and use quantitative data

- Put these skills into a context of time management

_____ References _____

Bowring-Carr, C. and West-Burnham, J. (1997) *Effective Learning in Schools,* London: Pitman.

Broadfoot, P. (1995) 'Performance assessment in perspective: international trends and current English experience', in H. Torrance (ed.), *Evaluating Authentic Assessment,* Buckingham: Open University Press.

Crozier, G. (2000) *Parents and Schools: Partners or Protagonists?,* Stoke-on-Trent: Trentham.

Education Reform Act 1988, London: HMSO.

Gipps, C. (1994) 'What we know about effective primary teaching', in J. Bourne (ed.), *Thinking Through Primary Practice,* London: Open University Routledge.

Her Majesty's Chief Inspector of Schools (2002) *Annual Report of HMCI: Standards and Quality in Education 2001/2002,* London: HMSO

Kerry, T. (2000) *Surviving the Future: Changing Education in a Changing World*, Working Paper no. 40, Lincoln: University of Lincoln.

Kerry, T. (2001) *Plowden: Mirage, Myth or Flag of Convenience?*, Working Paper no. 43, Lincoln University of Lincoln.

Kerry, T. (2002) *Learning Objectives. Task Setting and Differentiation,* Cheltenham: Nelson Thornes.

Kerry, T. (2003) *Learning Objectives, Task Setting and Differentiation,* Cheltenham: Nelson Thornes.

Lovey, J. (2002) *Supporting Special Educational Needs in Secondary School Classrooms,* 2nd edn, London: David Fulton.

Mortimore, P. (1992) 'Quality control in education and schools', *British Journal of Educational Studies*, 40(1).

Ross, A. (2001) 'What is curriculum?', in J. Collins, K. Insley and J. Solar, *Developing Pedagogy: Researching Practice*, London: PCP.

chapter eight

The accountable teacher

Monitoring, evaluation and professional progression

Levels of accountability

Formal dimensions

The performance management framework

General Teaching Council (GTC)

Active participation – professional engagement with the process of accountability

Planning for a successful lesson observation

Beyond the formal framework – responsibility to yourself

In this chapter you are invited to:

- Consider different levels and dimensions of teacher accountability

- Develop your understanding of the key requirements and components of the formal Performance Management Framework

- Think about how you can actively participate in, influence and make the most of this 'opportunity'

- Undertake self-evaluation and career planning within and beyond the formal framework

Chapter 3 challenged you to consider what 'being a teacher' means and what makes an effective or master teacher. We established that one element of the role that attracts us to the profession is that it is an 'important' job. The power and influence education has over children's future life chances means that we should not be surprised if we are expected regularly to prove our competence to carry out our duties effectively. The social and economic implications and costs of the national education system also mean that we cannot be surprised at the extent to which government concerns itself with the teaching profession.

Levels of accountability

Informal dimensions

It is human nature that we all continually form judgements about the people around us. Teachers have a range of stakeholders or 'audiences' continually forming a view of their effectiveness, some examples being:

1 Pupils will indicate their judgement on you as a teacher through their general classroom and on-task behaviour and the quality of their work.

2 Parents respond to the way they see you working with their children; the level and regularity of homework set; formal and informal discussions; the quality of reports; what their child reflects back to them about their experience in the classroom; how you compare with teachers they have dealt with before.

3 Colleagues will judge you by comparing the way you work in school and the way you interact with themselves and other colleagues. They will notice the time you spend in school compared with them, whether you are on time for assembly, duties and so on. Generally, they will notice whether or not you are pulling your weight.

4 The way governors make judgements about you will depend on the relationship of a particular governor to the school. A parent governor will shape their view mostly as a parent. Additional information available to governors that will colour their view is how your participation in school is termed in head's reports, performance analysis related to your classes over time, what they see on 'visits' to your classroom, how you conduct yourself in any joint governor/staff training or presentations.

5 Your head teacher will be making judgements about you as he/she is monitoring planning, when he/she 'pops in' to your classroom: how you relate generally to pupils around the school; when they see you on duty; in relation to your timekeeping; reliability in doing what you say you will; the way you participate in staff meetings; your commitment to wider school events.

Of course, as we discussed in Chapter 1, the most important person you are accountable to as a professional is yourself. As a reflective practitioner (see Chapter 2) you will be evaluating yourself continually and seeking ways to improve your effectiveness for your pupils. A self-aware teacher is sensitive to the implications of his/her actions in relation to all the above stakeholders, framed within personal aims and values. As it is imposssible to please all of the people all of the time, integrity based on sound principles has to be the filter for external accountability.

The formal or managerial aspects of accountability (Reeves et al. 2002: 4) are those we are most conscious of, but the informal elements are integral to and form the main evidence that will focus and drive the formal. Both are subject to what West-Burnham, O'Neil and Bradbury (2001: 4) call 'professional ethics' and the 'shared moral purpose' of the school.

Formal dimensions

Ofsted

School (and thereby teacher) accountability was dragged (some might say 'kicking and screaming') into the public eye from the inception of the Office for Standards in Education (Ofsted) statutorily enshrined in the School Inspections Act 1992. Although there have been many adjustments to the original procedure, it is still the main impetus for an unprecedented opening-up of schools to external and, more importantly, public scrutiny. The nature of the process has in recent years become less punitive, particularly in view of the push towards and development of school self-evaluation. The fact that Ofsted inspections are now carried out on a six-year cycle actually raises the stakes for schools, since an unsatisfactory or even a mediocre report impacts on the school's reputation for a more protracted period.

REFLECTION

How do you react to being observed? Do your reactions differ according to who is doing the observation and for what purpose? What are the negative and the positive outcomes of being observed, in your view?

An impending Ofsted inspection puts fear into the hearts of teachers, even though it is no secret what inspectors are looking for (e.g. Ofsted 1995) and despite the fact that classroom observation has become a much more regular and accepted aspect of everyday teaching (Doyle 2001: 154). It is the very personal nature of teaching that means that such a public process of accountability leaves even the most effective and talented teacher feeling vulnerable.

However, in reality, if you are a self-aware and reflective practitioner, working within a self-evaluating school, an Ofsted inspection is unlikely to tell you anything you don't already know (Ferguson et al. 2000). If you are unfortunate enough to work within a school that does not self-evaluate effectively, then you can still make sure the lessons you are observed teaching validate your individual effectiveness. Although, however effective you are as an individual, if you are in a school that receives a poor Ofsted report it is still bound to impact on your professional morale and self-esteem. The problem for inner-city schools particularly is highlighted in Ferguson et al. (2000: Chapter 9).

The key aspects of teaching on which you will be judged during an Ofsted inspection will be:

- management of pupils
- teaching of basic skills
- knowledge and understanding
- use of time, support staff and resources
- effectiveness of teaching methods
- effectiveness of planning
- expectations
- quality and use of ongoing assessment
- use of homework.

These elements are consistent with those recommended to be scrutinised in ongoing monitoring and evaluation of teaching in the annual cycle of performance management (see below) and we will consider later on in this chapter how you can plan actively for and ensure a positive lesson observation.

Performance management

Monitoring of teaching and learning has always been a key feature of effective school management. A system of ongoing appraisal (Poster and Poster 1991) has been the main process of monitoring and evaluating individual teacher effectiveness over many years and is still the basis of the current formal process, despite the change of terminology since September 2000 to performance management.

The underpinning legislation for performance management still uses the terminology of 'appraisal' – Education (School Teacher Appraisal) (England) Regulations 2001. Indeed, the principles behind the requirements in the earlier Education (School Teacher Appraisal) Regulations 1991 were much the same as those of performance management. However, the 1997 government Green Paper, *Excellence for All Children*, laying out government's main plans for raising standards in education, marked a turning point in the formality and central control of appraisal as a means of holding individual teachers accountable for their performance.

The main thrust behind the Green Paper was an overarching concern about standards of attainment and teaching nationally, and there was plenty of evidence to support and validate such concerns. The Green Paper laid out a compelling vision to 'create an education service second to none':

> At the heart of this vision is the school which takes responsibility for improving itself and which challenges and works with every pupil to reach ever higher standards. The school of the future, working in partnership with parents and the community, will often be a centre of lifelong learning. It will offer pupils excellent teaching in the basics and a wide range of learning opportunities, some provided at the school site and others elsewhere. It will be outward looking, constantly seeking to learn from other good schools, drawing on libraries and other sources of learning and examining the evidence of what works. It will be well-led and managed, rewarding good performance and it will offer pay, conditions and training for all its staff that reflect the central importance of education to society. Above all it will seek continuous improvement, expect change and promote innovation.
>
> (DfEE 1997)

The introduction of a performance management framework was one of the main initiatives for achieving the vision, recognising the centrality of individual teachers within the context of well-led, self-evaluating schools.

REFLECTION

What is your personal view of performance management? What has it added to your professional life and understanding? What are the drawbacks? Are you broadly in favour of the government's policy? If not, why not?

Appraisal prior to 'performance management' was certainly not at odds with this vision. However, the earlier appraisal systems were often criticised for lack of rigour and consistency. Indeed, most individual teachers' experience bore this out and demonstrated that the effectiveness of the system relied very much on the individual relationship with and effectiveness of their appraiser and the degree to which the appraiser had been trained effectively (Dean 2002: 81).

Problems were compounded further by the lack of access to or resourcing for quality continuing professional development (CPD). Most important of all was the fact that appraisal was only really effective in raising standards of teaching when it was linked with effective whole-school development planning. So what mechanisms does the performance management framework have for overcoming the weaknesses of former systems? Perhaps the following:

- national standardisation and explication of processes, key principles and criteria
- guaranteed minimum of monitoring and evaluation of teaching
- clearer entitlement to CPD and funding to support it
- clearer mechanisms for complaint in cases of disagreement
- high levels of investment in training for leaders and funding for implementation
- potential financial reward for good performance, or withholding of pay progress for poor (or, post-threshold, mediocre) performance.

The overall aims of performance management are to drive forward the model of individual and school continuous self-review within a framework of accountability, which is laudable enough. Unfortunately, the downside with any large-scale attempt to institutionalise good practice seems to be inevitable proliferation of bureaucracy (Preedy, Glatter and Wise 2003: 64).

In practice, the quality of the experience for individual teachers is still heavily influenced by the skills of and their relationship with their team leaders. Also there is a great deal of debate as to whether or not the overall financial invest-ment and increased time allocation to the process have yet been justified in terms of overall impact on the quality of teaching and learning. Although the system may not yet be perfect or foolproof, nevertheless we believe that a well-managed professional appraisal cycle should be seen by teachers as a professional entitlement, rather than something to be feared.

The performance pay element is still highly controversial (Reeves et al. 2002: 39). Pressure from the teacher unions in particular is aimed at diluting the judgement of relative teacher effectiveness being reflected in teachers' pay and at broadening the concerns into areas like teacher shortage (Mansell and Slater 2003: 1). The problems of recruitment and retention are a further inducement to the new scales being seen as virtually an automatic increment due to time in service (except in cases where competency is at issue). Although teachers have long felt they deserve better pay to bring them closer to the pay of other profes-sions, many still feel uncomfortable about performance pay. This is due mainly to the fact that they see themselves as part of a team and fear the divisiveness of true performance pay.

_____ The performance management framework _____

All schools have a legal requirement to have an agreed performance management policy, which is reviewed annually (Activity 8.1). A model policy is available (www.teachernet.gov.uk). In effect, most of the policy is non-negotiable or strongly recommended. The external monitoring of policy and implementation means that in reality schools have very little choice about the policy content – only really to go beyond its minimum requirements (which many do in particular in terms of number of classroom observations and clarity on interim review meetings). The basic framework in relation to teachers consists of these elements:

1 Teachers will be appointed to a team leader (effectively their appraiser) – often their line manager but certainly someone who has a good overview of the teacher's work and the ability to provide support to the teacher.

2 At the beginning of the annual cycle (generally the autumn term), teachers meet with their team leader to agree objectives.

3 A minimum of three but no more than six objectives is set and must include pupil progress as well as ways of developing and improving teacher's professional practice.

4 The objectives should relate to the school development plan or any team plans, etc., as well as to individual professional needs.

5 In setting objectives, support and training needs should be identified and planned for.

6 If objectives cannot be jointly agreed, then teachers have a right to add comments to the written record of objectives.

7 Progress will be kept under active review over the year, using a minimum of one classroom observation and other relevant information.

8 A team leader must consult the relevant teacher before obtaining oral or written information from others relating to their performance.

9 At the end of the performance cycle a meeting must be held to review the objectives (in reality, the review meeting for the last cycle and the planning meeting for the next cycle often take place at the same time).

10 Teachers receive a performance review statement, written by their team leader (within ten days of the meeting).

11 Teachers then have ten days in which to add any written comments they may wish to make to the review statement.

12 If teachers are dissatisfied with aspects of the review and these cannot be resolved with their team leader, they can raise their concerns with the head (or the chair of governors if the head is their team leader). If a teacher's concerns are upheld, a new team leader may be appointed.

13 The teacher keeps one copy of the review statement and the head teacher keeps one copy on file, which is only accessible to the head, team leader and governors responsible for making decisions regarding pay.

14 Performance reviews will be used as part of the supporting evidence for an annual increment on the lower pay scale if the teacher is performing at least satisfactorily or if he/she is put forward for double increments for excellent performance. They will also form part of the evidence for completing the threshold application and for any subsequent move on the upper pay scale. (However, it must be stressed that the performance review is not the sole deciding factor.)

ACTIVITY 8.1

Examining your school's performance management

Look at your own school's performance management policy and compare how it equates to the minimum requirements.

How does the policy relate to your experience of the actual process?

What is good about it?

What is less good? What would you like to improve?

How effectively does it work in practice?

What are the practical strengths and weaknesses?

Threshold assessment

We have already looked at the standards and dimensions required in Chapter 3. This is an important part of the overall national framework for supporting teachers' career and professional development, with the intention of raising educational standards in schools (West-Burnham et al. 2001: 116).

What is particularly notable about this element of the framework is that the onus is on the individual teacher to apply and to provide the evaluation and evidence to support their application. Originally one could apply after seven to nine years' teaching, depending on whether one had a good honours degree. In line with changes to the main teachers' pay scale, this has been brought forward to six years' service. The main outcome of this process is moving on to the upper pay scale.

Although the onus is on the individual to apply, the applicant is entitled to guidance and support. One of the biggest problems for teachers has been that they have not traditionally been good at self-evaluating, especially in terms of recognising what they do well. However, changes in training and the Performance Management Framework are building up these skills. Indeed, with the embedding of performance management, the evidence will have been continually developed since QTS, and therefore will be an integral part of the process of CPD rather than an intimidating bolt-on. Effective teachers have always reflected on their performance, although not necessarily in such a formalised way.

It is the head teacher who is then responsible for the assessment of the application (subject to monitoring and sampling by an external assessor). The progression on the upper pay scale, which potentially has three more steps, hinges on the statement that a teacher's achievements and contribution to a school have to be 'substantial and sustained' (HMSO 2002). There is no formal application process, as is required for initial threshold assessment, but rather the judgement is largely informed by the performance management process. The funding and criteria for the upper pay scale are still major areas of concern at the time of writing.

A more difficult issue to reconcile is whether a teacher who is not making a substantial and sustained impact in a school is indeed effective enough to be teaching.

General Teaching Council (GTC)

The legislative machinery to form a professional regulatory body for teachers was put into place in the Education Act 1998 and came into effect from 1 June 2001. There are three strands to the GTC's remit: advisory, regulatory and to promote the profession. This was to bring teaching in line with other professions, although the traditional power and role of the teacher unions do not sit comfortably with these intentions.

Teachers are required to register with the GTC if they are employed in any post that requires Qualified Teacher Status (QTS). As we saw in Chapter 1, the GTC has a Code of Professional Values and Practice for Teachers, which is meant to be a useful reference point and benchmark for teachers. However, by far the most important power of the GTC is that of regulation of the profession. In the areas of professional conduct and competency, the council has the power to issue a reprimand, attach conditions to registration or remove a teacher temporarily or permanently from the register.

Teachers subject to these regulatory sanctions would normally have already been found to be below accepted standards by their employers and the employer's procedures would normally have been completed. Employers have an obligation to report cases, for example of misconduct, to the GTC.

REFLECTION

What has been your experience of the GTC? Has it been favourable or unfavourable? To what extent do you understand its working? How has it worked for you?

There is an informative website about the work of the GTC (www.gtce.org.uk).

ACTIVITY 8.2

Reflecting on your response to accountability

Consider your own experience of the formal dimensions of accountability (or, if you personally have not experienced these, discuss the following questions with someone who has):

■ What concerns did you have prior to engaging with the process?

■ How did your concerns relate to the reality of the experience?

■ How fair did you feel that the evaluation of you was compared with your self-evaluation?

■ Did you get credit for what you did well, as well as identification of areas for development?

■ What was the balance of these, and did it raise issues that you were not previously aware of?

■ What contribution were you able to make to the process?

■ What were the overall strengths/weaknesses of the process?

■ In retrospect, what would you have changed about the process?

■ In what way did the process influence or change your subsequent teaching practice?

■ Did you receive appropriate opportunities for CPD following the review of your needs?

Active participation – professional engagement with the process of accountability

Preparing yourself for appraisal (review and planning) meetings

However well one knows and trusts the team leader/appraiser, the teacher needs to have given a great deal of thought to what he/she wants out of the appraisal meeting. Indeed, the more relaxed one feels about the appraiser, the more vigilant one needs to be in making sure one has a professional dialogue that supports career development, rather than just a 'pleasant chat'.

Throughout the chapters of this book we have encouraged the reader to reflect upon the many facets of teaching and future trends. This type of thinking will greatly help you to take full advantage of the opportunities presented by performance management/appraisal (Dean 2002: 114–15). We feel strongly that such professional dialogue and review should be considered an entitlement to be welcomed. In the busy life of a school, this is one guaranteed opportunity when you are at the centre of the agenda – when you are guaranteed the full attention of your line manager and/or head teacher.

This meeting will set the tone for personal development over the forthcoming 12 months. By this we do not just mean that it will decide which courses one might be allowed to attend, but what you say could lead to you being given opportunities to lead or participate in particular projects or initiatives of interest to you; for your personal views or concerns to be taken into account; for you to demonstrate your potential and your enthusiasm, etc.

Here are some questions and issues it will help you to think about prior to your annual meeting. The order they are given in may not be the best order for you. Some may prefer to start from themselves and then work out to the 'big picture'. Others might like to think about the 'big picture' in education and then funnel down to a personal perspective within that. Whichever way works best for you, it is the process of thinking and reflection that matters (Activity 8.3).

ACTIVITY 8.3

Preparing for appraisal

Jot down your initial thoughts/response to the questions and issues as you read through them.

Me and my values

- What are your core values for teaching and learning?
- Why? Are these still sufficient or do recent initiatives and developments challenge you to rethink or adjust your vision?

Me and my career

- What do you want to be doing professionally in three to five years' time?
- What skills have you already got and which ones will you need to develop to get there?

Thinking about this and sharing this appropriately with your team leader can ensure that he/she keeps you in mind for relevant opportunities. This keeps you focused on the issues of 'where am I now?', 'where do I want to get to?' and 'how am I going to get there?' – just as a school has to have a vision, so do you.

Me and my classroom

- What is going well in your classroom at the moment in terms of:
  - relationships, behaviour and classroom management
  - areas and aspects of learning
  - individual children or groups of children
  - strategies, approaches, activities
  - available assessment data?
- What isn't going so well in your classroom at the moment in terms of:
  - relationships, behaviour and classroom management
  - areas and aspects of learning
  - individual children or groups of children
  - strategies, approaches, activities
  - available assessment data?

Me and my school

- What are the current identified priorities in the school development plan (SDP)?
- What are the trends and issues arising from performance analysis, in comparison to schools nationally, with similar pupil profiles, locally?

- What are the key values in the school and how does your practice reflect or link to these?

- Are there any school issues not identified in the SDP that you think should be?

- Are there any resource or organisational issues that are impacting on your effectiveness at the moment?

Me and the wider world

- Are there any particular characteristics in the community which influence/ impact on the way you work?

- Are there any LEA level initiatives that are influencing or may influence the way you work?

- Are there any central initiatives that are placing particular demands or expectations on your teaching phase?

- What are the current national educational issues and trends?

Useful ways to keep up your awareness are through the *TES*, the annual report of the Chief Inspector of Schools, professional journals, teachernet website, DfES website, etc. Given the limited time you have available, browsing the *TES* and DfES website and documents like the annual report are an efficient way of keeping a feel for trends and anything that really catches your interest can be researched further if you wish.

- What are the current key political and socio-economic issues?

Even if these are not of direct relevance to education, there are not many key issues that do not have some influence over school life.

This already sounds a long list, but use the opportunity as a good time to pull together the threads of thought so that you can then think about the final two important issues:

- Review what you think your progress and achievement have been against last year's targets.

Make sure you have thought about what evidence you are basing your self-evaluation on – planning, lesson observations and feedback, examples of pupils' work, feedback from colleagues, parents, etc., making sure you could justify your view if there is any discrepancy between your own and your team leader's judgements.

■ What do you think your targets should be for the forthcoming year?

Think in terms of the following key areas:

– teaching and learning in the classroom

– pupil progress (this is a statutory aspect – see model Performance Management Policy Sept 2001)

– coordinator and management roles

– personal professional aspirations.

Think also about what support and development opportunities you might need to meet the targets. Most need to link to school development planning, but not all.

The planning and review meeting

Even if you know your team leader well, you are still bound to feel a little nervous at the beginning of the meeting. However, it is important to bear in mind that if you have thought through the issues above and have been honest with yourself, then there should be no major surprises in the meeting.

The most important thing is not to go into a review meeting on the defensive, but be prepared to listen and then be confident and assertive in participating in the professional dialogue. Most of the time these meetings actually affirm the positives of what you are doing and are an opportunity to say 'well done'. If there is a real problem with your teaching, you are likely to have been informed about it outside the performance management meeting, but for the purposes of the intended audience of this text we assume that this is not the case.

However, you do need to be confident and assertive in making sure you get what you are entitled to from the meeting. Again, this is where considering the issues listed above is so important. It is possible to use this checklist as an agenda. A good team leader will welcome the appraisee's active participation in the process and consider it a positive that he/she is developing the essential professional characteristic of reflective self-evaluation and awareness. It is very important to make sure that the outcomes of such meetings are clear:

■ confirming your essential tasks and objectives

■ identifying the judgement of your progress and achievements against former objectives

■ setting and agreeing new objectives

■ establishing the criteria for success and what professional support can be expected to help meet these.

If anything is unclear, ask for clarification. It is much better to come to a mutual agreement through discussion and negotiation during the meeting.

Within ten days of the planning and review meeting, the teacher will receive a written statement covering the main points from the meeting. Within ten days or so of receiving the written statement, one has the right to add written comments to the statement. Both the team leader and appraisee should then sign and date the statement. Only two copies should be kept – one by the teacher and one by the head teacher. Only the team leader or governors responsible for making decisions regarding pay may request access to your review statement. In practice, the governors will rarely ask for access as they will usually accept the verbal recommendations of the head and/or team leader, unless there appears to be a discrepancy.

What if a teacher is unhappy with the outcome?

The right to add written comments to the review statement is one way in which one can record dissatisfaction with any or all of the outcomes or processes. However, if there are concerns and they are not able to be resolved with the team leader, then the individual has the right to raise these concerns with the head teacher. Where the head is your team leader, then concerns should be raised with the chair of governors.

In the event of a complaint, this should be stated clearly and supported by clear evidence and examples to back the case. An individual teacher must be careful not to overreact to constructive criticism or identification of needs, as long as it is fair. What feels comfortable to discuss and agree in verbal form can look rather blunt when put in black and white on a sheet of paper. Team leaders should always (and generally do) give very careful thought to wording development needs in a concise, fair and non-emotive way.

REFLECTION

How do you react to undergoing a review of your teaching? What experience have you had of it? What have been the negative and positive outcomes?

Planning for a successful lesson observation

Lesson observations are one of the most important aspects of monitoring and evaluation in a school and are one of the most important ways that you can demonstrate and showcase your effectiveness as a teacher. In the past, teachers could go several years without a formal observation of their teaching; thank goodness this is now no longer the case.

As indicated above, one observation per year is the minimum. With more involvement of subject coordinators in monitoring and schools becoming involved in innovation through action research, the frequency of observation and range of participants is increasing. Although teachers generally feel nervous about observations, again we believe that they should be viewed as a professional right (and equally, one should take any opportunity to observe other people teach in order to build on experience).

There is no secret about key elements that an observer is looking for in a lesson observation (the Ofsted criteria are set out in Ferguson et al. 2000: 17). As we have seen in Chapters 3–7, there is now a considerable body of work that identifies key traits and characteristics of effective teaching. The balance of these may change for different subjects and activity types, and the individual personality and style of a teacher will obviously influence the classroom climate. However, the key aspects identified are mostly necessary for teaching to be effective. Therefore, if one is planning a lesson that is going to be observed, it makes sense to ensure thought is given to these aspects.

A good starting point for planning teaching/learning for an observation is to look at the exemplar observation guidance from the model Performance Management Policy referred to above (Fig. 8.1).

FIG. 8.1 Lesson observation guidance

Lesson observation: guidance

1 **The teacher plans effectively and sets clear objectives that are understood.**

   (a) Objectives are communicated clearly at the start of the lesson.
   (b) Materials are ready.
   (c) There is a good structure to the lesson.
   (d) The lesson is reviewed at the end.
   (e) The learning needs of those with IEPs are incorporated with the teacher's planning.

2 **The teacher shows good subject knowledge and understanding.**

   (a) Teacher has a thorough knowledge of the subject content covered in the lesson.
   (b) Subject material was appropriate for the lesson.
   (c) Knowledge is made relevant and interesting for pupils.

3 **The teaching methods used enable all pupils to learn effectively.**

(a)   The lesson is linked to previous teaching or learning.

(b)   The ideas and experiences of pupils are drawn upon.

(c)   A variety of activities and questioning techniques is used.

(d)   Instructions and explanations are clear and specific.

(e)   The teacher involves all pupils, listens to them and responds appropriately.

(f)   High standards of effort, accuracy and presentation are encouraged.

(g)   Appropriate methods of differentiation are used.

4 **Pupils are well managed and high standards of behaviour are insisted upon.**

(a)   Pupils are praised regularly for their good effort and achievement.

(b)   Prompt action is taken to address poor behaviour.

(c)   All pupils are treated fairly, with an equal emphasis on the work of boys and girls, and all ability groups.

5 **Pupils' work is assessed thoroughly.**

(a)   Pupil understanding is assessed throughout the lesson by the use of the teacher's questions.

(b)   Mistakes and misconceptions are recognised by the teacher and used constructively to facilitate learning.

(c)   Pupils' written work is assessed regularly and accurately.

6 **Pupils achieve productive outcomes.**

(a)   Pupils remain fully engaged throughout the lesson and make progress in the lesson.

(b)   Pupils understand what work is expected of them during the lesson.

(c)   The pupil outcomes of the lesson are consistent with the objectives set at the beginning.

(d)   The teacher and pupils work at a good pace.

7 **The teacher makes effective use of time and resources.**

(a)   Time is utilised well and the learning is maintained for the full time available.

(b)   A good pace is maintained throughout the lesson.

(c)   Good use is made of any support available, e.g. learning assistants and older pupils.

(d)   Appropriate learning resources are used, e.g. ICT.

8 **Homework is used effectively to reinforce and extend learning.**

(a)   Homework is set if appropriate.

(b)   The learning objectives are explicit and relate to the work in progress.

(c)   Homework is followed up if it has been set previously.

These areas will all be relevant to threshold assessment, especially knowledge and understanding (2); teaching and assessment (1, 3, 4, 5, 7, 8); pupil progress (6); and professional characteristics (1, 3, 4, 5).

Some of the prompts have a strong inference towards the structures of the 'three-part lesson' – as exemplified in the literacy and numeracy strategies. However, developing knowledge about learning shows that this is not the only or always the best structure (see Chapters 5, 6, 11). Nevertheless, most of the prompts are still relevant generic statements against which to cross-check planning. The key items in the proforma ensure that the basis is there for a professional discussion against which the teacher observed can explain their teaching choices. This is the key point: you need to be able to explain why specific choices were made.

Effective everyday planning documentation should be sufficient for a lesson observation (see Chapter 7). However, some teachers prefer to write a detailed lesson plan for these occasions. The downside of planning in too much detail is that it can entrench the teacher mentally in what he/she thinks will happen rather than being sensitive to what is actually happening during the lesson (this theme is pursued below). What must be addressed clearly in lesson plans, whatever the degree of detail, are:

- the learning objective/s (which must be appropriate to the subject area, age and broad attainment in the class)
- activities and strategies that are appropriate to teaching/learning for this objective
- how the needs of all pupils will be met (differentiation).

A little bit of nervousness is to be expected when being observed. One is in effect giving a 'performance'. That is not to say that one should be planning anything very different or out of character for this occasion. Indeed, given the raised nerves created by the situation, a formal observation by the team leader/line manager is not the ideal time to experiment. One needs to keep in mind the issue of being 'interesting', but it is not the time to try something totally radical (especially if it is an Ofsted observation).

If the school is focusing particularly on developing an aspect of teaching – e.g. appropriate use of ICT, visual, auditory and kinaesthetic education, peer evaluation etc. – a lesson observation is a useful opportunity to show that this is being included in the teaching. Alternatively, if the aspect is omitted, it is useful to have very good reason why it is not appropriate on this occasion. Again, it is the issue of being reflective, showing one is making professional choices about teaching and learning and that the reasons for these are understood.

To ensure that one can focus on teaching well, one of the main aspects that can be controlled and made secure are the resources used in the lesson. With heightened nerves, it is important that one is confident that everything needed by teacher and pupils is at hand (and in working order). During the lesson, if it becomes clear that what has been planned is not working and if one would adapt it or change direction if one weren't being observed, then do so. It takes a lot of confidence, but it is the ultimate indicator of 'assessment in action' and professional focus on the needs of the learner.

Follow-up/feedback

After you have been observed, it is certain that you will be asked your opinion of how the lesson went. Make sure you have thought about it and been honest with yourself. If something did not go well, say so and say why you think that was the case. Do acknowledge what did work and why. Lesson observations are not about proving we are perfect and infallible, but that we are competent professionals. As teachers we are dealing with a class of around 30 individuals; it will be rare to get everything right for every single one. Master teachers have to show that they understand the needs of the pupils and how to strive continually to respond to the needs of each one.

Make sure that in the feedback discussion you give an indication of what your next steps to follow up this lesson will be, based on your assessment of pupils during the lesson and based on task outcomes marked following the lesson.

The main thing that an observer is looking for is that you understand what is going on in your classroom, that you have the skills and understanding, and will to be able to solve the problems you come across in the complex role of a teacher. In Activity 8.4 you are asked to reflect on a recent lesson observation that you have experienced.

ACTIVITY 8.4

Reflecting on a recent lesson observation

Think about a recent lesson in which you were observed at work. With respect to the issues raised in the section above:

- How did your preparation compare?

- How did the lesson unfold – did it go according to plan?

- If not, why not?

- How did you feel during the observation?

- To what extent were you able to use some of the skills of self-analysis and self-awareness discussed elsewhere in this text?

- How did your self-evaluation relate to the feedback you received?

- Did you feel you had some control over the process?

- What would you change next time?

Beyond the formal frameworks – responsibility to yourself

What the formal frameworks do is to ensure that professional development is firmly at the heart of school development and that it is not left to chance. In this chapter we have concentrated on the performance management and attendant issues from the perspective of the individual master teacher (by contrast, the school's perspective is recorded by Wintle 2001). That does not mean that, as an individual, you can be complacent about your career development. If you have clear ambitions about what you want to achieve in and through your teaching, you still need to be proactive in your professional development. As indicated above, the majority of your development through the formal processes is embedded in the school context in which you happen to be teaching. The priorities and development needs of your school may not necessarily link to what you need to meet your aspirations. (We discuss these issues in more detail in Chapter 9.)

So what else can you do or consider? Within the formal frameworks there are opportunities such as Fast Track and Advanced Skills Teaching, as well as working your way up through taking on additional responsibilities within your school. Information about educational initiatives and opportunities has never been more widely available, thanks to the internet. Just as for your pupils though (see Chapter 6), the issue is not the availability of information, but rather what response we have to it – how it is used.

REFLECTION

How have observation, appraisal and performance management shaped your attitudes towards your career? What ambitions do you have at this time, and how do you intend to pursue them?

Chapter 9 is aimed at widening awareness of what CPD can be and what it can contribute to your career. But we argue that the most powerful tool in teaching is the understanding of pedagogy and its ongoing development (Chapter 2). It is the understanding of why we work in particular ways to meet particular needs and how we combine strategies and balance constraints that are at the heart of truly 'effective' teaching or the work of the master teacher. The push to restructure and redefine the teaching workforce, as well as the impact of ICT, will make this high-level knowledge all the more important – the big shift is to managing learning rather than imparting knowledge.

At the end of this chapter you should have:

■ Gained an insight into the dimensions of accountability

■ An understanding of the key aspects of performance management

■ Considered how you can be professionally active in this crucial process

————— References —————

Dean, J. (2002) *Implementing Performance Management: A Handbook for Schools*, London: Routledge Falmer.

DfEE (1997) *Excellence for All Children*, London: HMSO.

Doyle, M. (2001) 'Head teacher development and performance management', in J. West-Burnham, J. O'Neill, and I. Bradbury, *Performance Management in Schools*, London: Pearson.

Ferguson, N., Earley, P., Fidler, B. and Ouston, J. (2000) *Improving Schools and Inspection: The Self-evaluating School*, London: PCP.

HMSO (1991) *Education (School Teacher Appraisal) Regulations*, London: HMSO.

HMSO (2001) *Education (School Teacher Appraisal) Regulations*, London: HMSO.

HMSO (2002) *Schools Teachers' Pay and Conditions Document*, London: HMSO.

Mansell, W. and Slater, J. (2003) 'Teachers likely to get pay rise of 2.9 per cent', *Times Educational Supplement*, 7 Febuary: 1.

Ofsted (1995) *Handbook for the Inspection of Nursery and Primary Schools*, London: HMSO.

Poster, C. and Poster, D. (1991) *Teacher Appraisal: A Guide to Training*, London: Routledge.

Preedy, M., Glatter, R. and Wise, C. (2003) *Strategic Leadership and Educational Improvement*, London: PCP Open University.

Reeves, J., Forde, C., Obrien, J., Smith, P. and Tomlinson, H. (2002) *Performance Management in Education: Improving Practice*, London: PCP.

West-Burnham, J., O'Neill, J. and Bradbury, I. (2001) *Performance Management in Schools*, London: Pearson.

Wintle, M. (2001) 'Performance management and the giant teddy bear', in J. West-Burnham, J. O'Neill, and I. Bradbury, *Performance Management in Schools*, London: Pearson.

chapter nine

The self-developing teacher

Continuing professional development in action

In this chapter you are invited to:

- Consider the nature of professional development and its role in making teachers more effective

- Understand its main areas and forms of access, and how to get the most from them

- Assess the value of various forms of professional development to your own situation

- Relate professional development to improved personal performance and career advancement

 Introduction

In Chapter 1 we entered the debate about professionalism. Without revisiting that debate, we should note that Hoyle (1997: 53) identifies a number of professional characteristics, among which is specialised knowledge. According to Hoyle, this knowledge, for teachers, embraces subject knowledge, pedagogic knowledge, reflection on practice and research-based knowledge. He further points out that these areas do not exhaust the knowledge areas that teachers need:

While it is right that the quest for further exploration between cognitive knowledge and classroom practice should be given priority, it should also be recognised that teachers have a wide range of professional responsibilities in addition to the transmission of knowledge and skill. Pastoral care, social education, curriculum development, departmental management, etc., are underpinned by forms of theoretical knowledge other than those relating to pedagogy, and require much further exploration.

(Hoyle 1997: 53)

In the present context, Hoyle's list does set one of the agendas for this chapter (except in relation to departmental management, which is covered in another text in this series, Tranter 2000). Here we shall concern ourselves with the teacher as manager and leader *in the classroom* only, rather than of a department or of a year group. But first, we need to examine some of the theoretical perspectives of professional development.

────── Professional development as a process ──────

Though it sounds a crude question, the fundamental issue in considering the nature of professional development is whether professional development is something done by teachers or done to them. The debate reflects the one we have articulated earlier about whether teachers are 'technicians'. This debate is shot through the whole of government's thinking and its pronouncements about teacher 'training', as is evidenced in reports such as Thornton (2003). For the last two decades successive administrations have attempted to move teachers down this road (e.g. Department for Education and Employment (DfEE) 1992), and the concept (sometimes referred to as 'the empty vessel theory') rests on a number of assumptions:

- that teaching consists of a number of individual competences that can be taught and imitated
- that rehearsing these competences in class will guarantee effective teaching
- that such competences can be learned or acquired by a range of people otherwise untrained
- that the apprenticeship model will suffice as a training model: watching a master at work will provide the vehicle through which competences are conveyed.

The competence model is essentially behaviourist in philosophy; it looks at the simple level of cause and effect: if the teacher does *x* is the desired result obtained? Zeichner and Liston (1987) express it more theoretically when they assert:

> *At the first level of technical rationality, the dominant concern is with the efficient and effective application of education knowledge for purposes of attaining ends which are accepted as given. At this level, neither the ends nor the institutional contexts of classroom, school, community, and society are treated as problematic.*
>
> (Zeichner and Liston 1987: 24)

Let's take a simple example of this. The teacher sets a test: ten questions about mathematical tables of the kind $3 \times 3 = ?$ The test is competent (the questions are all valid and the teacher can score the answers accurately). The purpose of the test is to see who has done their homework. The test is effective at a *technical* level. It measures what it is designed to measure and answers the teacher's intended need. However it does not address the following:

1 *At the level of the classroom* it does not identify the reasons why some children have problems with some answers; why Jane can cope with $3 \times$ but not $4 \times$, or why Jamie can't read the questions. It does not look at alternatives to tests to gain the same outcome.

2 *At the level of the school* it may not take into account aspects of the school's policy on testing.

3 *At the level of the community* it may not address the views of parents about setting homework, or take into account the differing social contexts that make homework more problematic for some children than others.

4 *At the level of society* it may not reflect a view that children are being over-assessed or relate directly to the long-term goals of mathematical proficiency.

The efficacy of this approach is accurately, and somewhat dramatically, summed up by Hill (1997). In this quotation he calls the approach we have described 'technical reflection' and he is describing the movement to replace initial teacher education by school-based, on-the-job training:

> *For technical reflection, trial and error and mimicry based on an apprenticeship competence-based approach ... could be enough. Hence, no theory would, at first sight, be required. Rather like an apprentice butcher, the apprentice teacher could learn her or his cuts and strokes by copying the 'master butcher', and by having a go, getting better through practice. This is the 'tips for teachers' approach, the tips being primarily related to execution and presentation within a teacher-dominated stimulus–response framework, with no development or understanding of the 'why' of teaching, only of the 'how to'.*
>
> (Hill 1997: 194)

This is not an approach we espouse or would countenance; nor is it one on which we intend to spend more time. So what are the alternatives?

Marion Dadds (2001)has a phrase that we like that sums up our approach to professional development: 'nurturing the expert within'. She goes on:

> Teachers ... do not enter into CPD as empty vessels. They bring existing experiences, practices, perspectives, insights and, most usually, anxieties about the highly complex nature of their work. They usually enter into CPD courses brimful of thoughts and feelings; with implicit or explicit beliefs about education and their work with children. They come with differences, disagreements, preconceptions, uncertainties, missions. These are all useful resources which can be drawn upon and studied in CPD processes.
>
> (Dadds 2001: 51)

So the question becomes what to do with these resources and how they can be harnessed. Higgins and Leat (2001) explore this question, trying to synthesise the many overlapping views of the answer. They try to extract models from a range of writers and trace the connections between them. The models they identify include:

- *the expert/novice model* – fundamentally this is the apprenticeship model we have discussed using Hill's constructions
- *the reflective model* – though varying in interpretation from author to author, this model stresses the process by which teachers analyse the processes of teaching and their effects on students
- *the socialisation model* – sees the induction of the teacher into the culture of the school and the staff as central to the learning process
- *the personal model* – operates largely in the affective domain and is concerned with autobiographic accounts of how teachers develop
- *the craft model* – a variation on the expert/novice model, which is concerned with 'recipe knowledge' and the 'technology' of teaching
- *the subject knowledge/pedagogical knowledge model* – stresses the dimensions of knowledge as the focus of teacher effectiveness.

What Higgins and Leat discovered through this process was that fundamentally no one model could be sustained in its entirety to do justice to the conceptualisation of professional development. Models overlapped, but often not significantly. In an attempt to overcome these problems the cited authors developed their own model based on the questions:

- What develops?

- How and why do the developments take place?

- What influence does context have?

These basic questions led them to place the self at the heart of thinking about professional development. But even they admit that their conceptualisations are incomplete. What is clear is that there is some form of continuum for under-standing the processes, though exactly how one would label the arms is unclear.

FIG. 9.1 A possible continuum of professional development

Action research-orientated<-->Training course-orientated

In Fig. 9.1 we see two approaches that are about as far apart as one can get. The first, action research, puts the teacher at the centre of the process. It assumes that teachers conceptualise their own classroom problems and needs, devise investigative approaches for solving them and operate a range of solutions to make their work more effective. The second, the training course, epitomises some recent government approaches. It begins from the assumption that there is a 'right answer' to meet some kind of predetermined general need. It imposes a schedule of 'training' on the participants based on the view that 'correct' action will lead to the 'desired' result. It is essentially outcome-orientated as opposed to process-orientated.

In this section we have attempted to set the scene for more detailed discussions of some of the major forms of professional development that follow. What has emerged so far is a lack of consensus. Those who oppose the dogma of 'training' would claim that the teaching profession is being 'led by the nose' by politicians. Those who oppose more open and investigative approaches complain of wasted time, wasted money and woolly solutions. Your decision about where you stand in this debate will determine your view of teachers' professionalism and your own self-image as a professional.

———— Subject and curriculum knowledge ————

Teachers teach something. What they teach – the content – is the subject knowl-edge that is bound up in the curriculum. Of course, the curriculum is wider and deeper than the sum of all the individual subjects studied, involving as it does the hidden curriculum, the extracurricular activities of the school, and so on. So in addition to expertise in teaching a subject or subjects, teachers need skills in curriculum building.

Until 1988 this last statement would have been a sine qua non of every teacher's life. Part of the role of teachers was to build the curriculum for their classes and share in determining the overall curriculum of the school. The 1988 Education Act imposed a National Curriculum: put simply, the state built a common curriculum for all on teachers' behalf. The arguments for and against this need not detain us in this chapter, but the constraints of National Curriculum – now so readily accepted by those who have known nothing else – took many teachers of a previous generation by surprise. As one of us has summed it up elsewhere, what teachers expected was a statement of entitlement for all pupils; what they got was a prescribed syllabus with testing attached.

But let us be clear about a few things before we pursue this discussion, because we would not want our book to be confined to the same dungeon of myth as was the Plowden Report (Kerry 2002). So here are some assertions:

1 *Subject knowledge is important for teachers*: a major component of teaching is to explain material clearly to pupils and students. It is impossible to explain what you do not know and understand yourself. One of the most fundamental qualities of a teacher is to know their material.

2 *Subject enthusiasm is a critical teacher quality*: almost any examination of what makes a teacher memorable in the mind of an adult looking back on his or her education will place at or near the top of the list of attributes the ability of a favoured teacher to 'bring the subject alive', 'to fire the imagination', e.g. of far-away places in geography, or to 'make me want to find out more – I've never lost the interest'. This assertion matches with our advice to new teachers: one of the twin pillars of the profession is to be interesting.

3 *Subjects change and teachers must keep up with the changes as part of their professional development*: the chemistry, language or theology we learned at undergraduate level moves on. There are new pieces of information coming to light, new theories being developed, new interpretations of events, new perceptions and laws surfacing all the time. To teach effectively the teacher must keep up with this change. This assertion matches with the other twin pillar of our advice to new teachers: be interested.

4 *Subjects build into a curriculum and knowing how to match work into an overall framework is essential*: the critical things are the balances between subjects and the links that make them interrelate. The watchword here is: integration is better than segregation.

This is not the moment in which to enter into a deep debate about the nature of knowledge, though we discussed the issue briefly in Chapter 3. But there is a modicum of theory that may help to illuminate what teachers need to know about subjects. Subjects consist of information – sometimes referred to as propositional or substantive knowledge (Turner-Bisset 2001) – and ways of proceeding within the discipline, sometimes called procedural or syntactic knowledge. At its simplest, propositional knowledge consists of statements like 'The battle of Hastings was fought in 1066' or 'Male birds often have brighter plumage than females'. Procedural knowledge would look at evidence for the process of the battle or its motivations, or at the reasons why evolution had equipped male and female birds with differentiated plumage. Propositional/substantive knowledge is about 'facts', procedural/syntactic knowledge about interrogating the facts.

Teachers need knowledge, but they also need to understand knowledge and how it develops over time. A factor in professional development then must be to keep abreast of subject knowledge. But it goes beyond that even – never more so than for teachers in primary schools who cover large swathes of curriculum knowledge – to embrace extending our range of knowledge. It means broadening the general or overall knowledge of the world around us and its debates, being alert to learning opportunities, to new experiences, to things that interest our children (even though they may not interest us), to the world beyond the village, the street, the town, even the narrow parochialism of the country to become in a very real and intellectual sense citizens of the world.

REFLECTION

Re-read the last paragraph slowly and carefully. How closely does it reflect your own beliefs, and where does it deviate from them?

Pedagogic knowledge and skills

In a nutshell, pedagogic knowledge consists of two key understandings: how children learn and therefore how to teach them more effectively.

How does learning occur?

There are numerous theories. Here we will sift out the bones of some of the most relevant.

Behaviourist models

Most people are familiar with the behaviourist models. They had their genesis in Pavlov's experiments with animals: a dog trained to come to food at the sound of a bell would salivate to the bell even when lunch was not provided. This kind of thinking was developed by Skinner and Thorndike into classroom theories, which emphasise the role of drills (such as saying tables or reciting French verbs), value practice and point to the importance of reinforcement.

Behaviourism has its problems as a theory. It does not place much value on starting from where the student is and using existing knowledge. It is low on teacher interaction with students and ignores the range of abilities that occur in most classrooms. It focuses more on content than on the learner. It is a way of teaching that has value for certain activities that are suitable for reduction to rote learning, but is often inadequate as a way of furthering learning and stretching the intellect.

Constructivist theories

These suggest that students learn through an interaction between thought and experience. This is a very valuable step forward since it takes us into the realm of child-centredness. But the variation called social constructivism is more productive still. Social constructivists tell us not only that we must begin from the pupil, but also that the social interactions of learning (between teacher and pupil, and pupil and pupil) are also significant. The theory underpins collaborative classroom working, group-based activities and discussion methods.

Social constructivist theories depend on a view that places language at the heart of the learning process. Through talk the developing child moves towards the development of intellect and the higher cognitive processes. An extension of the theory is the concept of the 'zone of proximal development' (ZPD). Effectively, this theory says that pupils learn incrementally; beginning from what they know they 'scaffold' new knowledge onto this base.

These theories promote a debate about National Curriculum, centred on the relative values of what pupils should know as opposed to what they should understand. The National Curriculum is too obsessed (it is argued) with subject knowledge rather than the connections between subjects that lead to real insight.

Developmental theory

To deal with the problem of progression in learning we move to Jean Piaget. His work identified developmental stages in pupils – sensorimotor, preconceptual, intuitive, concrete operational, formal, operational. But such a theory is only a rough guide in that children progress at different paces and with overlapping skills. Bloom took this theory on a step and talked about higher-order and low-order thinking skills. Thus revision and the rote repetition of work are at a low order, while application, analysis, synthesis and evaluation are at a higher order. What now becomes significant is the kind of tasks we set, or the kind of questions we ask.

More recently, Howard Gardner (1993) has talked about seven 'intelligences', a view he revised to nine in later work. This view clearly has implications for curriculum building. He suggests that children possess and need educating, in all of these seven:

- verbal/linguistic

- logical/mathematical

- visual/spatial

- body/kinaesthetic

- musical/rhythmic

- interpersonal

- intrapersonal/self-knowledge.

Clearly, the stance one takes about how children learn will affect how and what one teaches. In turn, it will affect the kinds of professional development we consider to be appropriate and valuable. What emerges from our brief survey of how children learn is that there is no single theory that does total justice to this complex area, and there can therefore be no single statement that encapsulates how to teach effectively. Many writers have noted that one factor that makes it difficult for teachers to claim professional status is the lack of a rationale for their activity in the form of a single accepted theory of pedagogy. But some educationists also believe that we rely too much on the detail of how individual children learn in trying to construct pedagogy, rather than on the broader insights that a generalised study of human learning can bring (Gipps 1994: 27). In the absence of a single rationale, continuous exploration and refinement by teachers are needed of the questions about how learning and teaching take place. This, in turn, leads us to theories of professional development that involve notions of reflection, and of the teacher as researcher. It is to these that we now turn.

Reflection on practice

Reflective teaching has become the buzzword of professional development inherited largely from the 1990s. Schon (1983) is credited with much of the pioneering thinking in this field. Phelan (1997) describes the phenomenon, albeit wryly:

> *Throughout the last decade, the discourse of reflection has reverberated ... The discourse resounds with promises of greater insight, sharpened self-awareness, ethical and political sensitivity and more balanced and reasoned self-awareness skills ... The teacher education literature is littered with descriptors such as 'teacher as action researcher', 'teacher as scholar', 'teacher as change agent', teacher as participant observer', 'self-monitoring teacher' ... Despite the odd cautionary note ... the discourse of reflection appears to have been embraced wholeheartedly (perhaps uncritically?) ... 'reflective practice' has become the unquestioned contemporary standard of the good teacher.*
>
> (Phelan 1997: 169)

McLaughlin (1997) attempts to define the phenomenon:

> *At its core, reflection is a process of becoming more conscious: about purpose, about action, about conditions and about social consequences of actions.*
>
> (McLaughlin 1997: 183)

He goes on to look at how reflection might work in professional development. First, reflection is about retelling events. For this reason, many exponents of the method ask teachers to keep journals or logs of their experiences through which banks of experience (what happened, how one acted or reacted, what went well, what went badly, what one might do better next time, how the events relate to theories and bodies of knowledge) are constructed.

Second, he notes Schon's view of reflection as a kind of inner dialogue: the reflective practitioner converses with the self about experience in order to learn from it. Third, reflection interrogates experience; it asks about the nature of the problem reflected upon and how to respond to it in more effective ways. Fourth, Schon talks of 'reflection in action', which is a kind of internalised dialogue that leads to refined behaviour. Finally, reflection includes an emotional element that allows learning to emanate from experience as opposed to emanating from authoritative external instruction.

REFLECTION

Which of Schon's models in the previous paragraph fits most closely the reflection you have been doing as you have worked through this text?

Hill (1997) divided reflection into types – indeed his first level (technical reflection) has been described already (p.186). He adds two more 'levels' of reflection to his analysis: situational or contextual reflection, and critical reflection. Of these, the situational/contextual reflection consists of looking at:

> The theoretical and institutional assumptions behind, for example, curriculum and pedagogy, and ... the effects of teaching actions, goals and structures.
>
> (Hill 1997: 194)

Critical reflection, Hill suggests, contains:

> A consideration of the moral and ethical implications of pedagogy and of school structures.
>
> (Hill 1997: 196)

It can readily be seen that situational reflection is more 'domestic' in its nature, while critical reflection is 'global'. In other words, the former deals with the internal concerns of the classroom, while the latter asks the 'big' questions concerning theories about society, social stratification, power, ideology, and about the interrelationships of these things. As you will have gathered from your reading of this text, we are very much at home in using both these levels of reflection to define teachers' professionalism and hence their professional development. There are other ways of defining reflective approaches to teaching, and just one further example will suffice. This is based on the work of Zeichner and Liston (1990) and shown as Table 9.1.

TABLE 9.1 Models of reflective approaches to teaching

- *An academic model*: stresses reflection on subject matter, and the construction of subject matter knowledge in order to promote learning

- *A social efficiency model*: applies research into learning/teaching to the practical teaching situation in a thoughtful way

- *A developmentalist model*: prioritises as important teaching that is sensitive to pupils' interests, pupils' thinking and developmental growth

- *A social reconstructivist model*: puts its main emphasis on the social and political context of schooling, and values classroom actions in so far as they promote greater equity, social justice and humane conditions within and beyond school

Reflection as a way of construing professional experience and activity is now embedded in many professional development activities, from one-day courses to higher degree studies. Often, the reflective act takes the form of writing a journal or log. Bain et al. (2002) studied this process to probe its benefits and concluded:

> *The benefits achieved through a focus on the level of reflective writing are not merely 'surface' changes to the structure or writing style ... but represent real changes in the way students view the relationship between reflective writing and reflective teaching. Students who achieve the highest levels of reflective writing report that their ideas develop as they write, they are not simply recording ideas they have already developed ... In this way the journal becomes a learning tool rather than a record of events.*
>
> (Bain et al. 2002: 193)

Reflection, then, alters practice, and it does so through a conscious and self-conscious process, embedding the new actions firmly in the teaching situation of the teacher and also within his/her internal mental processes. This argument takes us back to the earlier sections of the book, where we labelled this situation rather more loosely as that of being 'self-aware'. This reflective view is a valuable contribution to understanding teacher development, but one that must resist reduction to the situational/contextual, devoid of critical reflection. As we are reminded by Kompf et al. (1996), if these processes are confined to the personal and practical, they become detached from other important elements: the historical, social, political and economic.

Research as professional development

Reflective teaching has within it the germ of the concept of the teacher as researcher, but as researcher of a specific kind. In reflective teaching we are talking almost exclusively of action research, in which the teacher formulates a classroom problem, sets out to act as participant/observer, puts in hand strategies to remedy the problem and gathers data to monitor the outcome. There are other models; for example, a diary or log can be used as a tool to identify personal strengths, weakness, training needs, and so on. This is certainly from a legitimate tradition, and has an immediate professional application, but it does not delimit the kinds of research in which a teacher might be involved. Table 9.2 sets out just a few typical alternative research options for teachers.

Not everyone is enthusiastic about teachers becoming researchers within their own classrooms. An Ofsted report criticised teacher-based research as often partisan rather than objective in its construction, weak on methodology, not mainstream to educational policy and practice, and carried out in a vacuum (Hargreaves 1996; Tooley and Darby 1998).

TABLE 9.2 Some kinds of research in which teachers might be involved

Type of research	Example	Value
Case study	Most teachers carry out a case study at some time – they may look at a job role (such as pastoral care) or the use of a new teaching space	Of immediate value in the workplace, with potential for sharing professional knowledge with colleagues as well as for influencing one's own performance
Statistical studies	An analysis of SATs or GCSE/A level scores over time	Can provide hard evidence of trends and alert the school to potential problems and remedial action
Curriculum research	Usually the devising and trialing of a new piece of subject curriculum	Has potential value for self, colleagues and pupils

Type of research	Example	Value
Evaluation studies	A form of case study designed to take an innovation and subject it to scrutiny, e.g. the effectiveness of a new merit system	May help to throw up issues, e.g. the bias towards girls of merits awarded, or the uneven effect on pupils where some teachers operate the system and some don't
Child development studies	Need stringent confidentiality, but the study of individual children over time, e.g. those with special needs, may help to identify improved remediation	Practical value for pupils, and for feedback to parents, but must be handled ethically
Linguistic analysis	A study of children's writing to discover their access to a range of forms	Designed to improve teaching and learning through the teacher's greater insight
Research for higher degrees	Not a form of research but an application of it that many teachers access at some time	Research projects for courses may or may not be job-related. While the former may be attractive, the stretching of the mind by exploring new subjects should not be underestimated

As often, however, with educational issues the forked tongue licks. Until 2003, the DfES put substantial money and energy into promoting its Best Practice Research Scholarships (a scheme whereby teachers were awarded small sums to undertake school-based inquiry in collaboration with an institution of higher education). This suggests that research is seen as valuable. Indeed, it could be argued that the 'vacuum' in which teacher research is conducted represents a valuable dimension since every school is different. The direct involvement of a research-based higher education institution with the school ensures the calibre of the work, thus overcoming issues of bias and poor methodology. Whether teachers carry out small-scale research in-house (preferably with external support) or work for research-based higher degrees, there is plenty of evidence of the value of such working. Multiple examples can be accessed in Middlewood, Coleman and Lumby (1999), though they relate specifically to teachers following the Leicester MBA course, and also in Nutbrown (2002) in relation to studies in early childhood.

However, control over research and research topics is a more contentious issue. This is not a manual of research practice and this is not a place to rehearse all the arguments. Suffice it to remark that the aim of every researcher is to investigate a problem that he/she perceives as important, and to do so without a biased agenda. When research is funded in any way or by any agency, there may arise ethical issues about the choice of topic and the objectivity of the outcome. Even small-scale teacher researchers need to be aware of these matters. Something of the debate about the ownership of research is recorded in Pritchard's (1997) account of the attempt under the Education Bill 1994 to hand over control of all research into teacher education to the TTA.

Hancock (2001: 127) argues that teachers are reluctant to get involved in research because society has little expectation that they will. Teaching is a hands-on activity, government marginalises teachers from the discussion of the changes that might be informed by research, and research methodologies are often alien to them and their way of working in classrooms. Yet the trend over recent years has been for increasing numbers of teachers to access research-based higher degrees and for heads to do so also. Thus the mood in schools is changing and a more research-orientated culture is emerging (as in Bubb et al. 2002), though the two activities – research and classroom teaching – may sometimes be kept at arm's length from one another, even by individuals who themselves pursue both activities. Benson and Blackman (2003) suggest that one problem may be that research is not seen as 'interesting' by those who carry it out, and they suggest some (albeit fairly common-sense) ways in which this problem can be addressed, including closer supervision by tutors of developing research proposals and good topic selection.

Insofar as research can be seen to inform teaching, either at the micro-level of the classroom or at the macro-levels of school or LEA, it remains a potent weapon in the armoury of professional development experiences and techniques. As well as informing practice, it may serve as a route to promotion and evidence for professional advancement.

ACTIVITY 9.1

Auditing your involvement in professional development

This is an opportune moment at which to take stock of your personal involvement in professional development. Using headings generated from this chapter, identify your current professional development activities:

- subject and curriculum knowledge

- pedagogical knowledge and skills

- reflection on practice

- research

- other kinds of activity.

Are there things missing from this profile that ought to be present?

How does this profile fit your career aspirations?

What is the balance in this profile between the aspirations of the school and your personal interests?

Where do your professional development interests need to go from here?

_____ Appraisal, performance management and _____ inspection as professional development

At first sight the title of this section might seem rather unlikely, but it is the intention here to suggest both that these processes are interlinked and that they serve a useful developmental function. As we saw in Chapter 3, appraisal was introduced into schools from 1988 as a means for teachers to develop and self-develop against a background of accountability. LEAs set up appraisal training teams within their professional development provision and the process got under way in the 1990s in most schools. Success was variable, the commonest complaint being that professional development needs identified during appraisal were not met subsequently because of a failure of resources at the school level. Nevertheless, the intention of appraisal was a laudable one: that every teacher's performance should be scrutinised by a peer or manager (details of the schemes varied). As a result of this observation and an initial appraisal interview, following an appraisal statement and formal outcomes-related interview, appropriate development activities should result. Other good intentions for appraisal included matching teachers more effectively to specific roles and modifying or improving their career paths. Gunter (2002) traces the history of the appraisal process from 1988 to 1998 in one fairly typical LEA and notes what it eventually evolved:

> It seems that the choices identified by the writers of the Green Paper (DfEE 1998) were either to acknowledge the humanistic approach to improving developmental appraisal at local level, through which teacher experiences could be valued and built upon, or to kill it off in favour of the shift to site-based management ... The marketisation of education required human resource management processes based on scientific approaches to controlling labour and work, and this enabled external inspection, league tables, and target setting to be introduced.
>
> (Gunter 2002: 70)

The government's view is somewhat different. It concluded (Ofsted 2002: 1) that the original appraisal scheme was operating below par, a judgement that was borne out by independent research (Kerry 1997). Thus, out of appraisal came forth performance management, which had as its themes:

- more strongly focused targets, now called objectives
- higher-quality classroom observation
- an involvement of school governors in overall performance monitoring in the school
- a closer relation between appraisal and school management
- clearer links between appraisal and pay.

This is not the moment to debate the merits of the system. Our purpose is to link the system to professional development. Like the original appraisal system, an intention of performance management has to be to identify training needs, translated into training plans, to effect a match between actual teacher performance and the skills necessary to achieve the formal objectives. This process is described by Ofsted (2002: para 42), but ominously the previous paragraph notes that:

> Whilst there has been some improvement in this linkage, with about half of the teachers' training plans now of good quality, it remains one of the weakest features of performance management practice.

The literature of performance management is remarkably light on identifying effective links between this process and tangible professional development activities, though Murphy (2001) makes some sound suggestions for bridging the gap:

- abolish meetings and use the time for training
- set up a truly interactive training intranet
- invest in a 'super-sub' (really reliable teacher who was de-timetabled and used to cover in order to free up time for training).

So both appraisal and performance management have potential for professional development subject to their being carried out effectively (i.e. identifying needs with insight) and then being managed well (so that needs are met). We would add that a third factor is that of the teacher him/herself taking some control of the situation to ensure that these two conditions are fulfilled. This requires some of the skills that have been reviewed earlier in the chapter, such as reflection, journal writing and class-based action research, to prepare the ground.

Hand in hand with performance management – albeit separate from it – goes inspection. This can be regarded as a form of external appraisal. Through feedback from the inspectors and via the inspection report, there is once again the potential to identify areas for development. Many teachers fear inspection, but a more positive approach is to view it as a chance to get an alternative view of one's own work and performance. Furthermore, the extra effort that most teachers make to prepare, document and teach lessons that will be inspected allows them an opportunity to revisit and refine their skills as described in other chapters in this text.

REFLECTION

In your own experience, what contribution have appraisal, performance management and inspection made to your professional development?

While many may feel that the systems described in this section are flawed or threatening, what we have attempted to communicate has been a sense of opportunity. In professional development terms these systems are just one more channel through which teachers can examine and adapt their performance on the road to continuous improvement in the constant quest for better learning experiences for pupils.

_____ Getting the most out of professional _____ development

Despite the comments made above about resourcing, the fact remains that most teachers access a broad spectrum of professional development opportunities every year. We would want to argue the case for a range of opportunities, and for matching the type of experience in an informed way to the required outcomes. A teacher who only attends practically-based in-house training is likely to have, after a while, a stultifying experience of professional development – however good the activities are to begin with – because horizons inevitably narrow with time. By contrast, a teacher who only accesses external conferences may have broadened horizons but will not be sharing experience with colleagues.

In Table 9.3 we look at the advantages and disadvantages of various kinds of professional development events and what they may contribute to the teacher's professional understanding. None of the items listed (and the list is not exhaustive, so you may care to add your own items and an assessment of them) is a solution per se to professional development. Some that have been mentioned already – such as research and reflection – do not feature in the table. Each has its place; over time one might try to access all of these experiences. When you do, however, you should be realistic about what you are likely to get from them. For example, if you access a short course, read the small print before you apply about what the course will cover and what its intentions are. It is no use complaining that a given course fails to give practical solutions if it is billed as an awareness-raising theoretical day, or that an event is aimed at generic special needs when what you needed was only information about dyslexia. If in doubt, check with the provider beforehand.

Remember, too, that in evaluations of the 'happy sheet' variety half the respondents at training events say they would have appreciated more group work and sharing of experiences; the other half say they wanted to listen to more of the presenter and less from self-opinionated members of the audience. Attendance at any event can only be a compromise because that kind of professional development experience cannot, by definition, be built around your individual need. If you want a tailored experience, opt for one of the self-help activities such as professional reading or involving yourself with a professional association. Such associations tend to be subject-related (e.g. the Association for Science Education or the National Association of Teachers of English), generic (e.g. the College of Teachers), or phase-related. Some have local branches or focus groups, which operate rather as teachers' centres once did.

Professional development parallels life in one important respect: what you get out of it depends on what you put into it. Too often one hears the lament that 'this school/association/website/event has done nothing for me'. The real question is what have you done for it. You control your professional development, it should not control you. Some aspects of it may be mandatory, but how you deal with the rest is up to you. Only you can decide how you want to shape your own learning.

TABLE 9.3 The contribution to professional understanding of a range of professional development activities

Type of activity	Advantages	Disadvantages	Contribution
Short courses	Often rack up enthusiasm for a topic; immediate improvement in knowledge/skills; awareness-raising	Many question the lasting effects; without dissemination may not alter practice in own school	Valuable for providing networking opportunities and as a source of ideas that can be adapted
National and local day conferences	May give access to 'experts' and the latest thinking	May not seem immediately applicable to own situation	Broaden intellectual horizons
In-house training days	Offer the chance for colleagues to share good practice; potential to generate better working relations	Can become inward-looking	Provide a sharing environment when not an exclusive method
Professional reading through libraries, internet, etc.	Malleable to personal needs; subject to control so time-efficient	Sources may be time-consuming to track down	A 'must' for any thinking teacher, but one that is widely neglected

Type of activity	Advantages	Disadvantages	Contribution
Professional memberships	Give access to sources (e.g. journals, newsletters, etc.); may provide a network of contacts or access to expert advice	Limited if confined to trade-union-only data – user must look to professional associations	One of the marks of a professional, but often neglected; time-demanding if the teacher takes an active role, e.g. in committees
New experiences, e.g. visits to other schools	A very practical way of comparing practice across situations; provides practitioner self-help; shows that there are multiple ways of construing and solving problems	Quite time-consuming, and costs may be involved; the market economy means schools are less ready to share practice than they were	A relatively economic and very practical way of looking at alternative solutions to problems through good practice
Overseas experience	Has the edge in providing new perspectives and gaining access to different ways of thinking	Expensive	Personally enriching while retaining potential for honing practice and boosting confidence
Personal development portfolios	Cheap and easy way to track personal progress in a systematic way	Some time demand in compiling the data; needs a disciplined approach	Good for building evidence of personal development for use in seeking promoted posts

Type of activity	Advantages	Disadvantages	Contribution
Work placements outside teaching	Like overseas experience, these can open eyes to different ways of handling problems	More valuable for those without employment experience beyond teaching; maybe costly and with high time demand	Broaden the mind and provide greater sensitivity to issues of society as they affect teaching
Advanced qualifications	Can provide long-term systematic stimulation to think about pedagogical and professional issues	Very high demand on time and self-discipline; often require deadlines to be met	Strong on value for promotion, learning from research and personal satisfaction
Access to self-help and similar groups at professional development or teachers' centres	A good source of practical information and a way of sharing views with colleagues	Very few of these exist in the present funding climate	Where available, activities in these settings provide a sense of ownership
Career planning	Essential from time to time to take stock of personal achievements and identify needs	Some people feel this is self-indulgent – we would dispute this; may encourage some dissatisfaction with current experience	A good thing to review one's professionalism – and one's life – from time to time

Learning leadership and mentoring as professional development

Master teachers are called upon to support others; they become leaders and mentors of new teachers or inexperienced colleagues. Indeed, their leadership in classrooms is even more fundamental than this:

> *Teachers practise a form of pedagogical leadership directly since in schools they stand first and closest in a caring relationship to children.*
>
> (Sergiovanni 1996: 93)

In the present context our intention is not to explore the concepts of leadership and mentoring, which are well documented in the appropriate literatures (e.g. Kerry and Shelton-Mayes 1995), but to pass comment on the benefits of these processes of guiding others to one's own professional development.

Mentoring and leading other staff require skills that have already been developed through professional experience and training:

- being a good listener
- making oneself available as a result of good time management
- being reflective on one's own teaching
- being a good observer of the teaching of others
- being a good communicator
- being organised so as to fit in the administrative and other related chores
- studying the skills required of the mentoring process.

West-Burnham and O'Sullivan (1998) argue for coaching as a pervasive concept of learning. Coaching is closely related to reflection and consists of:

- observing performance
- analysing that performance
- measuring performance against standards
- identifying remedial strategies where apposite
- evaluating strategies against change
- consolidating improvements.

These are key components in the teaching of good teachers in relation to their pupils and are, without exception, transferable to the mentor role. Implicit in these components is the ability to reflect on the work of oneself and others, and thus to improve one's own performance alongside that of the mentee, thus transforming the process into a developmental activity.

—— Judging quality in professional development ——

This chapter has surveyed the theoretical underpinning of professional development for teachers and has examined some of the means by which such development is delivered. This then is the time to look at issues of quality. As subjects of professional development, teachers are effectively consumers. Thus the overriding question about any professional development event or activity has to be in terms of its fitness for purpose: the same concept that underpins consumer legislation. But it has to be borne in mind that, for any activity, its fitness must be judged by individuals to match their individual needs. In Table 9.4 we have tried to encapsulate some of this thinking into the form of a checklist that might help you to evaluate development activities with more insight than is embedded in those dreadful 'happy sheets' we referred to earlier. Though compiled so as to be used with courses and similar events, you can easily adapt it to activities such as your involvement with reflective practice or with higher degree work.

REFLECTION

If, as we have argued previously, pupils have preferred learning styles, then it is also true to say that teachers have preferred learning styles of professional development that are individual to each person. What are your preferred learning styles for professional development? Why do you find these conducive? What do you find unconducive about other styles?

TABLE 9.4 Judging the effectiveness for you of professional development activities

Key issue	Some elements to interrogate
Audience	Is this identified? Do you fit the profile?
Title and subject matter	Are these specific to your need?
Intentions	Are these clearly spelled out? To what extent do they meet your needs?
Provider	What are the qualifications and profile of the provider? Do these match the intentions?

Key issue	Some elements to interrogate
Learning style	Is there information about the intended learning styles? If so, do these accord with your preferences?
Content	Do these, and the age/phase profile, match your needs?
Practical application	Where appropriate, do the intentions of the session seem to be designed to make a contribution to improved practice? Will there be demonstration, modelling, simulated classroom practice or hands-on experience on which to draw?
Theoretical content	Is the session intellectually demanding or merely 'tips for teachers' lacking substance and transferable skills?
Change	Is there any evidence that suggests the session is capable of helping to bring about desirable change? Is the likelihood for change in the home institution such as to support the learning gained?
Presentation	Is the event well presented? Is it interesting? Provocative? (The most stimulating events are sometimes the ones you most disagree with – disagreement is not bad!) Is it well prepared? Does it engage attention? Does it challenge? Are activities varied? Well balanced?
Cost-effectiveness	Remember, cheap is not always good. A good professional development leader is worth his/her weight in gold.

Advanced qualifications and status

As a postscript to this chapter we wish to add a note about gaining qualifications such as higher degrees, or enhanced status such as that of Advanced Skills Teacher. There is some negative prejudice within the profession about such activities – the equivalent for teachers of the 'swot' mentality adopted by a minority of pupils towards high-achieving peers. Despite this, professionality demands pride in achievement, demands indeed achievement itself. Only when all teachers adopt this core professional attitude will society take teachers' professionalism seriously.

For some teachers, as we have seen, their progression in the profession leads them to the Advanced Skills Teacher route. For others, their careers build on the management skills that they acquire as teachers – to which we turn in the next chapter.

At the end of this chapter you should have:

- Acquired an understanding of the many routes to improved professional development

- Understood the theory that underpins professional development

- Considered your own involvement in professional development

- Taken stock of what identifies high-quality professional development

---

References

Bain, J., Mills, C., Ballantyne, R. and Packer, J. (2002) 'Developing reflection on practice through journal writing: impacts of variation in the focus and level of feedback', *Teachers and Teaching: Theory & Practice*, 8(2): 188–6.

Benson, A. and Blackman, D. (2003) 'Can research methods ever be interesting?', *Active Learning in Higher Education*, 4(1): 39–55.

Bubb, S., Hellbronn, R., Jones, C., Totterdell, M. and Bailey, M. (2002) *Improving Induction: Research-based Best Practice for Schools*, London: Routledge.

Dadds, M. (2001) 'Continuing professional development: nurturing the professional within', in J. Soler, A. Craft and H. Burgess, *Teacher Development: Exploring Your Own Practice*, London: PCP Open University.

Department for Education and Employment (DfEE) (1992) *Initial Teacher Training: Primary Phase*, London: DfEE. Curcular 9/92

Department or Education and Employment (DfEE) (1998) *Green Paper: Teachers Meeting the Challenge of Change*, London: DfEE.

HMSO (1998) Education Act 1988, London: HMSO.

Gardner, H. (1993) *Frames of Mind: the Theory of Multiple Intelligences*, New York: Basic books.

Gipps, C. (1994) 'What we know about effective primary teaching', in J. Bourne (ed.), *Thinking Through Primary Practice*, London: Routledge Open University.

Gunter, H. (2002) 'Teacher appraisal 1988–1998: a case study', *School Leadership & Management*, 22(1): 61–72.

Hancock, R. (2001) 'Why are class teachers reluctant to become researchers?', in J. Soler, A. Craft and H. Burgess, *Teacher Development: Exploring Your Own Practice,* London: PCP Open University.

Hargreaves, D. (1996) 'Teaching as a research-based profession: possibilities and prospects', Teacher Training Agency Annual Lecture, London: TTA.

Higgins, S. and Leat, D. (2001) 'Horses for courses or courses for horses: what is effective teacher development?', in J. Soler A. Craft and H. Burgess, *Teacher Development: Exploring Your Own Practice,* London: PCP Open University.

Hill, D. (1997) 'Critical reflection in initial teacher education', in K. Watson, C. Modgil and S. Modgil, *Educational Dilemmas: Debate and Diversity, vol. 1 Teachers, Teacher Education and Training,* London: Cassell.

Hoyle, E. (1997) 'Teaching as a profession', in K. Watson, C. Modgil, and S. Modgil *Educational Dilemmas: Debate and Diversity, vol. 1 Teachers, Teacher Education and Training,* London: Cassell.

Kerry, T. (1997) 'Knowing me, knowing you, and our institution too: the art and science of appraisal', *Education Today,* 47(4): 2–5.

Kerry, T. (2001) *Plowden: Mirage, Myth or Flag of Convenience?,* Working Paper no. 43, Lincoln: Faculty of Business and Management, University of Lincoln.

Kerry, T. (2002) *Explaining and Questioning,* Cheltenham: Nelson Thornes.

Kerry, T. and Shelton-Mayes, A. (1995) *Issues in Mentoring,* London: Routledge.

Kompf, M., Bond, W., Dworet, D. and Boak, T. (eds) (1996) *Changing Research and Practice: Teachers' Professionalism, Identities and Knowledge*, London: Falmer.

McLaughlin, H. (1997) 'The nature and nurture of reflection', in K. Watson, C. Modgil and S. Modgil, *Educational Dilemmas: Debate and Diversity, vol. 1 Teachers, Teacher Education and Training,* London: Cassell.

Middlewood, D., Coleman, M. and Lumby, J. (1999) *Practitioner Research in Action: Making a Difference,* London: PCP.

Murphy, A. (2001) 'Performance management and the Church school', in J. West-Burnham J. O'Neill and I. Bradbury, *Performance Management in Schools: How to Lead and Manage Staff for School Improvement,* London: Pearson.

Nutbrown, C. (2002) *Research Studies in Early Childhood Education,* Stoke-on-Trent: Trentham.

Ofsted (2002) *Performance Management of Teachers,* London: Office for Standards in Education.

Phelan, A. (1997) 'When the mirror crack'd: the discourse of reflection in pre-service teacher education', in K. Watson, C. Modgil and S. Modgil, *Educational Dilemmas: Debate and Diversity, vol. 1 Teachers, Teacher Education and Training,* London: Cassell.

Pritchard, R. (1997) 'Some international perspectives on British teacher training', in K. Watson, C. Modgil and S. Modgil, *Educational Dilemmas: Debate and Diversity, vol. 1 Teachers, Teacher Education and Training,* London: Cassell.

Schon, D. (1983) *The Reflective Practitioner,* London: Temple Smith.

Sergiovanni, T. (1996) *Leadership for the Schoolhouse,* San Francisco: Jossey Bass.

Thornton, K. (2003) 'Generation excellent', *Times Educational Supplement,* 7 March: 16.

Tooley, J. and Darby, D. (1998) *Educational Research: A Critique,* London: Ofsted.

Tranter, S. (2000) *From Teacher to Middle Manager,* London: Pearson.

Turner-Bisset, R. (2001) *Expert Teaching,* London: David Fulton.

West-Burnham, J., Bradbury, I. and O'Neill, J. (2001) *Performance Management in Schools,* London: Pearson.

West-Burnham, J. and O'Sullivan, F. (1998) *Leadership and Professional Development in Schools,* London: Pearson.

Zeichner, K. and Liston, D. (1987) 'Teaching students to reflect', *Harvard Educational Review,* 57(1):

Zeichner, K. and Liston, D. (1990) *Traditions of Reform and Reflective Teaching in US Teacher Education,* Issue Paper no. 90-1, East Lansing, MI: National Center for Research on Teacher Education.

The managing teacher

In this chapter you are invited to:

- Define more closely your role as manager, leader and follower

- Apply the insights of these definitions to your relationships with parents, senior colleagues, support staff within the school, and external authorities such as inspectors and governors

- Analyse aspects of home–school relations using case studies

- Scrutinise the processes of followership at work in your own school and your own relations with your senior colleagues

- Take greater control over your work through understanding how to manage adults better

Managing and leading

There are confusions and ambiguities in the words 'managing' and 'leading'. First it is important to clarify some ways in which these terms are used here. For the present purpose, the words 'managing' and 'manager' are used mainly in an organisational sense. 'Managers' are people who operate systems, provide structures and organise others into the structures thus created. 'Leading' and 'leaders' are about essences beyond structures: they are about gaining hearts and minds, about showing the path, about enthusiasm, about personality and about charismatic or entrepreneurial activity, and above all about power.

Teachers both manage and lead. At the leadership level they set the tone of the classroom, act as good examples, provide enthusiasm for pupils to emulate, facilitate and bring out the best in teaching assistants, inspire some students to intellectual heights, and so on. As managers, they operate the merit point system, divide the available time to achieve curriculum ends, write reports and letters home to parents. Much of this book is about skills that are the component parts of leadership. Here we concentrate more specifically on the management, and that managing role as it affects other adults with whom the teacher comes into contact. It is important to recognise at the outset, however, that these managing roles may include elements of leadership, and our dichotomy is one of convenience rather than one to be pursued to exclusivity.

In particular it must be remembered that all our dealings with adults and peers, while they may be ostensibly about systems and structures (as if these were objective and tangible, which they are not), are also about overt or covert operations of power. In these the teacher may be, as it were, in the driving seat – as when dealing with a parent, perhaps – or may be the object of someone else's power role – such as that of an Ofsted inspector.

In an earlier chapter we have also discussed professionalism and discovered the problems associated with this concept. We would do well to remind ourselves of some of the dimensions of professionalism (Table 10.1), since they impinge on what this chapter has to say.

REFLECTION

By scrutinising the six models in Table 10.1 what can you say about your own roles as a professional manager and leader?

The models in Table 10.1 condition the way in which we think about teachers' relationships with other adults whom they contact in the school. This chapter attempts to examine some of these relationships and to provide some thoughts about how the master teacher can handle these relationships with a high level of expertise, just as he or she will manage other aspects of the job. To begin, we look at relationships with parents – one of the most changed and changing of all the teacher–adult relationships in recent times.

TABLE 10.1 Dimensions of professionalism and their effect on managing peers

Dimension	Description	Implications
Public administration model	The implementation of government directives	Teachers are seen as the agents of government will: they implement a required curriculum, to required standards, in required ways – and are accountable for the outcomes

Dimension	Description	Implications
Organisational model	Operationalising the resources – people, equipment, data – that lead to educational ends	Teachers manage whatever budgets and personnel (e.g. teaching assistants) that are assigned to them; they do this on behalf of the head
Democratic model	Delivering what the public wants for its children and young people	Teachers are accountable to the community – parents, LEAs, local politicians – for the quality of classroom performance
Market economy model	Educational quality provides the powerhouse for parental choice and thus resources for individual schools	Teachers are the operatives who churn out performance, whatever the odds, in order to sustain the school's place in the market
Professional model	Accountability is through the strictures of the lead body representing teachers	Teachers are judged by their peers and perform against codes of conduct and according to a body of professional knowledge and expertise
The model of self-motivation	Accountability is through personal ethics and self-imposed discipline	Teachers are people of personal integrity, respected in society, who can be trusted to teach and behave appropriately to high personal standards

Parents

The back cover blurb to Crozier (2000) sums up the situation with respect to teachers and parents succinctly and accurately:

> *Parents' relationships with schools are changing. No longer the passive recipients of a bureaucratic allocation system they are increasingly making choices, negotiating and challenging authority – all with a wealth of information that would have been unthinkable in even the recent past.*
>
> (Crozier 2000)

Despite the obvious truth of these remarks, however, relations generally between parents and schools vary widely. This variety forms the background to how teachers and parents interact, so it needs to be explored in a little more depth.

At the 'highest' level parents may take an extremely active part in the life of the school. The school may have an open-door policy; there may be a teacher on rota each morning to stand at the school gate to be available to parents with immediate concerns. Parents may run extracurricular activities as well as support them. There may be an active PTA that not only raises money but is consulted about its allocation. Parents may be proactive in putting on events such as concerts. The parent-governors may be vocal and active in seeking parents' views about events and activities within the school. Parents may support at close to the 100 per cent level opportunities such as the annual parents' meeting and the Ofsted meeting for parents. In the most empowering of schools, parents will be actively encouraged to give opinions and their views will be trawled prior to any major decision being taken that may affect their children's life in school.

At the 'low' end of the spectrum, parents may play little part. They may elect members of the governing body with difficulty. The elected members may contribute little or nothing. There may be no PTA. Attendance at parents' meetings may be less than a handful. Parents may take no part in fundraising or extracurricular work. They may not support – may even resist – efforts of the school over issues like uniform, PE kit, homework, and so on. Communication may be rare and one-way.

For most schools, relations between the parents and the institution will fall somewhere on a continuum between these two extremes. Typically, parents will have access by arrangement. Some will participate in groups or committees; a minority will turn up for Ofsted meetings and the like; a couple of keen people will involve themselves in coaching for sports. There will be a limited exchange of views on non-curriculum issues. Vincent (1996: 476) concluded that 'teachers routinely send out messages that involvement beyond the role of supporter/learners is not appropriate to parents'.

As an individual teacher you will not have control over these things, but it is important to understand the processes that underpin them. Often they are attitudinal. Attitudes involve taking stock of how we view others. In Fig. 10.1 we look at some ways in which we may view parents in relation to schools and classrooms (right-hand captions), and suggest that participation by parents relates importantly to how they are viewed (length of the bars). This is certainly not an attempt to quantify involvement parental in any statistical sense, but it serves as an indicator of attitude in relation to participation.

FIG. 10.1 Levels of parental participation in school activities

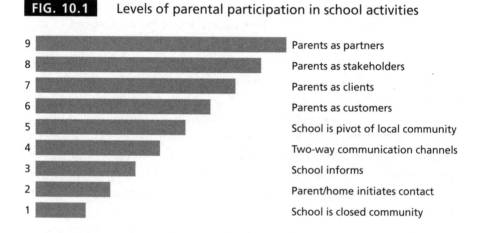

9	Parents as partners
8	Parents as stakeholders
7	Parents as clients
6	Parents as customers
5	School is pivot of local community
4	Two-way communication channels
3	School informs
2	Parent/home initiates contact
1	School is closed community

Bearing in mind some of these theoretical considerations you are now invited to move on to work out some of the implications in practice. In Activity 10.1 you will find some case study scenarios. We would emphasise that they are all true, although names have been changed. We would also point out that we have chosen negative scenarios for the purpose of the exercise. They are not necessarily typical of individual schools and do not imply that only negative events happen. Read the scenarios and carry out the activity.

ACTIVITY 10.1

Analysing the nature of home–school attitudes

Read each of the short case studies below. In each case suggest:

- how you, as a teacher, react to the case
- what you might have done to make things better had you been involved and/or
- what advice you might have given to the head about possible action
- the underlying attitudes and models that are at work in each incident, where appropriate

Case study 1

Simon is 10 years old and in a mixed-age class in a small rural primary school, with many children younger than he is. He always comes to school in Doctor Marten boots. You notice that, among the group in which he sits, a child will often shout out spontaneously as if in pain. Simon is an inveterate liar – you can watch him do something and yet when he is challenged he will swear that he has not. One day the parent of one of Simon's group comes up to you in the car park and shows you three black bruises on her son's ankles. The child says that Simon has kicked him when he would not let him copy the answers to an exercise. The parent asserts that, according to her son, Simon does this to other children too. It is a Church of England school and Simon is the child of a leading light in the parish church. In the past the head teacher has been reluctant to report or challenge his bad behaviour.

Case study 2

In this comprehensive school a good deal of stress is placed on examinations. Every year there are end-of-year exams, and the marks are totalled to give a hierarchy of pupils in the class. One of your class, who is normally a good historian, comes to you and says that the history teacher, Mr Hunt, has made an error in adding up the marks on her history paper. He has missed the marks for two questions because the pages had become stuck together. Instead of 37 per cent the student now has 71 per cent; the rise in marks means that in history the student rises from 27th in the class to 3rd, and overall in the class this student rises from 8th to 2nd across all subjects. Mr Hunt admits the error but has refused to change the results, and the student's parent is distressed.

Case study 3

You are invited to a day's training course at the nearby Tuckby primary school. Tuckby school is hosting a delegate from every school in the LEA at a conference on 'Improving Relationships with Parents' to be led by its head and some staff members. You are not very impressed with what you know about Tuckby and its relations with its parents, but your head teacher is insistent you attend. You turn up as required. As you enter the main door of the school you find yourself in a tiny entrance lobby facing a set of double glass doors into the school interior. On these are pasted two notices. The first, a temporary notice, reads: *'Improving Relationships Conference straight on'*. The second – obviously a permanent fixture – proclaims: *'No parents beyond this point'*.

Case study 4

At the local comprehensive school, North Steven College, Mrs Jones's son is not making the progress of which he is capable. After several low-key attempts to resolve her concerns, Mrs Jones decides to be more proactive. Her first concern is whether her son is genuinely as able as she believes he is. She has his intelligence tested by a qualified educational psychologist selected from a list supplied by the British Psychological Society, the national qualifying body. Young Jones has an IQ of 162, which puts him in the top half of one per cent of the population. Armed with this information Mrs Jones returns to the school. Here she is presented with a list of rather low percentages written on a scruffy sheet of paper torn from an exercise book. Mrs Jones asks what these numbers represent: what kinds of tests they are – on what topics, normative or summative, and where the marks stand with respect to other marks (not pupils) in the class. The head of year rounds on Mrs Jones and accuses her of being a troublemaker. Offering no explanation, he insists she leave the premises under threat of police action if she stays. She is banned from the school premises henceforth.

Activity 10.1 should have helped you to analyse some difficult issues that arise in dealing with parents. In practice the most difficult and stressful situations involving parents are probably those in which it is necessary to deal with problems relating to the child. These may be things that you need to say (such as reporting poor progress at a parents' evening to a disappointed mother or father), or issues that are raised by a parent with you (such as a report of alleged bullying). In some schools you may have the support of a senior colleague, especially in incidents resembling the latter example; in others you may not. What follows is an attempt to provide some general advice that will raise your game in this important area of relationships.

In a study in Cyprus (Peshiardis 2001), teachers rated highly the head teacher who, in dealing with parents, 'put my justification about an issue on the table to be judged by everyone, I will tell the truth and will not beautify the situation for anyone; albeit taking care not to hurt someone personally'. Most British teachers would likewise do well to begin their dealings with parents from a position of evidence-based honesty coupled with gentle tact.

However, we have noted that leadership has, as one of its characteristics, an element of manoevering for power. In this process Hodgson (1996: 3) recommends the qualities of being resourceful, patient and firm. In his now famous management text, Covey (1989) discusses the options for the outcomes of contentious situations:

- win/win
- win/lose
- lose/win
- lose/lose
- win
- win/win or no deal.

Let us take the scenario of the child Simon in Activity 10.1, case study 1, and use some of Covey's categories to analyse it. The teacher might press for Simon's isolation from other children for a period and for the parent to be informed. This is a *win/lose* situation – the teacher may win the battle for discipline in the class but lose the attempt to socialise Simon since he is now isolated.

Worse, the head may not back the teacher, so the teacher loses face, other children go on being bullied, and Simon is free to carry on his bad behaviour without his parent's knowledge and effectively supported by the school. This is *lose/win*.

Alternatively, the decision may have been made merely to isolate Simon to work away from other children in the class (which doesn't address his relationship problem), but the teacher might have been made aware that Simon's behaviour is regarded as her failing of class control. This is *lose/lose*.

The teacher may, of course, engineer a meeting with Simon's parent and by mutual agreement have Simon removed from the school. That's a win for the teacher, who then has no interest in what happens to Simon - a *win only* situation.

The *win/win* outcome here may be that Simon on the one hand is censured for his bullying and made to sit alone, with the parent's agreement, for a short probationary period close under the teacher's eye, while the teacher on the other is publicly supported by the head teacher in her stand against antisocial behaviour between pupils.

Covey's model is a useful one to apply to conflict situations and serves as an analytical tool to explore the progress that the teacher is making towards appropriate resolution of issues. The aim of Covey's model in the quoted incident is towards win/win – though he himself is sanguine enough to suggest (p. 211) that this is not always the best outcome. The actual outcome of the Simon incident was lose/win, which seemed hardly the best option.

REFLECTION

Have you experienced a conflict situation such as the case of Simon? If so, use Covey's model to analyse it. What is your conclusion on the effectiveness of the outcome?

Revisiting Simon's case has opened up some of the problems in dealing with parents and children. In interviews with parents, teachers need particular skills. Table 10.2 examines some of those skills. In it we have pulled out 30 of the most important pieces of knowledge, skill and understanding that a master teacher needs in dealing with parents. Of course, in relatively informal situations not all of them will apply. This is a list that will allow you to plan for interviews with parents at various levels of seriousness and formality by being selective.

TABLE 10.2 Thirty key understandings for dealing with parents in interviews

Knowledge, skill or understanding	Commentary
1 Always prepare thoroughly	Never go into an interview without proper forethought; take a summary of the data you might need. Of this, share what you can but be aware of any remark that breaks confidentiality, e.g. directly or indirectly identifying another pupil as a comparison.

Knowledge, skill or understanding	Commentary
2 Cultivate confidence	Try to dress appropriately, feel calm and communicate goodwill. Make it clear you are taking the lead without making the other person feel inferior or wrong-footed.
3 Be conscious of covert messages	These can be conveyed through a range of signals, e.g. the placement of chairs in opposition across a table or by keeping the interviewee waiting after the appointed meeting time. Avoid things like this that may get the session off to a negative start.
4 Keep a win/win philosophy	Go into the session determined that everyone will get something from it.
5 Pre-plan a range of acceptable solutions	Despite the previous item, interviews are like a chess game – you need to know your moves ahead and to have alternatives up your sleeve. Know your best solution and your absolute bottom-line position.
6 Keep notes	You won't remember the conversation after the event; agree with the interviewee to keep notes on the session to use in your summaries (see below).
7 Listen first, and really listen	You may need to set the scene briefly, but then listen – and listening means not just hearing the words but receiving the underlying messages and interpreting the nuances. The stated problem may not be the real problem.
8 Listen first and talk afterwards	Don't be tempted, e.g. through nervousness, to talk first or to fill the silences; let the interviewee do that.

Knowledge, skill or understanding	Commentary
9 Set out the problem clearly	Begin the session with a clear but succinct statement of the issue to be addressed and what the broad outcome of the session needs to be (not the solution, but the principles at stake).
10 Identify an agenda	Often it is helpful to agree a batting order to tackle sections of the issue; if nothing else, this means that you can move towards a solution in a planned manner – it gives you a form of control.
11 Ask insightful questions and try to empathise with the other person's position	Questions will provide you with information or an expanded picture from the other person's perspective. Careful questions can guide the discussion.
12 Consider the whole range of options or solutions	Set out a range of possible outcomes, not just one or two. It is much easier to reach an amicable agreement with someone who feels that they have had choices.
13 Use agreement	Capitalise on any areas of agreement by emphasising them, recording them and using them as signposts towards the next step in the journey. Recap on them if the interviewee shifts ground later.
14 Think 'on your feet'	Often you have to think quickly, creatively, or change tack – another good reason for pausing rather than overtalking.
15 Assertive not aggressive	People confuse assertiveness and aggression: it is assertive to say that a solution must be reached today, aggressive to say 'or else'.

Knowledge, skill or understanding	Commentary
16 Don't lose energy	This is a serious point. Interviews can go on a long time and they sap mental energy. Make sure that you go into the session with enough calories in your system to survive.
17 Summarise from time to time and note progress made	In longer sessions and more contentious ones, pause at intervals (keep a watch on the time) and summarise the progress made, gaining agreements wherever possible.
18 Keep cool under pressure	It is almost never a good idea to get angry; at best it gives an advantage to the other person and at worst it is unprofessional.
19 Rehearse your tactics	There are things you can do to control a situation that is slipping away from you, e.g. you can adjourn, bluff, impose a deadline. *Never threaten.* Even if you can carry out the threat (usually not possible), the threat becomes a barrier to further discussion.
20 Soft man, hard man	One useful tactic in a difficult session is to shift your ground by playing the soft man, hard man game. At one moment you may spell out the letter of the law, the next you may say that you are trying to help the interviewee to get around the law – you can be authority figure and hero at the same time.
21 Praise the positive	Never miss a chance to reinforce any positive statement or progress.
22 Be ready for anything	Be aware that the person you are dealing with may not have revealed all the information available at the beginning of the session; be wary of the googly when things get tough.

Knowledge, skill or understanding	Commentary
23 Move blockages	If you get to a sticking point don't let it block continued progress; put the item on one side and agree to return to it later. Often you don't need to.
24 Rule out the impossible	Do state clearly what cannot happen and is not open to discussion – it saves so much time. But always keep something up your sleeve that you are prepared to concede so that you can keep the win/win philosophy alive.
25 Use word pictures and other verbal ploys	Reflect the interviewee's ideas back to him/her: 'If we were to take this solution, then *x* would happen; is that really what you want?'
26 Know about emotion	Don't ever get angry for real; there are just a very few occasions when a display of feigned emotion can be productive. Dangerous area: approach with care.
27 Watch your intonation	Don't give away your real, or convey the wrong, feelings by an unguarded tone of voice. Quiet, calm speech is best. Keep things gentle and don't make jokes in tense situations (any given joke is offensive to 50 per cent of its hearers).
28 Remain professional	Above everything, you must be the consummate professional: you have everyone's good at heart and have to convey that in tone, manner and attitude.
29 Draw up an agreement	When you get to one, write down the final agreement at the time; if possible get the interviewee to sign it.
30 End pleasantly – whatever the outcome	Try to end on a smile, a handshake, reassuring words that communication will be continued.

Some readers may react negatively to Table 10.2, construing it as cynical and calculating. Elements of the management role are like that or, as it was once put, leadership is about getting people to do things they would prefer not to do. But the fact remains that in this chapter we have argued for enhancing the status of parents in the education process and one's sight of that basic stance should not be lost. Nevertheless, there are inevitably moments of issue or conflict. Teachers need to know how to deal with these. The Table provides raw advice: it needs interpretation in specific circumstances.

Thus, while we have dealt with issues of social class in other contexts (see Chapter 1), it is also one of a range of factors that impinge on parents' perceptions of and relations with schools and teachers. Among others, it can cause problems. As an example we leave the last word on parents with Crozier (2000):

> At a very basic level, within school, parental involvement that is based upon understandings of participatory democracy can only be brought about if mutual trust and respect is established. This will require parents trusting the teachers but likewise teachers trusting the parents. For all concerned it will incur a level of risk. With respect to working-class parents, before any trust can be placed, there will be a need to challenge the negative attitudes, negative stereotyping and, albeit unintentional discriminatory practices levelled against them. Linked to this is the need to address cultural diversity and the politics of difference. There has been much discussion of how democracies can deliver on equality while accommodating and welcoming difference ... but only limited answers ... This would seem to be the major challenge.
>
> (Crozier 2000: 125)

So handling these relationships won't be easy, then!

____ Senior managers and the role of followers ____

From dealing with a major external stakeholder, the parent, we turn our attention to the master teacher's ability to manage relations with a major internal stakeholder – the head teacher or senior colleague (deputy, head of faculty/ department, head of year).

We began the chapter with an introduction about the teacher as leader/manager; we proceed to a consideration of the teacher as follower. While many would doubtless reject this actual descriptor, the fact remains that most of us – even those in managerial positions – are also the followers of those in authority above us. Followership, especially in education, has been little studied, but it is opportune to summarise here some of what we know about the concept. Thody (2002) pulled together the major research on the issue. Her stance is interesting:

> *Most of the few other writers and researchers in the field focus on leader–follower interaction, see the value of followers just within the leadership relationship and as having a life that is determined by leadership. In contrast, this author hypothesises that the territory of followership has a life of its own too … followers must be seen as their own persons; what they do is at least as much an outcome of their personalities, their positions, their purposes and their own planning, as it is of leadership. Followers are as much independent actors as leaders [are].*
>
> (Thody 2002: 162)

Thus, while the life of the head teacher is determined (from his/her perspective) by issues of leadership, the life of (even the master) teacher is determined from his/her perspective by issues of followership. So what are these issues? Thody trawled the literature to establish a typology of followership, and this we have attempted to encapsulate in Table 10.3.

TABLE 10.3 Models and descriptors of followership roles

Model	Description
Positive models	
Aspirant, mentee or apprentice	Aspires to leadership and thus works consciously and closely with leaders to learn leadership skills
Coordinator	Works to make connections between the strategic and operational levels of an organisation – interprets the vision into action
Disciple	As in the Bible, is concerned to learn from a 'master' and then pass on that learning
Gatekeeper, filter	Undertakes voluntarily a role as the person who relieves the burdens of the leader/head by filtering out unnecessary information or actions

Model	Description
Muse	Suggests ideas and stimulates the leader's head's thinking
Rescuer	Covers up the failings of the leader/head, often at personal risk
Resnatronic	Supports without seeking personal advancement
Second-in-command	(Often a deputy head rather than a teacher) acts as the loyal supporter and message carrier in each direction between head and staff
Sidekick, partner, comrade	A helpful person who has little if any formal status
Toxic handler	Heads off trouble before it reaches the leader/head
Negative models	
Communication distorter	The negative models are mischievous types, in this case someone who distorts information to cause confusion
Saboteur	Indulges in micro-politics to undermine the leader/head
Toxic creator	Deliberately casts doubt on the leader's/head's decisions and competence

REFLECTION

In what ways and to what extent do you recognise these 'followership' roles in yourself and in your colleagues?

Of course, while the individual teacher may adopt one of these followership roles more or less consciously, for more or less of his/her time, there will be occasions when he/she deliberately changes role. The roles we choose as followers have an effect on our ability to manage our relations with those in authority and the kind of relations we have. Consider this scenario:

James is a teacher at Damien's School, where the head is Mr Diamond. James is given a pretty free rein to run his subject – drama – as he is the only drama teacher in the school. Mr Diamond is keen to enhance the reputation of the school in the community: the local population of young people is dropping and this is putting pressure on the school to gain a larger percentage of the age cohort. Mr Diamond puts much emphasis on exam results as a marketing tool but is conscious of the need to take school-based activities to the community too as a way of enhancing the school's profile. To this end he has been generous in his allocation of funding to James to support the annual school production. James responds by acting as a coordinator/follower: he translates the school's vision of community involvement into the reality of sold-out performances on all three nights of the lavish annual production. James and Mr Diamond apparently get on well.

However, in 2003, a number of students leave from the school because the local military personnel are withdrawn from their camp following a reorganisation by the Ministry of Defence. The school suffers financially. James has his share of the school budget cut, meaning that he will have to cut back on the school production. Rather than looking for economies in order to mount an equally impressive production at lower cost, he is resentful that his previous hard work has been undermined (as he sees it). He drops in some hints of his frustration about incompetent budget management at school level to a friend he meets in the pub, whose girlfriend, he knows, is a reporter on the local paper. As a result of this (toxic creation) the paper runs a news item about the cuts at Damien's school. Mr Diamond's public profile is lowered and his credibility in the school is undermined. At the time of writing it is not clear whether Mr Diamond will discover the source of the newspaper's information.

In this scenario you can see two of the followership models at work. The chances are that you recognised other models in the behaviour of yourself and your colleagues when you carried out the last Reflection. In Activity 10.2 you are invited to undertake a more in-depth analysis of your own school.

ACTIVITY 10.2

Followers and their behaviours

Using the prompts below, think back over:

■ first, your own actions

■ then the actions of colleagues

over the last year or so.

In each case identify an instance of the behaviour in the role listed.

When you have completed this list summarise what you have learned, especially about yourself, in the process.

Role*	Example of your action in role	Example of this role played by a colleague
Aspirant, mentee, apprentice		
Coordinator		
Disciple		
Gatekeeper, filter		
Muse		
Rescuer		
Resnatronic		
Second-in-command		
Sidekick, partner, comrade		
Toxic handler		
Communication distorter		
Saboteur		
Toxic creator		

* Refer back to Table 10.3 for definitions of the roles.

Finally, what would you conclude about schools as micro-political organisations from your findings?

Whatever your conclusions from Activity 10.2, this section about the teacher's relations with those in authority cannot be allowed to pass without some mention of desired behaviours. Teachers have a duty to uphold professional standards in all aspects of their work; perhaps this section has revealed that this is not always a duty fulfilled. Furthermore, much emphasis is placed in some quarters on team-working in schools. Gronn (1996: 12) has criticised 'barren models of followership' on the grounds that they emphasise the role of leader unnecessarily, ignoring the distributed nature of leadership in organisations. Team-working is one medium through which leadership is distributed and actioned by teachers. Others would push the objections even further, perhaps. In a later paper Gronn (1999) cites the instance of Moosewood – a US restaurant collective – which rotates leadership. If you think that is alien to the educational scene, then think again because there are similar systems in operation (e.g. in Israel in the kibbutz school tradition).

For most people in the teacher role – as opposed to a middle manager – team-working is a way of exercising some leadership. This leadership both moves on the institution as a whole and influences the senior managers. Peter Senge (1990) remains the most eloquent and influential exponent of the value of teams to what he calls the life of the learning organisation:

> *Team learning is the process of aligning and developing the capacity of a team to create the results its members truly desire. It builds on the discipline of developing a shared vision. It builds on personal mastery ... But shared vision and talent are not enough ... Individual learning, at some level, is irrelevant for organisational learning. Individuals learn all the time but there is no organisational learning. But if teams learn, they become a microcosm for learning throughout the organisation.*
>
> (Senge 1990: 236)

He goes on to cite three 'critical dimensions' of team learning:

- the need to think insightfully about complex issues
- the need for innovative, coordinated action
- the need for learning teams to influence other teams in turn.

For Senge, team-working is about dialogue and discussion and about how to 'deal creatively with the powerful forces opposing dialogue and discussion', i.e. the opponents of change.

So what have we learned about the teacher's relations with senior colleagues? Certainly that they can be either positive or negative; that followers can influence the life of an institution for better or worse. Second, that professionalism is a factor in individual behaviour and relationships. Third, that the teacher can influence change and provide leadership in that role alone, above all through team-working. These are important messages for anyone aspiring to be a master teacher.

_____ Support staff (teaching assistants, LSAs, _____ administrators and technical staff)

The one group that classroom teachers – even NQTs – manage in today's schools are support personnel. At the time of writing the government is training a hundred ASTs to manage support staff.

In this section we shall examine the management process but first it is important to define the groups about whom we are talking. They include the job roles listed above in the subtitle; but in research (Kerry 2001) it has been found that over 70 job roles exist and are labelled in schools. To make things easier it is probably worth drawing on one distinction now favoured by the Department for Education and Skills (DfES) (2002):

1 *Classroom-based*: support personnel who have direct contact with learning, e.g. teaching assistants (TAs) and learning support assistants (LSAs – often one-to-one workers with children with special learning needs) or any member acting as a learning mentor (Kerry, C. 2002).

2 *Curriculum-based*: those who support the curriculum, e.g. technicians working in science laboratories, or those who run ICT systems and translate lessons into intranet learning.

3 *Administration-based*: support personnel whose tasks are primarily administrative or financial such as secretaries, receptionists, bursars.

Most management by teachers is of the first group and it is on these that we shall concentrate attention.

Adults assisting in classrooms do not constitute a new situation: there have always been volunteers who have washed the proverbial paintpots. But the support phenomenon has been thrown into relief by recent debates about teacher overload, teacher shortage, poor retention rates of teachers especially in urban areas, and 'teachers on the cheap'. These are not debates for this text, but you can follow them in Kerry (2002a) and Kerry and Kerry (2003).

Who are the support staff in your school? Who manages them and their day-to-day work? How effective are these systems?

It is important that we take a stance on the role of support personnel. At present they suffer, in too many cases, from lack of initial training, poor pay, lack of national conditions of service, poor access to continuing professional development, and consequent failure of status (Kerry 2001; Lee and Mawson 1998; O'Brian and Garner 2001). The fact that most are women perpetuates these inequalities (Bonner 2002). There is limited opportunity for advancement (Foulkes 2002). The view of this text is that they are more appropriately treated as para-professionals, and that the inequities listed above should be addressed by national government. While national government wants them to have a pivotal role (Department for Education and Skills (DfES) 2002) in fulfilling the political dream of 'world class schools', there is currently no sign that it will grasp this nettle.

There is thus a real danger that support personnel (especially those who are classroom based) will emerge as a second-rate teaching force for second-rate students (Kerry and Kerry 2003). It is incumbent on teacher-managers of support staff to prevent this negative development. Perhaps teachers do not give enough thought to the issues surrounding the growing use of support personnel and need to understand these employees better. To this end Table 10.4 sets out the 'propositions' that emerged from the research carried out by Kerry (2002a). These remain to be tested on a wider sample, but the list might serve as a means to examining more closely practice in your own school.

Management of the work of classroom-based support staff by teachers is sometimes well done and sometimes not. While virtually no older teachers will have been trained in this way, the Teacher Training Agency (TTA) (2002) has a passing reference to the need to train NQTs in the skills of managing support personnel in their classes. Yet Golze (2002) in an unpublished study, albeit of just one secondary school, found that support staff themselves found younger teachers less capable of managing their work. Support staff (Kerry 2001, Kerry 2002a) were often content with their management; but when it went wrong, it went really wrong:

I have left education to go into the care sector. Much as I greatly loved working with children – indeed the comment made regarding my work by an Ofsted team was 'exemplary' – until the attitude of teachers changes towards support staff I feel I must look elsewhere to be valued.

(Support staff employee, quoted in Kerry 2002a: 25)

TABLE 10.4	Collected propositions emerging from Kerry's (2002a) research
P1	Support staff roles attract mainly female employees.
P2	Support staff typically stay in the role for at least 6–10 years.
P3	The majority of support staff work in the primary phase.
P4	For many support staff continuous professional development is not provided, and is infrequent for many others.
P5	The most effective training may be self-sought and self-funded.
P6	Union membership is a growing, but by no means universal, phenomenon.
P7	Membership of non-union professional organisations is minimal.
P8	Half of all support staff do not read any professionally orientated literature.
P9	Among those who do read, a proportion take advantage of a spouse's professional literature rather than seeking out their own.
P10	Nursery nurses are both the group most likely to be professionally trained and also the most likely to read professional literature.
P11	The large majority of support staff, in a range of job roles, not only support learning but claim to 'teach' groups of pupils; most of these personnel teach classes regularly or occasionally.
P12	More than half of support staff have a role in the pastoral care of pupils in their schools.
P13	A substantial minority of support staff are involved in either lunchtime supervision of pupils or of lunchtime clubs or activities.
P14	A substantial minority of support staff cover for teaching staff absence occasionally or regularly, even for long periods.
P15	A substantial minority of support staff do not cover for teaching staff absence and feel that it is wrong to do so.
P16	A sizeable minority of support staff has a low opinion of supply teachers and their ability to substitute adequately for teacher absence.
P17	Support staff are generally supportive, but sceptical about the realism, of government policy about their deployment.
P18	Support staff believe training and continuing professional development to be inadequate or unavailable.

P19   Support staff believe that the major barriers to implementing government policy are the failure to put in place:

- a national conditions of service agreement
- a professional pay structure
- fair contracts for support staff.

P20   Support staff regard the extension of learning through ICT as unlikely to succeed until there is adequate resourcing, especially in the primary sector.

P21   There is a need to define and differentiate support roles and teaching roles.

P22   School plant is not capable of taking the extension of adult roles envisaged as there is inadequate accommodation in most schools to house the personnel.

P23   Most support staff accept the need to shoulder some of the administrative burden of teachers/schools.

P24   Many support staff think that there is too much administration and paperwork in schools overall.

P25   The Secretary of State for Education should increase school funding to allow for increased deployment of support staff – up to one per class in every school.

P26   Support staff roles in schools need clarification and definition.

P27   There should be a national pay scale and conditions of service for support staff.

P28   Training for support staff in their specific roles is crucial.

P29   Teachers need to be educated to use support staff effectively.

P30   In secondary schools, support staff may need to be tied more closely to a subject specialism.

So, if most support staff feel well-managed, but a few do not, and if some teachers are trained in managing them but others not, the question remains: what exactly constitutes good management of support staff? Table 10.5 provides an overall answer to the question as it emerged in Kerry's (2001) research. Many of the issues raised in Table 10.5 are outside the control of the class teacher, others are not, but it provides a useful checklist against which to examine your own and your school's management in this field.

TABLE 10.5   Issues in the effective management of support personnel

Managers need to ensure, in relation to support personnel, that they:

- Provide clear job descriptions prior to appointment

- Provide written guidelines for unpaid personnel

- Review and update job descriptions regularly

- Understand what they, as managers, want from each support role

- Ensure post-holders do not (willingly or under pressure from others) expand or amend the roles in practice without authority

- See that all staff (support/teaching), as well as parents and governors, understand the parameters that govern each support person's role

- Provide a single, named line manager for each post-holder

- Provide a mentor for each post-holder (not the line manager)

- Provide adequate resources for the efficient execution of the roles

- Review the work of, and provide appraisal opportunities for, the post-holders

- Identify and provide initial and continuing training wherever appropriate

- Put in place a system of accountability, e.g. a log of work done

- Capitalise on the post-holder's enthusiasms and individual skills

- Identify elements in each support role that are part of the learning resource of the school

- Use these learning elements to maximum effect

- Provide time for post-holders to reflect on what they are doing

- Provide (literal and metaphorical) space for post-holders to operate

- Ensure the status of support personnel in the eyes of the pupils and others

- Listen to the views of support staff

- Regularly review value-for-money issues around support roles

- Reward jobs well done

- Deal with post-holders who are ineffective and let down the team

- From time to time, carry out self-assessment of their management strategies

- Do not relinquish power to a zealous individual (e.g. a personal assistant).

At the classroom level it may help to look at what motivates and what demotivates support staff, since management strategies can be drawn from this knowledge. To this end we quote a section from a research study by Kerry (2002b), through the summary Table 10.6.

TABLE 10.6 Demotivating factors for support staff

- Too heavy a workload
- Poor communication/information structures in the school
- Resistance to support staff by teachers
- Lack of recognition
- Negative attitudes by other support staff
- Negative comments (sources unquoted)
- Low pay
- Inefficiency with the school
- Lack of appreciation
- Poor working environment
- Poor professional development opportunities
- Receiving contrary instructions
- Others claiming ownership of one's work
- Lack of support from the head teacher
- Insufficient resources
- Unrealistic expectations
- Negative attitudes from outside agencies
- Colleagues who are not team players.

Table 10.6 summarises what constitute demotivational factors in the work of support staff in schools. However, the tone of all the responses in this research remained positive. There were some other clear messages that emerged from this research, and it may be worth drawing these out at this juncture. They are:

- self-motivation is important
- achievement of motivation can come through being valued
- a challenging, even busy, working environment is good
- motivation results from one's investment in and ownership of the school
- targets, goals and missions play a part in clarity of direction

- the main source of motivation is in promoting children's satisfaction with school, especially where there is a dimension of social deprivation that can be compensated for.

All of these views are very positive. So management of support personnel is about enhancing motivation and limiting demotivation. It is about proper conditions of service and about appropriate understandings by all parties of the expectations of the job. It is about professional respect. It is about ensuring that the role is planned into classroom activities and that there is proper scope for preparation. There is an increasing literature of effective support (Balshaw and Farrell 2002; Lovey 2002; Watkinson 2002) and teacher-managers of support staff need to become familiar with it. These aspects of management are largely in the control of the teacher in the classroom, but the management of our next group of personnel may be rather harder to achieve.

_____ Inspectors, advisers and outside experts _____

The relations with inspectors, Ofsted or LEA (who may conduct 'mock' inspections), are often laced with foreboding. The way in which we shall consider them is first, briefly, to establish a principle, and then to look at the timescale of before, during and after inspection.

The principle is this: master teachers are able professionals. They should not view themselves, and should not be viewed, as inadequate. Inspection provides an opportunity not only to be judged on what they can and do do; it provides the chance to show it off to a fellow professional. It is up to you to put on display the very best of your work both practically as a teacher in the classroom, and on paper through the quality of your professional records. These things are, after all, the basis of your expertise. Furthermore, if you are questioned about what you are doing, you should be ready to discuss it and the reasons for it, and the background of your children, as one professional to another.

As an aside we should say that we recognise that, in a minority of instances, this ideal cannot be achieved. We too object to inspection teams where the expertise of the inspector is questionable. Indeed, one of us was inspected not too long ago teaching mathematics to a mixed-age group. We had worked hard on the lesson and on all the background materials. The lesson was observed by the lay inspector.

But having established the basic principle, what of the timescale? This consists of before, during and after inspection. Before, there is no face-to-face contact with the inspector; but this is the time of preparation of lessons and background paperwork. During the inspection there is face-to-face contact, often quite fleeting. However, inspectors are required, if possible, to speak to you about the lesson when it ends; and this is where your professional knowledge has a chance to show itself. The largest single complaint from teachers is still that inspectors' comments are not useful (Ferguson et al. 2000). After the inspection, the teacher's role will be to play a part in implementing any changes identified in the key issues – again, not a face-to-face activity.

REFLECTION

What positive and negative experiences have you had of inspection? What have you learned as a result?

Relationships with other education professionals who come into the school are usually less strained than those with inspectors. These professionals include, for example, psychologists, speech therapists, nurses, community police, education welfare officers and social workers. Here, the emphasis is usually on professional sharing and there are few conflicts that arise.

Governors

It would not be right to leave this chapter on relations between the classroom teacher and other interested personnel without a mention of the relations between teachers and governors. In the experience of most teachers, even the highly able governors probably play little part. What part they do play will usually fall to one of the following circumstances:

- where the teacher meets governors at school-based social events such as the annual carol service or the PTA
- where the teacher (more frequently in a primary school) has a responsibility for, say, the coordination of a subject – he/she may then be asked to present a report to a governors' meeting
- where the governors have a policy of visiting classrooms on an occasional basis
- where the teacher is an elected staff representative on the governing body.

Of these, we shall assume the teacher has enough small talk to cope with the first and we shall deal only with the remainder.

It is very unlikely that a teacher will be asked to present a report to the governing body about some area of responsibility unless there is careful liaison with the head about precisely what is required. Indeed a teacher in this position should not avoid the opportunity (it may be a good way of bringing one's ability to the notice of the governors). But he/she should certainly seek the fullest briefing on what is required in terms of the scope of the data to be supplied, the paperwork to be produced, and the time allowance for presenting the information. Preparation is the key and all the usual advice – about pithy and professional presentation, exuding confidence, working to time and keeping to the point – applies. There may well be a question-and-answer opportunity at the end of the presentation, so don't make the mistake of preparing a good presentation but having little to offer beyond this.

Some teachers stand for election and are voted on to school governing bodies. They have to face the fact that their fellow governors will not (usually) be well versed in educational matters. They will include local politicians, business people and parents, plus some individuals co-opted for their knowledge or contacts. Teacher governors will be excluded from parts of meetings that deal with sensitive issues such as the pay of the head and other staff. Teacher governors have to play a role in relation to the governing body not unlike that of the deputy in relation to the head: they have to represent the governors to the staff, and the staff to the governors. Many of the things we have said earlier about attitudes to parents can be transferred to attitudes to governors and the business that governors transact.

Governors have enormous powers and responsibilities within schools: many of their responsibilities are statutory. Most governors are really pleased to be with and talk to teachers, to accept their help and guidance. Governors need to be consulted about many issues within schools, though this will usually happen directly with the head teacher or be facilitated by the head. Middlewood and Lumby (1998: 12–13) argue that the extent of consultation with governors should be conditioned by three factors: whether they have jurisdiction over the area (e.g. a statutory responsibility, as in the case of special needs); whether they have something relevant to contribute; and whether they possess relevant expertise. These decisions are beyond the remit of the teacher governor to make. What is certain is that in governing bodies where the teacher governor turns the role into a micro-political battle between governors and staff, things usually go horribly awry (a case study of conflict between school and governors appears in Menter et al. 1997: 71–5, and epitomises the issues). Positive relationships can and should be established for the good of the school.

How might teacher/governor relationships be promoted and improved?

The other sensitive area is that of the head and the staff representative talking at cross-purposes with one another in governors' meetings. In an ideal world, the head and the staff governor should consult about potentially difficult issues before meetings, though ideally neither would want to constrain the other from expressing a contrary view. The manner in which this is done should always be professional and restrained, with arguments based on logic and evidence rather than dogma and emotion.

On the issue of governors visiting classrooms, again feelings often run high, and negatively, in the profession. It really is the duty of head teachers to spell out the ground rules of this process. Typically, there would include the following principles:

- Visits by governors should always be prearranged and with reasonable notice.

- Governors' visits are never to judge the quality of teaching – most governors are not professionally qualified to carry out this role.

- The purpose of the visit must be indicated in advance and relate to the governor's remit (for example, as the governor with responsibility for multicultural education to observe a lesson on a relevant topic, or as a finance committee member to see how new equipment is being used).

- The governor should report to the head any comments on what is observed.

- Governors should behave with decorum in the classroom, e.g. not talking to an individual pupil or a member of support staff while the teacher is speaking.

- Governors must operate codes of confidentiality and avoid gate gossip about teachers and pupils.

- A parent governor should not visit the classroom of their own child.

If there is a code of conduct like this, agreed by the head teacher with the governing body, few problems will arise.

———— Conclusion ————

This chapter has surveyed a wide field of personal relationships between the effective teacher and other adults in the school, involving leadership, management and followership. Schools are becoming increasingly open and increasingly accountable; these skills must be seen as potentially increasingly important.

But while interpersonal relationships are critically important, for our final chapter we return to the teacher's ability to reflect on their own learning and to assist pupils to do the same using the techniques of meta-cognition.

At the end of this chapter you should have:

■ Examined your approaches to a range of relationships in which you are involved, in the classroom and in school

■ Appreciated the management and leadership roles you play, for example in relation to support staff

■ Understood that 'followers' can have a significant effect on the development and well-being of their organisations, and that followership carries professional responsibilities

■ Recognised the need to examine closely your skills in human relations as they impinge on parents, colleagues and outside agents

References

Balshaw, M. and Farrell, P. (2002) *Teaching Assistants: Practical Strategies for Effective Classroom Support,* London: David Fulton.

Bonner, F. (2002) 'Why are almost all support staff female? Does it matter?', *Education Today,* 52(3): 20–27.

Covey, S. (1989) *The Seven Habits of Highly Effective People,* London: Simon & Schuster.

Crozier, G. (2000) *Parents and Schools: Partners or Protagonists?,* Stoke-on-Trent: Trentham.

Department for Education and Skills (DfES) (2002) *Developing the Role of School Support Staff: The Consultation,* London: DfES.

Ferguson, N., Earley, P., Fidler, B. and Ouston, J. (2000) *Improving Schools and Inspection,* London: PCP.

Foulkes, P. (2002) 'Teaching assistant to qualified teacher', *Education Today,* 52(3): 28–33.

Golze, S. (2002) 'The perception of support staff in school', unpublished MSc dissertation, University of Lincoln.

Gronn, P. (1996) 'From transactions to transformations', *Educational Management and Administration,* 24(1): 7–30.

Gronn, P. (1999) *The Making of Educational Leaders,* London: Cassell.

Hodgson, J. (1996) *Thinking on your Feet in Negotiations,* London: Pitman.

Kerry, T. (2001) *Working with Support Staff*, London: Pearson.

Kerry, C. (2002) 'Support staff as mentors: a case study of innovation', *Education Today*, 52(3) 3–12.

Kerry, T. (2002a) *Providing Support: A Review of Local and National Views on the Deployment and Development of Support Staff in Schools*, Papers in Leading and Learning, Lincoln: Lincoln University.

Kerry, T. (2002b) 'What motivates support staff?', *Managing Schools Today*, February: 25–8.

Kerry, C. and Kerry, T. (2003) 'Government policy and the effective employment and deployment of support staff in UK schools: democratic progress or knee-jerk reaction to the teacher shortage? A dilemma for school leaders', *International Studies in Educational Administration*, 31(1) 65–81.

Lee, B. and Mawson, C. (1998) *Survey of Classroom Assistants*, Slough: NFER.

Lovey, J. (2002) *Supporting Special Educational Needs in Secondary School Classrooms*, 2nd edn, London: David Fulton.

Menter, I., Muschamp, Y., Nicholls, P., Ozga, J. and Pollard, A. (1997) *Work and Identity in the Primary School*, Buckingham: Open University Press.

Middlewood, D. and Lumby, J. (1998) *Strategic Management in Schools and Colleges*, London: PCP.

O'Brian, T. and Garner, P. (2001) *Untold Stories*, Stoke-on-Trent: Trentham.

Peshiardis, P. (2001) 'Secondary principals in Cyprus: the views of the principal versus the views of the teachers – a case study', *International Studies in Educational Administration*, 29(3): 11–27.

Senge, P. (1990) *The Learning Organisation*, London: Century Business.

Thody, A. (2002) 'Followership in educational organisations: a pilot mapping of the territory', paper delivered at the Commonwealth Council for Educational Administration and Management Conference Umea, Sweden, 21–23 September. Reprinted in the Conference Guide (to which page numbers refer).

Teacher Training Agency TTA (2002) *Requirements for Initial Teacher Training*, London: TTA.

Vincent, C. (1996) 'Parent empowerment? Collective action and inaction in education', *Oxford Review of Education*, 22(4) 465–82.

Watkinson, A. (2002) *Assisting Learning and Supporting Teaching*, London: David Fulton.

chapter eleven

The sensitive teacher

Self-learning and meta-cognition

In this chapter you are invited to:

- Think analytically about the ways in which you learn at your own level

- Consider some further taxonomies of learning

- Understand the definition and value of meta-cognition in learning

- Apply the principles of meta-cognition to children's learning

- Understand the value of meta-cognition as a tool in the armoury of the master teacher

Much of this text has been about learning: about how master teachers can encourage effective learning through effective teaching. It has, at opportune points in the book, explored discrete issues such as theories of learning, organisation for learning and assessing learning. So it is appropriate in this final chapter to return overtly to the theme of learning. Some of what is said here is taken from Kerry and Kerry (2000). This chapter asks the reader to reflect on the nature and processes of learning, and to consider the reflexive process we call meta-cognition.

What is learning?

It is important to begin by rehearsing and recalling what learning is:

- A psychologist might describe it in terms of the functioning of the mind.

- A biologist could think in terms of electrochemical impulses in various portions of the brain.

- For a sociologist learning might be a process of adapting to the human environment.

- A historian would examine the way learning has changed over the centuries.

Each discipline has an insight to contribute to the way in which we understand learning; each is both valid and valuable. For the purpose of thinking about learning in this chapter, however, we will introduce the topic with a taxonomy. This simply means a way of dividing up and classifying different kinds of learning. The taxonomy is taken from Bowring-Carr and West-Burnham (1997: 24–25).

1 **Learning as memorisation**. *Some of such memorisation is important (e.g. the times table, the rules of spelling) as the rules memorised enable higher functions to be undertaken without conscious thought as to the foundation activities. Some memorisation, however, is important only until the next test or examination, and the material memorised can be, and indeed often is, discarded as soon as the test is over. We may therefore divide memorisation into functional memorisation, and shallow memorisation or shallow learning.*

2 **Learning as a quantitative increase in our knowledge on a topic**. *If I am becoming interested in gardening, for example, by experience, by talking to other gardeners and reading books and magazines on the subject, and of course, by gardening, I increase the body of knowledge that I have on the subject.*

3 **Learning as the creation of personal meaning**. *From our earliest conscious moment, we are learning about the people and things around us – what is safe and trustworthy and what is not, what is warm and what is repellent, and so on – because without this learning we cannot make sense of the world in which we live.*

4 **Learning which results in the creation of our reality**. *As a continuation of 3 above, from the learning about the people and things around us we create our sense of reality, which is shifting and uncertain over time, but which at any given moment allows us to know our world and function in it.*

5 **Learning which results in our changing as a person**. *This learning, deep learning, is what occurs when a new idea, a new perception, a new grasp on a topic fundamentally alters the way we are, the way we behave.*

Read over this taxonomy and keep it by you as you work through this chapter as we shall refer to it again later.

ACTIVITY 11.1

Reviewing your own learning

Think back to some learning you have done recently at your own level. It could be trying to learn a foreign language, mastering a computer, tackling a part of this book or learning to drive, for example.

Now take the five steps in the taxonomy, listed below, and jot down some notes about the part each played in your learning:

- Memorisation
- Acquisition of knowledge
- Creation of meaning
- Creation of reality
- Personal change

What has this process of review told you about your own learning?

——————— The teacher as learner ———————

Learning and teaching are two perspectives of the same process, like views from either end of a telescope and – just as a piece of fun – we quote an extract from a short story to reinforce the theme and to introduce the idea of the relationship of learning and teaching in the role of the teacher.

It appears that in the Sussexville Proprietary School, Plattner not only discharged the duties of modern languages master, but also taught chemistry, commercial geography, book-keeping, shorthand, drawing and any other additional subject to which the changing fancies of the boys' parents might direct attention. He knew little or nothing of these various subjects, but in a secondary [school] … knowledge in the teacher is, very properly, by no means so necessary as high moral character and gentlemanly tone. In chemistry he was particularly deficient, knowing nothing, he says, beyond the Three Gases … As, however, his pupils began by knowing nothing, and derived all their information from him, this caused him (or anyone) little inconvenience for several terms. Then a boy named Whibble joined the school, who had been educated, it seems, by some mischievous relative into an enquiring habit of mind.

(Hammond 1998: 103)

This little extract is the beginning of a story of which the moral is 'don't meddle with subjects you don't know about – especially chemistry'. But you can read the ending for yourself. For the moment we must concentrate on the need for teachers to be learners too.

REFLECTION

How do teachers become learners or sustain their own learning?

The answers to the question in the Reflection are many and various (refer back to Chapter 10), but would certainly include:

1 *Continuous professional development (CPD)*. Training days ensure that all teachers pursue some level of updating and, while some of this activity is undoubtedly useful, there are real dangers that schools may not maximise this opportunity, or simply that it is not adequate to cover the needs that individuals feel.

2 *Using training manuals*. Many teachers feel a need to augment training days with their own studies. This book provides one way of doing that – using an interactive text. Interactive texts or e-learning materials allow the reader not merely to acquire knowledge but also to become aware of, practise and improve upon skills of teaching.

3 *Audiovisual approaches and self-assessment*. Another approach is critically to review one's performance as a teacher by using audio or visual recording. For example, if one wishes to learn how to be a more effective explainer or a better questioner, one way is to record one's own performance. Then, using the replays, one can examine one's own work critically and compare it against specific templates of performance. This approach is sometimes referred to as micro-teaching.

4 *Peer appraisal*. These methods are all useful but they depend on one's own objectivity. Often it is more useful – if more salutary – to involve a colleague. We have long been exponents of team teaching, which provides spontaneous opportunities to observe others and have one's own teaching observed. Failing this, colleagues can agree to form 'buddy pairs', as the Americans say, to watch each other and fulfil the role of critical friend for one another. Formal appraisal opens up the same opportunity, but with a more judgemental flavour.

5 *The professional log*. What these approaches to self-learning share is a conviction that reflecting on one's own work can improve one's learning of teaching capability. It is to Schon (1983) that we owe the insight of the value of reflective practice. He argues that it is when professionals 'reflect on the understanding that has been implicit in their actions and criticise, restructure and reapply that understanding, that they begin to create the knowledge which is of value to them in informing action'.

Keeping a log of one's learning over time (e.g. what happens in the classroom, what goes well or badly, what one tried to do to alter one's behaviour to achieve better results, what the outcomes are) is a good way through which to enter into the reflective practitioner model.

ACTIVITY 11.2

Learning yourself

At the very beginning of this book we suggested that one way of using it was to record your responses to each of the activities as you tackled them. If you have done this you might now look back over this log.

- What have you learned in the process?
- More importantly, what have you learned about your own learning and about how you learn best?
- If you haven't kept a log, carry out the reflection below.

REFLECTION

Think back over your reading of this text.

What have you gained from it? What insights have you gleaned? What attitudes have you modified? What knowledge have you acquired? What new connections have you made?

_____ Meta-cognition _____

An ugly word for a useful process, meta-cognition is the process of reflecting on your own learning, just as you have just done in Activity 11.2 or the reflection above. But it is important to add here that your pupils need to learn this skill too.

It is surprising, therefore, how little is said about it in texts that are overtly about learning; for example, in Stoll, Fink and Earl (2003) meta-cognition merits just two index references. Their definition is, however, useful:

> *Human beings can reflect on their own thinking processes. Experts describe their thinking as an internal conversation – monitoring their own understanding, predicting their performance, deciding what else they need to know, organising and re-organising ideas, checking for consistency between different pieces of information and drawing analogies that help them advance their understanding.*
>
> (Stoll, Fink and Earl 2003: 26)

Stoll et al. (2003: 70) note that using meta-cognitive processes in the classroom is an advanced teaching skill, but pupils will learn more effectively if they understand their own learning processes. In an interesting article with younger primary children, Wilding (1997) argues that almost every pupil can be helped to learn by using this process. Wilding introduced 'learning diaries' with children as young as six, to great effect. Her conclusion about both teachers and pupils using this method is hearteningly optimistic.

We are going to shift our perspective now from teachers learning at their own level to meta-cognition as a tool for master teachers in helping children to learn. Having experimented with various approaches to children recording what they had learned, including one-to-one discussions with the teacher, Wilding (1997: 20) concluded that a number of problems beset these approaches:

- The reviews were extremely time-consuming.

- Children generally only remembered and referred to very recent activities; also they used very general labels and imprecise language such as 'My maths was best 'cause it was good'.

- I found myself constantly drawn towards 'putting words in their mouths' as they struggled with the language.

- There was a wide spectrum in the level of sophistication in the responses of different children.

The issue of language is mirrored in Loughran (2002), who describes a meta-cognitive approach to teaching in an Australian setting, where learning the 'language of learning' was an important prerequisite in order to enable students and teachers to communicate about the processes of learning. For the reasons listed above, Wilding decided that a better solution to achieving meta-cognitive practice was to put aside some timetabled time on a regular and fairly frequent basis for the compilation of learning logs:

> I anticipated that, once the children were familiar with the task, it would only take up about 30–40 minutes ... I felt there was time available during Friday morning ... It could be justified in terms of the English National Curriculum as providing a meaningful purpose for Speaking and Listening, and Writing ... the majority of the children had the necessary writing skills (Y2/3 class) ... in the case of the four children who might struggle my ancillary or myself should be able to give extra support.
>
> (Wilding 1997: 20)

Each child was issued with an exercise book in which to write the log and some prompt questions were added to the front page:

- What have I enjoyed most during this week? Why?
- What have I done best during this week? Why?
- What have I found difficult during this week? Why?
- What am I going to try harder at next week? Why?

The sophistication of the children's learning diaries increased rapidly. The rather bald statements of the kind quoted earlier soon turned into:

> I have enjoyed writing on the computer. Why – because it is good but I did make some mistakes. I have been best at my stamp ready reckoner. Why – because it is a bit hard but I got used to it. I have found it difficult doing my Ancient Greece research. Why – because it is hard to get information. I am going to try harder not to shout. Why – because it is hard to keep it under control.

It is important to remember here that meta-cognition is not only about supporting the learning of the less able (Lovey 2002), useful though this is. It is a tool for all pupils including the very able. Wilding, in fact, went on to give a number of other examples of how the learning diary had not only helped the pupils understand their own learning processes – their strengths, weaknesses and distractions – but had also the teacher:

Example 1

'I have done my best at pot drawing this week because it is the only time you have said "Well done".' (This shows how important the teacher's response can be to children, and reminds us of the importance of being positive.)

Example 2

'I have found reading difficult because I am guessing the words.' (The teacher followed this up with the child and found that he was feeling very unsuccessful with his reading book; the book was changed to one he understood and enjoyed. It was also possible to explain that careful 'guessing' can be a very useful and appropriate strategy in reading.)

Example 3

'What I found difficult this week is swimming because Jamie kept taking the mickey out of me.' (The teacher was able to have a quiet word with the pupils involved.)

Wilding goes on to conclude that the aim of this process is to raise the pupil's stake in the learning process – to put the pupil at the centre of learning (see Chapter 4). To do this, it is important to show that what pupils say has an effect on what happens in the classroom. They need to 'see the point' of the activity and to see it expressed in action. The learning diary – the meta-cognitive process – was subsequently introduced throughout the school, in an oral version with the youngest pupils.

Though the examples given here have been from the primary phase of education, the process is by no means limited to use with younger children. Indeed, a parallel exercise could be carried out before or during the kinds of tutorials now used widely with year 10 and year 11 students in secondary schools.

There is widespread concern in the secondary sector about GCSE performance and the whole business of league tables. Much effort is expended in encouraging students in this age group to maximise their performance. Meta-cognitive processes and tools would significantly support this operation, giving a range of insights to teachers and to those support staff (Kerry 2002) who have responsibility for enhancing performance.

The same kind of needs and processes extend into the sixth form and on to universities at both undergraduate and postgraduate levels; this is the point of a tutorial-based approach. Even, perhaps especially, in initial teacher training the approach is important (Russell and Bullock 2001). These authors provide good examples of meta-cognition at that level of learning (Russell and Bullock 2001: 98f.).

ACTIVITY 11.3

Putting meta-cognitive processes in place

How could meta-cognition help your teaching?

How could it help your understanding of your pupils' learning?

How could it help pupils' understanding of their own learning?

How could it help pupils' understanding of your teaching?

In the light of the answers to these questions, how could you implement a classroom regime that depended more on meta-cognitive reflection and practice?

Implement your ideas and make an assessment of their effectiveness.

Meta-cognition and creativity

What you may have discovered from Activity 11.3 is that meta-cognition puts the learner at the heart of the learning process (Kerry 2001). Meta-cognition helps the pupil to own the learning. Pupils and students who own their learning are motivated and look for creative outcomes.

We are back to the classic triangle of learning in which the pupil and the curriculum are linked through the dynamism of the teacher. The curriculum itself needs to be relevant, interesting and exciting. This is especially important in an age of ICT (see Chapter 6) where young people can gain access to exciting and engaging images that may substitute for education if teaching fails to deliver a dynamic product. For example, a pupil might watch a stimulating set of materials such as a video of *Walking with Dinosaurs*. A few interesting facts or snippets of information may stick in the pupils' minds from this experience. However, this information-based teaching is limited (and – as we have seen – is the danger inherent in the National Curriculum).

Most teachers move on beyond this to engage thinking: to plan learning opportunities that get pupils involved in probing, questioning, expanding, contextualising and engaging in activity. To achieve truly *robust learning*, pupils must engage in the higher-level cognition and skills (Chapter 5) in a context of individualisation (described in Chapter 4). The danger is that learning stops at an earlier stage in the process and fails to move on to dynamic thinking. The master teacher will strengthen this element of what happens in the classroom, developing judgement, critical faculties, evaluating, creating fresh ideas and approaches to subjects, and so on – to become the conveyor of the message, not the recipient.

The master teacher provides first-hand experience, not second-hand experience.

Meta-cognition and the master teacher

Developing meta-cognition is a key element in maximising pupils' and students' learning. However, it is an equally important element in maximising teachers' own professionalism and quality of pedagogy. Teachers need to be aware of the processes of thought that underpin classroom practice if they are to direct it. The first step must be to think about what one is trying to achieve and why. It is essentially a change process. This is where one's ideological framework, one's philosophy, takes precedence, formulating the values on which change is based.

The second step in the process is to evaluate current practice in monitoring learning. One has to ask: is what is being done related to what one wishes to achieve? Are the pupils learning what it is intended they should learn? How do they respond to the learning activities? It is important to look for gaps between where we are and where we want and need to be. Having found the loopholes, they need to be addressed.

The third step is to consider the How? questions of change. How can one move from where one is to where one wants to be? How simple and cosmetic, or how root-and-branch and fundamental, are the changes likely to be? How can they be achieved? How can the barriers be overcome? But we also need to ask what are the targets, goals and advantages? Is there guidance – by consulting professional colleagues, professional associations, literature or research?

REFLECTION

What is the role of meta-cognition in helping to make children independent learners?

Change is challenging. But such a proactive approach provides teachers with the means to navigate their way through the unpredictable tides of educational change and gives them the discourse with which to justify their stance and avoid the pitfalls of feeling out of control, threatened and low in morale.

The learning organisation

It is not possible to draw this chapter to a conclusion without reference to the context within which learning teachers need to practise their learning – a context that Senge (1990) referred to as the 'learning organisation'. Teachers, even master teachers, do not operate in a vacuum. Many of the decisions that affect their work are taken at levels over which they have no direct control (though a full discussion of this issue is beyond the scope of this book). To be maximally effective it is ideal to work in a conducive setting such as Senge describes.

Senge (1990: 139) notes that 'organisations learn only through individuals who learn. Individual learning does not guarantee organisational learning. But without it no organisational learning occurs'. Senge defines learning in this sense as 'the ability to produce the result we really want in life' through creative approaches to problem solving in shared situations. Teachers need to be empowered so that, collectively, they can produce the shared goals of the school. In the process, they need vision and an ability to withstand emotional tension, along with a clear grasp of reality. What they produce then is 'personal mastery'. These aspirations seem to run counter to the imposed solutions beloved of our politicians.

At the end of this chapter you should have:

- Brought together some final thoughts on the issue of learning and teaching.

- Understood the place of meta-cognition in learning – at your own level and at the level of your students

- Considered some strategies for adopting practices in your own classroom that involve meta-cognitive processes and the gains that can accrue from these

- Placed these thoughts in the context of a learning organisation

———— References ————

Bowring-Carr, C. and West-Burnham, J. (1997) *Effective Learning in Schools*, London: Pitman.

Hammond, J. (1998) 'The Plattner Story', in *The Complete Short Stories of H.G. Wells*, London: Orion.

Kerry, T. (2001) *Plowden: Mirage, Myth or Flag of Convenience?* Working Paper: no.43, Lincoln. University of Lincoln.

Kerry, T. and Kerry, C. (2000) *The Management of Individual Learning*, Course text for the MSc in Educational Learning and Development in the International Institute for Educational Leadership. Lincoln: University of Lincoln.

Loughran, J. (2002) 'Understanding and articulating teacher knowledge', in C. Sugrue and C. Day (eds), *Developing Teachers and Teaching Practice*, London: Routledge Falmer.

Lovey, J. (2002) *Supporting Special Educational Needs in Secondary Classrooms*, 2nd edn, London: David Fulton.

Russell, T. and Bullock, S. (2001) 'Discovering our professional knowledge as teachers: critical dialogues about learning from experience', in J. Solar, A. Craft and H. Burgess, *Teacher Development: Exploring Our Own Practice*, London: PCP Open University.

Schon, D. (1983) *The Reflective Practitioner,* London: Temple Smith.

Senge, P. (1990) *The Fifth Discipline,* London: Century Business.

Stoll, L., Fink, D. and Earl, L. (2003) *It's About Learning (and it's about time),* London: Routledge Falmer.

Wilding, M. (1997) 'Taking control: from theory into practice', *Education Today?* 47(3): 17–23.

Postscript

The main intentions of this book have been to:

■ Provide a theoretical basis for teaching for those who aspire to be master teachers

■ Identify and discuss the skills that relate to highly effective classroom teaching in primary and secondary schools

■ Act as a source book for those who wish to become more knowledgeable and better read in the area of pedagogy and its related themes

Among the countless numbers of books that are written about schools, schooling, education, the administration, management and leadership of education, schools as organisations, or even the philosophy, psychology and sociology of education, only a small number deal specifically with the art and science of teaching. Of these, too many both in the UK and overseas fall either to the competence model (e.g. Zmuda and Tomaino 2001) that demotes teaching to a craft, or to the 'tips for teachers' genre that fails to do justice to advanced practitioners.

We have tried to redress that balance, but we have also had another aim. Because teaching is, in this age of technology and accelerating change, at a crossroads – where the act of teaching and the process of learning are having to be redefined – we have tried to keep a foot in both camps. We have tried to provide models of teaching for schools as they are and for schools as they will be.

Many writers (e.g. Beare 1998; Drucker 1989; Keichel 1994) provide long descriptions of how professions in general and the profession of teaching in particular will change, the conditions of service alter, the models of employment be reconfigured. These speculations are interesting if, as yet, largely unproven. But they are the periphery rather than the core of the issue. What matters, whatever the context or location of teacher employment, is the interaction between teacher and learner: its cognitive quality, social value and moral worth.

In the UK, the major professional newspaper for teachers runs a weekly column called 'Thank God it's Friday'. As an occasional feature this might be humorous; as a permanent fixture it is redolent of an outmoded attitude that belongs, in our view, to nineteenth-century unionism, stale performance and the moral tone of a defeated workforce. Readers of this book, we hope, would rather access a column called 'Hurrah! Every Day's a Learning Day!'

Few would shy away from the government's aspiration to create 'world class schools' even if the rhetoric is largely undefined. In their book of the same name Reynolds et al. (2002) set out five recommendations for reaching this target. The last of them seems a fitting mantra with which to end, with its undertones of confidence, pride, risk and sense of self-worth: *think the unthinkable*.

References

Beare, H. (1998) *Who Are the Teachers of the Future?*, Seminar Series no. 76, Victoria: Incorporated Association of Registered Teachers of Victoria.

Drucker, P. (1989) *The New Realities,* London: Mandarin/Heinemann.

Keichel, W. (1994) 'A manager's career in the new economy', *Fortune*, 11 April: 2–7.

Reynolds, D., Creemers, B., Stringfield, S., Teddlie, C. and Schaffer, G. (2002) *World Class Schools: International Perspectives on School Effectiveness,* London: Routledge Falmer

Zmuda, A. and Tomaino, M. (2001) *The Competent Classroom,* New York: Teachers' College Press.

Appendix
Managing a new teaching space

TREVOR KERRY and MANDY WILDING
The College of Teachers

This article examines the events surrounding the setting up of a new teaching space in a large primary school. It looks at the preparation and planning put into the scheme by those involved: governors, head and teachers. The effect on teaching style is explored. The views of pupils are probed. The role of consultants in assisting the scheme is analysed and discussed, and the consultants' report to the governors is summarised by way of illustration. Conclusions are drawn about the use of the new building, and about ways in which the project could have been managed more effectively.

Introduction

This study came about because the governors of a large suburban primary school in Middle England, Saxonvale Primary, decided to convert a disused building into an additional teaching space. Over a period of time the governing body and the PTA, assisted by the LEA, raised enough money for this significant capital project.

The resulting teaching space proved to be a very large open-plan area, detached from the main school building, equipped with a wet area, with cupboards and display surfaces on two walls, and two white-boards. There was a large walk-in storage area integral with the design, and some cloakroom areas attached. The level of equipment (chairs, tables etc) was very high, and the floor was carpeted. One external door led across a small courtyard to the main school, while the other gave access to the field and playground. This teaching space became known as the Viking Centre.

Problems arose almost as soon as it was occupied (by two classes and two teachers), because little thought had been given to how the space was to be used. As a result, soon after its occupation, the two authors were called in to act as external consultants to examine the potential use of the space to the maximum benefit of the school. Their brief was:

- to look at how the Centre was being operated by the two teachers in residence
- to consider ways of optimising teaching and learning in the Centre
- to take a 'whole-school' look at the future deployment and use of the Centre
- to report to the governing body.

Literature

This study of space and its use proved to be far more wide-ranging than might have been imagined. Our investigations led us to look at issues relating to strategic management by the governing body; at the management of teaching/ learning and class management by the teachers; at the ways in which change can be more effectively achieved; and at the use of consultants such as ourselves in support of management in school.

Davies and Ellison (1997) define strategic planning as:

The systematic analysis of the school and its environment and the formulation of a set of key strategic objectives to enable the school to realise its vision, within the context of its values and its resource potential. (p. 81)

For Davies and Ellison, the strategic planning process comprises four stages. The first is analysis, to give a view of the current and medium-term environment. The second is that of strategic choice: the generation of possible courses of action and their evaluation. Thirdly, there is the formulation of clear objectives; and finally the implementation phase. In the present case, we had been asked to involve ourselves in the life of the Centre during the implementation of it; the foregoing stages of the strategic plan had to be pieced together from our research.

Bush and West-Burnham's (1994) approach opens up other insights into strategic planning. They follow Marsh (1993) in pointing out the crucial role of customers in researching the nature of any strategic plan; and they place emphasis on linking that plan to the vision, mission and values of the institution. Caldwell and Spinks (1988) continue the theme, with the insight that strategic planning:

...secures appropriate involvement of people according to their responsibility for implementing the plans as well as of people with an interest or stake in the outcomes of those plans. (Quoted in Beare et al., 1989, p. 142)

In the current situation, we interpret the stakeholders to include both those who were likely to teach in the space, and those who were likely to learn in it, as well as the governing body which initiated the investment in the Centre.

Given that the customers and clients of the Centre are the teachers and learners, another useful insight into strategic planning relates to the concept of re-engineering. The development of the disused building into a teaching space was an opportunity to begin with a 'clean sheet': to aspire to fulfil the fundamental purpose of schools, which is to achieve effective teaching and learning (or as defined by Ofsted, to 'promote and sustain improvements in educational standards achieved and the quality of education provided' – Ofsted, 1995). Davies (1997) highlights the our key elements of re-engineering as:

■ fundamental re-thinking

■ radical re-design

■ dealing with business processes

■ dramatic improvement.

The 'conversion' project of redundant building to innovative teaching/learning space lent itself whole-heartedly to this kind of approach, and in what follows we look for evidence of re-engineering in the way the school managed the project. In Particular, we were looking for 'questions about the processes of learning rather than the structures of curriculum delivery' (Davies and West-Burnham, 1997, p. 89).

The management of teaching and learning is, then, high on the agenda of this study. In examining whether or not teaching and learning were taking place effectively, we decided to adopt a number of tested criteria. These related to the teaching strategies adopted by the teachers and their activities during lessons, along with analyses of the time pupils spent on-task and of the cognitive demands made by the questions asked by teachers, as a means of trying to gauge the effectiveness of learning.

The Open University (1994) encourages student teachers on its PGCE course to learn about the process and skills of being a teacher through critical observation of experienced practitioners. The materials referred to contain a simple proforma for observing a teacher at work; and we used part of this to examine what our studied teachers did in the Centre. However, the in-built assumption of this approach is that teachers act in informed ways when teaching – in other words, that they are indeed 'models' for emulation by trainees or, in our case, that they are making conscious adaptations to new situations. The shortcomings of this, model are discussed elsewhere (eg in Watkins and Whalley, 1993); but the purpose of our use of this form of open-ended observation was to tease out issues relating specifically to how the space was being used, in its formative period, to promote effective teaching and learning. In interviews, we also asked the teachers concerned to reflect on how their current practice had changed in the light of new opportunities offered by the open-plan Centre.

Two other ways in which we looked at the learning taking place in the Centre were to explore time-on-task and to analyse the cognitive demand of teacher questions.

Time-on-task is one way in which the concentration span and engagement of pupils with the tasks set by teachers can be measured. A number of studies have shown that time spent on-task is one factor in enhancing learning: concentration and practice are both means to improve performance. Bennett (1987) called time-on-task, and the match of task to pupil need, twin factors in the 'opportunity to learn' paradigm. We could make only broad impressionistic judgements about the latter, but there was opportunity to take time-samples of the former.

Teachers signal the level at which they wish their pupils to function through the cognitive demand they make on pupils – most significantly through the questions they pose. By analysing the questions our teachers asked of pupils in the Centre we hoped to make some broad judgements on this issue of cognition. To this end Kerry's (1982) methodology was used as it had the advantage of familiarity. This research showed that few teacher questions were of a higher order of cognitive demand, though primary teachers generally made more demands than those in secondary schools. More recent research (quoted by Brown and Wragg, 1993, as part of the Leverhulme project) confirms that this situation endures. Managerial questions accounted for 37 per cent of teacher questions in this latter study, while the percentage of higher-order questions (over all teacher questions) failed to reach double figures. Combined with the time-on-task and open-ended observation, we hoped this question analysis would help to form a picture of the effectiveness of teaching and learning in the new Centre.

A new space, and new teaching/learning strategies, require new methods of class management. This term is sometimes used to imply 'discipline', but here we use it to refer to organisational decisions made by teachers to promote learning efficiency and teacher effectiveness. In practice these come down to the way in which pupils are grouped: whether the work takes place in a whole-class context, whether children are organised into learning groups, or whether work is individualised. Kerry and Sands (1984) argued that genuine group work has to include pupils not merely seated in groups, but working collaboratively towards a shared end-product. They further suggested that individualised learning was characterised by pupils having tasks tailored to their specific needs, and did not include pupils working separately on a single task common to everyone in the class. These are the definitions used here.

We called these three organisational methods 'modes of teaching'. Research carried out by Kerry and Sands (1984) and Sands (1981a; 1981b) demonstrated that, in what are now Year 7 classes, group work represented substantially less than 10 per cent of pupils' experience, and individualised learning about 15 per cent. These figures were deemed to be low in mixed-ability settings. In the current study we are dealing with Year 4 pupils also in mixed-ability settings. Popular mythology would suggest that collaborative working and carefully differentiated work are widespread in the primary school, and such methods could be seen to be appropriate for two classes taught by two teachers in a large open-plan space. Part of the research project was designed to see how valid these assumptions were at Saxonvale. In particticular, we were aware of the stricture of Alexander *et al.* (1992) that:

> The organisational strategies of whole class teaching, group work and individual teaching need to be used selectively to achieve different educational outcomes. The criterion of choice must always be fitness for purpose. (p. 35)

We would have expected to find the teachers in our study dealing with change; the change of teaching style incumbent upon them because of the change in physical location. But we would also have expected that change to have been managed from 'above', ie to have been planned and prepared for by the senior management of the school; in this case the head and the governors.

Perhaps the most helpful insights here are those of Senge (1990). While most management concerns the bringing about of change, Senge's approach emphasises that institutions have to become 'learning organisations', and they do this through individuals who learn. What managers have to do is to live from a creative standpoint, being proactive, not reactive, to emergent situations. In the present case, the establishment of the new teaching/learning space challenged the school managers (head and governors), who had designed the building, to create a vision for the future that could be shared with those who would help to bring it to fruition (the teachers). This shared vision is itself evolutionary, and depends on those charged with managing a situation being able to listen as well as talk. For the head, there was a need to lead 'through designing the learning process' (p. 345), of moving from current realities (for us, the accepted teaching methods adopted in the school as a whole) towards that vision which the new situation demanded.

Finally, we had to reflect on our role as consultants in the process. We took the view, expounded by Cockman *et al.* (1992), that the ideal would have been to have worked with the school, over time (and from the inception of the project), and to have adopted a client-centred stance. Our research methodology could then have been based on action-research principles (Lomax, 1994). This would have involved looking at the desired teaching/learning in the Viking Centre and trying to perceive the situation more clearly (ie in a more detached way) than the clients, trying to devise alternative strategies, and evaluating some of these suggested alternatives in collaboration with the teachers in the Centre. In the event, because the head and governors felt vulnerable about the more experimental approaches, we were called in only after the Centre was operational, and we deemed it politic to work in what Cockman et al. call a 'prescriptive style'. This has four elements, and these represent what we were contracted to do, notably:

- listen to the client's problen
- collect the data required to explore it
- make sense of the data/problem from our experience
- present the client with recommendations.

In answer to Cockman *et al.*'s question 'Who is the client?', we had to conclude that we had two clients, with rather different agendas. The first client group was the head and governors, who were concerned to get the best from their investment in new school plant. The second group was the staff of the Centre, who had much to lose from any perceed 'weaknesses' in performance being revealed – through our researches – to the first group, yet who crucially needed some advice and direction about appropriate teaching/learning styles.

As we indicated at the beginning, this review has revealed the wide-ranging issues raised by the apparently straightforward act of creating a new teaching/learning space. In what follows we go on to describe how we set about providing some research on which to base our analysis and advice.

Methodology

We had at our disposal two researchers, who were allocated a total of six days of work within the Centre. Our aim was to get as broad a picture of the kinds of teaching/learning that took place there as was possible in this time. Emphasis had to be placed on identifying precisely what changes the two teachers working there had already made to their teaching styles and activities to match the demands and opportunities of the space, and to exploring what aspects of any unchanged practice needed some review. More generally, we had also to have some concern for global issues about effective use of the space in the Centre to benefit the whole school rather than just its immediate occupants.

To achieve these ends we compiled a battery of instruments which we thought would reveal as much detail about practice in the Centre as possible in a limited time. This battery consisted of:

1 A semi-structured interview schedule for use with the two teachers and designed to explore specifically any changes they had made consciously to cope with teaching in a new open-plan space.

2 A time-on-task analysis sheet to explore whether pupils could work effectively in the space.

3 A recording system for sampling the cognitive demand made by teachers' questions in order to estimate the quality of learning taking place.

4 An open-ended recording proforma for logging how, and how appropriately, the teachers operated within the space: this included the facility to gauge the proportions of time spent in whole-class teaching, group work and individualised learning. The emphasis here was to be on teaching strategies.

5 An open-ended proforma for shadowing a pupil during lessons in the Centre. The main interest here was in learning activities. Our aim was to shadow an able pupil, a less able pupil and a middle band pupil to see whether there were any problems caused by the learning space that were specific to these groups.

6 An open-ended interview with a cross-section of pupils selected at random, to triangulate with the views of the teachers and the researchers.

7 A summary sheet on which the researchers could record their thoughts and reflections about the current and potential use of the space.

This battery of proformas was compiled into a booklet, complete with instructions for use, in order to maximise the reliability and validity of observations from one observer to the other: the two researchers discussed their judgements using shared experiences of classroom observations prior to the study period in the Centre. Since a number of different methods were being used to investigate the use of the space, and both teachers and learners were being studied, the data were, we felt, being cross-checked for consistency and triangulated for perceptions of different audiences (Hammersley et al., 1994). A timetable for the study was drawn up, negotiated and agreed within the school.

The methods of study for use in the research phase of the project were selected against carefully articulated criteria. Semi-structured interview is a tested technique for gaining the views of participants in a situation about their experience of it: the structure enables the interviews to be consistent from one participant to another (that is, the same ground is covered and the interviewer can avoid bias in the way the questions are framed from one respondent to the next). But the option of pursuing leads set up by the respondent allows a closer analysis of personal views than is the case in a closed questionnaire. In compiling and analysing these data we followed the guidelines of Wragg (1979).

Time-on-task was measured by the simple device of observing each pupil in the class for a 60-second period and logging the number of seconds spent on and off-task. Thus 24 pupils can be observed in the same number of minutes and the percentage of time on-task gauged quite precisely to give an overall score (based on Wragg, 1978).

When the lesson being observed lent itself to question analysis – that is, when the teacher was engaged in dialogue and discussion with the class – the opportunity was taken to record each teacher question and to analyse it using a system adapted from Bloom (1956). This system has been used by Kerry (1986) and Wragg (1991) to assess the cognitive demand made by teachers on pupils.

The Open University PGCE training materials (1994) contain proformas for observing teachers at work, and for shadowing pupils of varying abilities (most and least able, and middle band) to gauge their learning and their involvement in lessons. These were used to compile open-ended descriptions of the teacher and pupil activities during lessons in the Centre. Though not strictly research instruments, these very open-ended proformas allowed recording of events to take place, which could later be scrutinised for evidence about the use of the Centre's specific facilities, for teaching strategy and for critical incidents or key issues (Faulkner et al., 1991, p. 98).

Finally, we compiled a summary sheet which could be used as a 'notepad' on which the researchers could either record ideas about the use of the Centre triggered by observations made, or on which they could write their reflections at the end of the day about opportunities taken or missed to use the Centre's facilities well and creatively.

This kind of research is in the overall genre of case study (Hitchcock and Hughes, 1994). It may have limited generalisability (Schofield, 1993), but that is not significant since the purpose is limited to a specific location and set of circumstances: the subject of our consultancy project. In a study of this kind we were also aware that it was impossible to achieve total objectivity; we hoped to form some views about teaching/learning in the Viking Centre and to use these to make suggestions to the governing body of Saxonvale school. We accepted Eisner's proposition that 'there is no single, legitimate way to make sense of the world' (Hammersley, 1993, p. 54). We were aware, too, of Toulmin's (1982) warning:

All of our scientific explanations and critical readings start from, embody, and imply some interpretive standpoint, conceptual framework, or theoretical perspective. The relevance and accuracy of our explanations can never be demonstrated with Platonic rigour or geometrical necessity. (p. 115)

The findings

We chose to collect our data during two weeks of the spring term, one of us working for two consecutive mid-week days in the first week and the other for four days in the following week. In this way we felt we would gain some view over time, however limited by the short-lived nature of the project.

Interviews with the teachers were carried out on the first morning of the research, before any classroom observation took place. Their responses were noted and the transcript checked with them later.

The teachers did not entirely share a perception about the use of the new teaching/learning area. Teacher B is more tentative about the stage of commitment reached in both planning and execution of combined work. Teacher B does not mention team-work and is sceptical about the managerial motives in setting up the space and the effectiveness of the management's consultation processes.

There is agreement about initial apprehension in colleagues working together so closely. Both teachers understand the need to experiment, but seem to have made little systematic or shared effort to do so. There is an accommodation between them to work formally in the mornings, and less so after lunch: this minimised problems of noise from each other's classes. Neither teacher has come to grips with appropriate teaching styles. Both enjoy the surroundings – their newness and sheer size. Neither has developed a distinctive philosophy of teaching to match the conditions.

Teacher A claims to be more involved in joint planning than Teacher B. Teacher A is more concerned to benefit professionally from the experience. Teacher A's methods of working have changed, inevitably, because in her previous year's role as science coordinator – she taught more of her specialist subject, but is now a generalist.

Thus the outcomes of this initial overview of the teachers' work in the Centre show some level of agreement, but significant differences that are worthy of further exploration.

Our next area for investigation related to whether pupils could work without disturbance in this large open-plan area. To this end we carried out the time-on-task measures described earlier. The results are shown in Table A.1.

TABLE A.1   Time-on-task

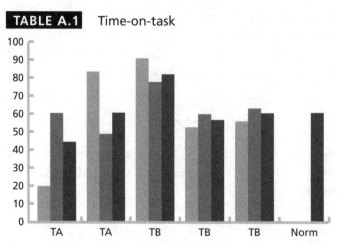

Note The Table shows the percentage of time-on-task by pupils during five observations in the Centre. Teacher A was observed twice for this purpose, and Teacher B three times. The left-hand column of each group is the score for girls, the centre the score for boys, and the right-hand column is the mean for all pupils during the observation period. The normative score is shown as the final single column.

Table 1 shows that pupils concentrated on their work equally well, or better, than pupils in more typical teaching spaces for most of the time. The exception was in one lesson taught by Teacher A. This was a technology lesson which failed to involve, or capture the interest of, most female pupils.

Because we were interested, too, in what pupils did when they were not on-task, a small amount of unplanned time was spent analysing this. The results are shown as Table A.2 might be expected, the commonest off-task behaviours (we called these 'deviant acts', though they were not necessarily of any significant seriousness) were chatting or staring around the classroom, apparently unoccupied. Queueing for teacher attention is not strictly an intentionally deviant act by a pupil, but the time spent on it does affect the overall time-on-task in class. It should be noted that there were no serious acts of bad behaviour during our observation period, and there is nothing of real note here about the ways in which these pupils behaved when off-task. The open-plan nature of the teaching space did not correlate at all with any deterioration of pupil behaviour over what might have been expected from observation of lessons in other, more conventional, school situations.

One intention of the investigation was to try to gain an impression of the cognitive demand made by teachers on children working in the Centre, using a system of question analysis described above. This attempt to collect data failed. Few dialogues between teachers and the class took place; of those that did none

TABLE A.2 Deviant acts

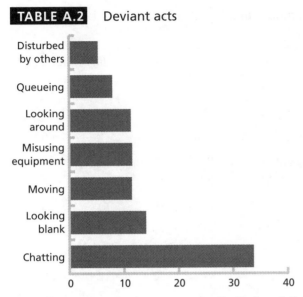

Note The Table shows, in percentages, the distribution of all deviant acts recorded ($n = 35$), broken down by category.

was sustained, and there was little evidence that pupils' thinking was being expanded through higher-order questions. Some questions from the teacher to individuals working alone were inaudible to us because the sound was lost in the large space. The results were thus entirely negative, and indicated that teachers were giving few verbal signals that children were required to respond to tasks in an analytical or creative way. (If this research were repeated it might be more productive – in terms of exploring cognitive demand – to attempt a task analysis of what children did over the observation period, rather than to explore what teachers said.)

We wrote lesson accounts of 19 lessons during the observation period. It was possible to analyse all of these for the proportions of time spent on the various teaching modes. Of these modes it was hypothesised (on the basis of previous research – Kerry, 1982) that whole-class teaching (W), individual work (Ii) and group working not involving collaboration (Gi) would be more strongly correlated with formal class teaching methodologies, and possibly with less cognitively demanding work. Individualised learning (Iii) and collaborative group work (Gii) were felt to be more logical modes for use in an open-plan space. An analysis of the 19 lessons observed is shown in Table A.3.

The results of the teaching mode analysis indicates that 25.3 per cent of time was spent on mode Gii and 9.4 per cent on mode Iii: a total of 34.7 per cent of all recorded lesson time. Thus about one third of all time was spent in the modes of

TABLE A.3 Teaching modes employed: an analysis of 19 sessions observed

Lesson	W	Gi	GH	h	lii	Total
1	24	0	13*	0	36	73
2	12	0	38*	0	0	50
3	59	0	1*	0	0	60
4	4	35	0	0	0	39
5	7	0	0	53	0	60
6	7	0	0	0	61	68
7	45	0	0	20	0	65
8	60	0	0	0	0	60
9	5	0	60*	0	15	80
10	25	0	0	50	0	75
11	10	0	50*	0	0	60
12	12	0	0	48	0	60
13	25	0	0	35	0	60
14	30	0	30	10	0	70
15	10	0	45	0	0	55
16	52	0	19	0	0	71
17	0	0	0	0	60	60
18	17	0	45	8	0	70
19	55	0	0	0	0	55
Total (mins)	459	35	301	284	112	1191
%	38.5	2.9	25.3	23.9	9.4	100%

Key

W   – whole-class teaching

Gi – pupils sitting in groups but working on identical tasks

Gii – pupils working in collaborative groups on shared tasks

Ii   – pupils working alone on a task common to all

Iii – pupils working on individualised tasks

* indicates that pupils were engaged on a mixture of Gii & Iii work.

teaching thought most likely to be matched to the open-plan nature of the learning space. Formal whole-class methods (W) predominated, with 38.5 per cent of time organised in whole-class activities, and 26.8 per cent in modes (Gi and Ii) which could be described as 'whole-class modes in disguise'. These modes fail to distinguish between the needs of individual children and imply differentiation of work by outcome only.

This picture was generally confirmed by the lesson accounts, both those concentrating on all the pupils, and those with a focus on pupils of specific levels of ability (most able, least able, and average). The key issues from these observations are to be found in Figure A1.

Pupils' views of the Centre were obtained through an open-ended interview with a random sample of youngsters who were not involved in a specific task. The opportunity was seized to chat informally with them. The group was of mixed gender and included pupils from both classes. Their comments are listed in summary as Figure A.2

Finally, the researchers had set themselves to pause from observing from time to time to fill in a reflective Use of Space Summary Sheet. This was intended to focus the researchers' minds on the specific uses of space witnessed in a lesson, or on thoughts which had been triggered by a lesson about opportunities lost in using the learning environment effectively. In practice this sheet was always intended to be a 'notebook' – not something to be compiled slavishly at the end of every session. Nevertheless, 14 of these summaries were completed, and the results are recorded in Figure A.3.

- Much teacher talk was centred around routine class management and administration
- Several sessions were used to administer Richmond and other tests
- A good deal of emphasis was put on keeping things tidy, and much time used up on this
- One area of the room was used as 'carpet area' for starting lessons off when the teachers shared an introduction to common work
- However, even where similar tasks were being carried out by both classes, the teachers often chose to work independently
- Seating of pupils was self-chosen and gender-divisive
- Much of the teacher input to lessons did not appear very focused: no learning aims were identified to us or the children
- Learning opportunities were often missed in dialogue with pupils
- The float teacher (available in one session) was not used or managed effectively
- Pupils' suggestions for lesson content were used twice (a video and a shell)
- Pupils did a lot of queueing
- Generally, there was a good social atmosphere in the room, and good pupil – pupil/teacher-pupil relations
- Praise was used
- Many pupils showed signs of boredom, eg repeated yawns
- There was very little challenge in any of the work
- There was little differentiation evident: more from one teacher than the other
- One very able pupil was withdrawn for maths lessons *
- Less able pupils were not engaged effectively in tasks

FIG. A.1 Key issues from lesson observations and from shadowing pupils of varying abilities

Pupils said:

- the Centre is good because it is roomy
- it is safer [easier groundfloor egress from building]
- we can work together more
- it is well decorated
- it is better for indoor playtimes
- it is warm and comfortable
- it has a technology bench
- the chairs are good
- we like joining with the other class
- it is easier to watch TV, do music

BUT

- it is noisy
- the second class can be distracting
- there is too much tidying up
- there are not enough toilets for the boys close by
- the cloakroom area is too crowded
- there is too much green colour in the room
- we do more spelling and number in here

FIG. A.2 Pupils' views of working in the Centre

1. *Pupil-related activities which made use of the whole classroom space in a distinctive way*

- 8 nil returns
- detached groups of pupils painted with the help of an ancillary/parent [3 times]
- one pupil used a computer [2]
- pupils performed playlets to the combined classes [1]
- Teacher A taught all pupils (Teacher B ill) [1]

2. *Pupil-related activities which could not have happened in a conventional classroom*

- 9 nil returns
- Teacher B supports Teacher A's pupil on computer [2]
- two classes combine to watch TV [1]
- one teacher supervised all pupils during a test [1]

---

3. Teacher-related activities distinctive to an open-plan space

- 3 nil returns
- spontaneous planning [5]
- combined notices/administration [3]
- teachers compared notes at end of session [3]
- combined lesson introduction [2]

---

4. Ways in which the space could be used more effectively for teaching/learning

- 6 nil returns
- no classroom displays
- no flexible use of furniture to create learning groups
- no use of space to create learning resource area, eg for science
- room too rigidly divided into two 'classroom' spaces
- long queues of pupils allowed to form at teachers' desks
- lack of large visual aids for combined group teaching
- opportunities to form cross-class groups lost
- opportunities for combined introductions to new work lost
- both teachers anchored to their desks
- teachers' planning does not generate opportunities for combined work

---

Notes
- Numbers in [ ] brackets indicate number of mentions, ie the frequency with which these events took place.
- In section 4 the number of mentions is omitted, since the purpose was simply to generate a list of ideas about lost opportunities.

FIG. A.3 Analysis of the 14 'Use of Space Summary Sheets' completed

What emerges from Figure 3 is that very few of the observed pupil activities (section 1) could not have been carried out in a conventional classroom, and few opportunities (section 2) were made to find new ways of teaching in the Centre. Teacher behaviour was conditioned by the space, but only to the extent that there could be instant (but basically trivial) planning to work together: this happened on five occasions in 19 lessons observed (section 3). The researchers noted (section 4) 10 ways in which opportunities to use the space creatively were lost during lessons: we felt this was probably only the tip of an iceberg.

Discussion

We were very tempted to sub-title this article: 'A study in failure'. The data we collected have catalogued significant areas where there are certainly failures of good management and pedagogical practice.

On the management front, it is clear that neither the governing body nor the headteacher had formulated, communicated, or prepared strategies and philosophies for the occupation of the Viking Centre and the changes its use would impose on the teaching activities of staff. There was, in short, no strategic planning of the kind described by Davies and Ellison (1997). There was no attempt to manage change, which Davies and West-Burnham (1997) call 'normal and persistent' in the education world of the 1990s (p. 6). There was certainly no evidence in our study that anyone had viewed the process of creating, and then using effectively, the Viking Centre as part of the school's role as a 'learning organisation' (Senge, 1990).

Though formal interviews with the chair of governors and the headteacher were not possible, the informal discussion with the latter and the meeting with the governing body to report our findings, along with the comments of the teachers (recorded above), demonstrated a total absence of any management plan. There was no evidence of leadership of the teachers by the head in reassessing their roles; and no opportunities were provided for realistic teacher preparation. Worse, no provision had been made for the teachers to gain insights from professional development opportunities – even after the occupation of the Centre exposed the weaknesses described. Once the space was occupied, the opportunity for consultation was (in turn) not extended by the teachers to the pupils who found themselves learning in the space.

The whole situation described here was a 'blank page' scenario. It would have lent itself ideally to the principles of re-engineering (Davies, 1997). Every opportunity' for this to happen was lost in the pragmatism to get something built as quickly as possible, and to worry about its rationale afterwards.

The open-plan nature of the space clearly hinted at the possibility of team teaching, but there was no expertise in this area in the school. Warwick (1976) in a dated, but insightful, analysis of this methodology, defines team teaching thus:

> *A form of organisation in which individual teachers decide to pool resources, interests and expertise in order to devise and implement a scheme of work suitable to the needs of their pupils and the facilities of the school. (p. 18)*

He points to the need for staff about to embark upon working in this way to be enthusiastic, but he clearly implies that some knowledge of procedures may help (Warwick, 1976, pp. 43–44). Indeed, he goes on (in chapter 10) to suggest that there are nine stages of preparation before a new building can be put to this use, including: understanding the theoretical underpinning of team teaching; preparation for it; identifying the framework of the curriculum; structuring the timetable; examining staff and pupil groupings; and bringing about changes in classroom procedure and organisation. The management did not attempt to bring any of these stages about at Saxonvale.

The approach of the teachers was no less naive than that of the managers. Comment from one of them ('Pupils work as two classes a lot, so there might as well be a wall down the middle really') provides clear evidence of an amazing lack of appreciation of the situation, its possible pitfalls and its potential strengths. As a result, there was less adaptation of teaching/learning methods to the new situation than was desirable. The pleasant surroundings were enjoyed by the pupils (Figure 2). The result was that they generally worked on-task in the Centre (Table 1), and their 'deviant acts' were of a minor nature (Table 2). Nevertheless Bennett's (1987) 'opportunity to learn' paradigm was neglected because there was little cognitively-extended task-demand (Figure 1, and the paucity of evidence collected from teachers' questioning of pupils). Work was rarely differentiated (Figure 1) and opportunities to cater for the most and least able were lost (Kerry, 1982; 1986). There was too much reliance (Table 3) on whole-class methods (Kerry and Sands, 1984): organisational strategies were too limited to provide good learning opportunities. Of pupils, Trott (1997) points out that:

> Whatever we provide at school its quality is primarily determined by clients, their achievement and level of satisfaction, not the teachers, the organisation or that of some outside body. (Trott, 1997, 167)

For her, the clients are the pupils; and this research has uncovered no evidence of their views being taken into account either about the use of the Centre or about the teaching styles adopted in it (apart, that is, from our own questions to them).

More positively, there is a very real sense in which this study is overtly 'of its time'. In just the brief spell since this research has been completed, there has been a massive expansion in the training of governors for their roles; we have seen the National Professional Qualification for Headship introduced, and a number of schemes have been piloted for accrediting the in-service efforts of teachers, such as the College of Teachers' Associateship in Professional Development for individual teachers and Institutional Membership for schools. In theory, therefore, the confluence of events which led to the failures described here should not occur elsewhere.

As we pointed out in our literature review, the role of a consultant in a situation like this is a delicate one. We had had Cockman *et al.*'s (1992) prescriptive model imposed on us. When the report was presented to the governing body it had to temper criticism of all parties (governors, head and teachers) with the need to gather all of them into a positive and purposeful partnership to improve teaching and learning in the Centre. We had also to be wary of our personal biases in accordance with Toulmin's (1982) admonition, quoted above. The result was that the report tried to emphasise, wherever possible, the better practice we had seen, appearing only to suggest changes of practice and direction in clear but tactful and open-ended ways. Extracts from our report follow.

Extracts from the report to the governing body

A common concern which the research uncovered was that the Centre – the inanimate criteria of building design and layout – seems to impose itself on the learning activities that take place in it. By contrast, the SMT [Senior Management Team] and staff should take a more aggressive stance to ensure that the physical plant is servant to the learning process. In practice this means that staff need to be more flexible and imaginative in using space to meet predetermined learning objectives. *It is suggested that a reappraisal of the layout and facilities of the Centre is now timely.*

How could children's learning be improved by extended utilisation of the space?

There is some use made of 'helpers' by the teachers who work in the Centre. However, team-teaching lends itself to a greater exploitation of the skills of 'helpers' to promote increased use of group work and individualised learning. The teachers, in this situation, would need to take an active managerial role in guiding the work of 'helpers'. (In this context 'helpers' may be student teachers, ancillaries, specialist teacher assistants, BTEC students, parents, visiting speakers etc.) *SMT and the teachers should explore what opportunities exist to use 'helpers' more extensively and productively.*

The move to the advanced skill of team-teaching and the increased use of 'helpers' would imply *a much greater degree of collaborative forward planning by the teachers* than is required in the present situation. *In a team situation staff would look to using their individual strengths to support the learning of all pupils* rather than working mostly as two independent groups.

What has been said above indicates a view that *the space lends itself to more opportunities for pupils to work in 'cross-class' groups* than happen at present. This should not preclude pupils from being allocated to 'tutor groups 'linked to a single teacher for organisational and pastoral purposes: both the teachers carry out these roles well in the present structure.

Team-teaching and enhanced group/ individualised learning opportunities sug-gest that *work could profitably be orientated more towards problem-solving by pupils*. This would make pupils more independent in their learning, able to proceed at their own pace, at their own level, and with less recourse to the teacher.

Thus working in the Centre – in a team-teaching environment – could *promote the kinds of differentiation* which are required by National Curriculum assessment and by the acknowledged teaching intentions to stretch all pupils' abilities. In the ways outlined above, teaching in the Centre could progress from the solid base already established to deliver the highest possible standards ...

What conclusions might be drawn from the investigation?

The time is ripe for a strong managerial steer, after consultation with the staff involved, to further the opportunities for learning provided by the Centre.

This managerial action should encompass decisions both about the use of the space and the appropriate in-service training for staff.

Any staff who teach in the Centre should be given access to training to develop and evaluate the advanced skills of team-teaching.

At an appropriate time the school should re-evaluate the best use of the Centre in the interests of all pupils ...

A note on the kinds of INSET implicit in this report

Throughout this Report the recommendation has been made that the staff work-ing in the Centre be given opportunities for in-service training (INSET) relative to their new roles.

The nature of this training is envisaged to include the following:

(a) Opportunity to meet with an appropriate consultant, in their present situa-tion, and time to discuss and experiment with a variety of room layouts and patterns of working to further pupils' learning.

(b) Opportunities to visit other schools where the plant and methods of teaching can throw light on maximising the potential of the Centre – these visits may be in or outside the county.

(c) Time to re-plan their approaches to teaching and learning in the light of the outcomes from (a) and (b) above.

These activities could be supported by Training Grant monies.

Postscript

This article has traced the history of a piece of consultancy aimed at improving the use of a teaching/learning space in a primary school. It has also attempted to establish some principles for handling more effectively the planning processes associated with establishing new teaching spaces. Despite the effort that went into this piece of work, the subsequent history of the use of the Viking Centre did not follow a predictable course.

At the end of the academic year, it was decided that the two teachers studied here should not continue to occupy the space, so the expertise they had gained was immediately lost. Two other teachers used the Centre to teach Y6. We were unable to study this process, but we were aware that they did make considerable efforts to plan together, though they never adopted a full 'team-teaching' approach, nor were they able to adapt fully to the open-plan nature of the space.

In the following academic year the local education authority, taking the new floor space into account, raised the intake of the school, with the result that the Centre had now to be occupied by three classes instead of two. Again, fresh teachers were allocated to use the Centre. No attempt was made by the governors or senior managers of the school to adopt any of the consultants' suggestions for training staff or developing the space for the benefit of the whole school.

References

Alexander, R., Rose, J. and **Woodhead, C.** (1992) *Curriculum Organization and Classroom Practice in Primary Schools*, London: DES.

Beare, H., Caldwell, B. and **Millikan, R.** (1989) *Creating an Excellent School*, London: Routledge.

Bennett, N. (1987) 'Changing perspectives on teaching and learning processes', *Oxford Review of Education*, Vol. 13, No. 1.

Bloom, B. (1956) *Taxonomy of Educational Objectives*, London: Longman.

Brown, G. and **Wragg, E.** (1993) *Explaining*, London: Routledge.

Bush, T. and **West-Burnhan, J.** (eds) (1994) *The Principles of Education Management*, Harlow: Longman.

Caldwell, B. and **Spinks, J.** (1988) *The Self-managing School*, Lewes: Falmer Press.

Cockman, P., Evans, B. and **Reynolds, P.** (1992) *Client centred Consultancy*, London: McGraw-Hill.

Davies, B. (1997) 'Reengineering and its application to education', *School Leadership and Management*, Vol 17, No. 2, pp. 175–85.

Davies, B. and **Ellison, L.** (1997) *School Leadership for the 21st Century*, London: Routledge.

Davies, B. and **West-Burnham, J.** (1997) *Reengineering and Total Quality in Schools*, London: Pitman.

Faulkner, D., Swann, J., Baker, S., Bird, M. and **Carty, J.** (1991) *Professional Development in Action: Methodology Handbook*, Milton Keynes: Open University.

Hammersley, M. (1993) *Educational Research: Current issues, Vol. 1*, London: PCP.

Hammersley, M., Gomm, R. and **Woods, P.** (1994) *MA in Educational Research Methods: Study Guide*, Milton Keynes: Open University Press.

Hitchcock, G. and **Hughes, D.** (1994) *Research and the Teacher* (2nd Ed), London: Routledge.

Kerry, T. (1982) 'Teachers' identification of exceptional pupils and their strategies for dealing with them', unpublished PhD thesis, University of Nottingham.

Kerry, T. (1986) 'Improving learning through classroom language', in B. Gillham (ed) *The Language of School Subjects*, London: Heinemann.

Kerry, T. and **Sands, M.** (1984) 'Classroom organization and learning', in E.C. Wragg (ed) *Classroom Teaching Skills*, London: Routledge.

Lomax, P. (1994) 'Action research for managing change', in N. Bennett, R. Glatter and R. Levacic, *Improving Educational Management through Research and Consultancy*, London: PCP.

Marsh, J. (1993) *The Strategic Toolkit*, IFS International. Ofsted (1995) *Guidance on the Inspection of Nursery and Primary Schools*, London: HMSO.

Open University (1994) *PGCE Course Manual: School Experience Guide*, Milton Keynes: Open University Press.

Sands, M. (1981a) 'Group work: time for re-evaluation?', *Educational Studies*, Vol. 7, No. 2.

Sands, M. (1981b) 'Group work: myth or reality?', *School Science Review*, No. 62, p. 221.

Schofield, J. (1993) 'Increasing the generalizability of qualitative research', in Hammersley (1993) *op. cit.*

Senge, P. (1990) *The Fifth Discipline: the Art and Practice of the Learning Organization*, London: Century.

Toulmin, S. (1982) 'The construal of reality: criticism in modern and post-modern science', in W. Mitchell. (ed) *The Politics of Interpretation*, pp. 99–118, Chicago: University of Chicago Press.

Trott,. C. (1997) 'The child as client', in Davies and West-Burnham (1997) *op. cit.*

Warwick, D. (1976) *Team Teaching* (4th Ed), London: Hodder & Stoughton.

Watkins, C. and **Whalley, C.** (1993) 'Mentoring beginner teachers: issues for schools to anticipate and manage', *School Organization*, Vol. 13, No. 2, pp. 129–38.

Wragg, E. (1978) *Nottingham Class Management Observation Schedule*, Nottingham: Nottingham University.

Wragg, E. (1979) *Conducting and Analysing Interviews*, Rediguide 11, Nottingham University.

Wragg, E. (1991) *The Leverhulme Primary Project*, Exeter: School of Education.

This article is reproduced by permission of the editor of *Education Today*.

Index